W9-ACP-812

VIRGIL'S MIND AT WORK

ANCHISES LEAVING TROY

Two detached scenes from the 'Trojan Picture' found on the site of Bovillae, after O. Jahn, *Griechische Bilderchroniken*, Bonn, 1873, plate 1, from an offprint kindly provided by Professor A. B. Cook

VIRGIL'S MIND AT WORK

An analysis of the Symbolism of the Aeneid

by

ROBERT W. CRUTTWELL

M.A. Oxon.,
sometime Classical Demy of Magdalen College, Oxford,
and Newdigate Prizeman

'pandere res alta terra et caligine mersas.'
Aeneid VI. 267

A MARANDELL BOOK

COOPER SQUARE PUBLISHERS, INC.
NEW YORK
1969

Originally Published 1947

Published in Agreement with
Basil Blackwell, Publisher, Oxford, U.K.
Published by Cooper Square Publishers, Inc.
59 Fourth Avenue, New York, N. Y. 10003
Library of Congress Catalog Card No. 68-58959

PREFACE

THE purpose of this book is outlined in the Introduction, which therefore requires reading first. Nor should what follows it be read otherwise than consecutively, since both evidence and argument are cumulative throughout.

Against a charge of presumptuousness in attempting so difficult a task, my defence must be lifelong study, as teacher and as taught, of that interplay between thought and word which links psychology with literature.

My particular thanks are due to the Virgilian scholarship of Mr. W. F. Jackson Knight, who both privately and publicly has given me much encouragement. To his mediation with Professor A. B. Cook's generosity, moreover, I owe the Frontispiece, together with valuable information relevant thereto.

For facility of reference I have quoted regularly, save for occasional modifications, from Professor H. Rushton Fairclough's translation of Virgil in the Loeb Classical Library, where it conveniently faces the Latin text.

R.W.C.

CONTENTS

N.B. The method of this book makes an Index quite impracticable.

ABBREVIATIONS

E=*Eclogues*
G=*Georgics*
A=*Aeneid*

INTRODUCTION

THE PURPOSE OF THIS BOOK

THE prosaic mind is one to which things mean nothing more than themselves:

> A primrose by a river's brim
> A yellow primrose was to him,
> And it was nothing more;

whereas the poetic mind is one to which things mean something more than themselves:

> To me the meanest flower that blows can give
> Thoughts that do often lie too deep for tears.

Thus anything, when once associated in the poetic mind with something else, can come to mean that other thing as well. Anything, that is to say, can become a symbol for the poet, and so through his poetry for others too; since, while a symbol is whatever means more than itself, a poet is whoever verbally communicates his symbols.

Mental association, then, is the creative principle of all poetic symbolism. But the creative principles of all mental association are those of human nature — (1) the self's organically assimilated heredity, as first determining the mind's functionally unconscious plane; (2) the self's organically assimilated environment, as first determining the mind's functionally subconscious plane; and (3) the self's organically assimilated identity, as first determining the mind's functionally conscious plane.

Therefore, since nature's threefold integration of an organically unique human self continues to determine that of a functionally unique human mind, it follows that a poem's symbolism will verbally communicate a poet's synthesis of things associated in his mind upon three levels — (1) that of unconscious relation to the poet's own heredity; (2) that of subconscious relation to the poet's own environment; and (3) that of conscious relation to the poet's own identity.

To apply these principles analytically to the symbolism of the *Aeneid*, and so to follow Virgil's mind at work upon his synthesis, will be the twofold purpose of this book.

CHAPTER I

VENUS AND CYBELE

illo Vergilium me tempore dulcis alebat
Parthenope, studiis florentem ignobilis oti.
(*Georgics* IV. 563-564)

WHENEVER Virgil left Rome by the Appian Way for his beloved Naples, the first stage of his journey took him across the Almo to Bovillae.

From Rome to Bovillae, a distance of some twelve miles, the Appian Way had long been paved throughout with hard basaltic lava, quarried locally and known as *silex*; this stretch of Rome's earliest highway being yet further memorable to travellers for its associations — those in particular of the Almo, a small bridge-spanned tributary of the Tiber; and of Bovillae, at the foot of the Alban hills, as the nearest stopping-place to Rome.

Bovillae, in Virgil's time almost suburban, had once been a venerable and independent city, one of the thirty of the old Latin League, founded originally as a colony from Alba Longa two miles away; whence the Bovillans derived their frequently recorded official name of *Albani Longani Bovillenses*.

Tradition told how, when in the seventh century B.C. Alba Longa was destroyed by Rome, the hallows (*sacra*) both of its Vestal cult and of its Julian clan (*gens Iulia*) were transferred for safety to its daughter-city of Bovillae; a belief attested by the discovery there both of inscriptions referring to the Bovillan Vestal Virgins as 'Alban' (*Virgines vestales Albanae*) and of an archaic altar bearing the words 'The Julian clansmen to Father Vediovis' (*Vediovei patrei genteiles Iuliei*) — Vediovis, or Veiovis, being a primitive Latin deity whose cult, being shared with Bovillae by the Roman Capitol, points to an Alban-Julian origin.

Nor had Bovillae, even in decay, ever lost its filial link with Alba Longa, where it still continued to participate in the Latin sacrifices on the Alban Mount, while certain of its ancient municipal privileges had never ceased to be recognized by Rome.

Bovillae was therefore memorable to travellers as perpetuating the early traditions, both ritual and mythical, of Alba Longa, itself at once Lavinium's daughter-city and the mother-city of Rome; these traditions being those not only of the Lavinian-Alban Vestal cult but also of that Alban-Roman Julian clan which included the patrician family of the Caesars — a clan, moreover, claiming direct descent from Jupiter's daughter Venus, and so from Jupiter's mother Cybele, through its eponym Iulus or Ascanius, founder from his father Aeneas' Lavinium of his own Alba Longa for those Vestal hallows of Troy whose virgin-priesthood was later inherited by the mother of Romulus, Rome's founder.

Thirty-three years after Virgil's death Bovillae was for this reason appropriately chosen for the temporary resting-place of the body of Augustus, as being adoptively a Julius Caesar, on the final stage of its progress from Nola to Rome; and it was at Bovillae, no less appropriately, that two years later in A.D. 16 his successor Tiberius consecrated or perhaps re-dedicated the shrine of the *gens Iulia*, in whose honour he there also instituted yearly Circensian games.

Consequently it is not surprising that at Bovillae were found the fragments of an earthenware tablet forming a 'Trojan picture' (*tabula Iliaca*), dated to the time of Augustus or Tiberius, whose details — to be examined in a later chapter — graphically illustrate precisely that myth of the Iulus-descended and Vesta-worshipping Julian clan, claiming descent both from Venus and from Cybele, which may be called the Alban-Bovillensian tradition, and which finds its supreme literary expression in the *Aeneid*.

This being so it is worth considering whether the *Aeneid* itself associates Iulus with Bovillae in an Alban context; and further, if so, whether this verbal association subconsciously records Virgil's own confused memories of travel from Rome across the Almo to Bovillae on his way to Naples.

Now the adjective *bovillus* is an ancient form of *bubulus*, 'belonging to cattle'; while the corresponding noun *bovilla*, perhaps surviving adjectivally in the place-name *Bovillanus fundus*, is explained by an early gloss as equivalent to the Greek βουστασία 'cattle-stall'.

It follows that the Alban place-name *Bovillae* originally meant 'Cattle-stalls' — nomenclature whose plural number at once recalls that of the *loci Albani* where King Latinus kept 'the royal cattle-herds' (*regia ... armenta:* VII. 485-486): 'the purlieus afterwards called "Alban" from Alba's name; in those days King Latinus had there his lofty stalls' —

> *... locos, qui post Albae de nomine dicti*
> *Albani; tum rex stabula alta Latinus habebat* (IX. 387-388);

a reference, clearly, to some easily identifiable and generally well-known place whose name somehow suggested the three-fold idea of Alba Longa, cattle-stalls, and early Latin origin — the city, in fact, of the *Albani Longani Bovillenses.*

Nor is this all.

For Virgil not only links Iulus explicitly with Latinus' 'Alban' cattle-stalls, and so implicitly with Bovillae's future site, by making him shoot a pet-stag which is kept in them (VII. 475-502) but twice actually gives the river-name Almo (VII. 532, 575) to the eldest keeper of this stag in these cattle-stalls (VII. 483-486); in both cases, moreover, coupling Almo with a companion who bears another Italian river-name, Galaesus (*Almo ... Galaesus:* VII. 532-535; *Almonem ... Galaesi:* VII. 575).

The stag's wounding by Iulus' arrow, too, is emphatically coupled with Almo's death from an arrow shot by one of Iulus' company (VII. 531-534) as together initiating the entire Latin war (VII. 479-482, 503-545, 553) and so, by logical implication, as together ultimately responsible for that war's results.

These results are partly immediate and partly prospective — immediate in the very purlieus of Bovillae itself (IX. 379-398), where death awaits Euryalus and Nisus (IX. 399-445) while each losing his way (IX. 366-378) as Iulus' own messengers to Aeneas (IX. 260-262, 310-313) at the site of Rome (IX. 192-196, 228, 241), in a context reaching from Iulus' Vestal cult (IX. 257-260) to the Julian dynasty at Virgil's Rome (IX. 446-449); and prospective in Aeneas' foundation of Lavinium, in Iulus' foundation therefrom of Alba Longa, and in Romulus' foundation therefrom of Rome (I. 5-7, 257-282).

Not only is such a use of the river-name Almo unexampled, but so strong an emphasis upon Bovillae, in connection both with the name Almo and with the idea of a momentous war, is hardly explicable apart from the influence on Virgil's mind — consciously planning, during his composition of the *Georgics*

(G. III. 8-41), that epic whose 'Kings and battles' already lured him during his earlier composition of the *Eclogues* (E. VI. 3) — of all those subconsciously recorded environmental impressions, at once psychologically vivid and topographically vague, which flooded it between the Almo and Bovillae on the way from Rome, with Alba Longa in the near distance to the poet's left and Lavinium in the far distance to his right; until at last with Naples, that nursing-mother of his Muse (G. IV. 563-566), their memory so sank into his being's unconscious depths as there, amongst hereditary influences, to mould the very matrix of the *Aeneid*'s symbolism.

It is fortunately possible at one point actually to follow the workings of Virgil's subtly associative imagination — that point being the significantly repeated coupling of the Italian river-name Almo with the Italian river-name Galaesus in a warlike context.

To begin with, Virgil's only mention of the river Galaesus (G. IV. 126) occurs in that same last book of the *Georgics*, written immediately before the *Aeneid*, which ends with his only reference to Naples (G. IV. 564).

Secondly, just as Rome adjoined the small stream Almo, so Naples adjoined the small stream Sebethus; while the Sebethus ran out into the Bay of Naples, just as the Galaesus ran out into the Bay of Tarentum.

Thirdly, Virgil couples the Galaesus with Tarentum under the name of 'the Oebalian citadel' (G. IV. 125) as being an 'Oebalian' or Spartan foundation; since Oebalus, a mythical king of Sparta, not only bestowed his name upon his kingdom, but led the Parthenians into Italy for their foundation of Tarentum.

Fourthly, this very name Oebalus is given by Virgil in the *Aeneid* to a native of the Neapolitan island Capreae; whose mother Sebethis was the eponymous water-nymph of the Neapolitan river Sebethus; whose kingdom covered the entire Neapolitan neighbourhood of Campania; and whose mention as a representatively foremost champion in the Latin war (VII. 733-740), on the side of Turnus against Aeneas for Lavinia's hand in marriage, follows closely after the mention of Galaesus and Almo as the two representatively foremost Latin victims of that war.

What, then, are the connecting links in Virgil's mind? The

answer, though somewhat complex, is illuminative of his mental processes.

For the Spartan King Oebalus begot Helen's father, Tyndareus, by a water-nymph Bateia; Bateia being also the name of Teucer's daughter, who by Dardanus was the common ancestress both of Helen's Paris and of Lavinia's Aeneas. Thus the name Oebalus, with its water-nymph associations transferred by Virgil subconsciously to his own Neapolitan environment during his conscious planning of the *Aeneid*, meant to him precisely that parallelism between Aeneas and Paris, Lavinia and Helen, by which the *Aeneid* would symbolize a parallelism between the Latin-Trojan war in Italy and the Graeco-Trojan war in Phrygia.

This explicitly repeated symbolism, moreover, is accompanied by an implicitly repeated parallelism between the legendary Latin-Trojan and the historical Roman-Carthaginian wars.

It is, in point of fact, Hannibal who links together in Virgil's memory the Roman river Almo, the Tarentine river Galaesus, and the Neapolitan river Sebethus. For Hannibal, who in 217 B.C. devastated the neighbourhood of Naples, in 212 B.C. encamped beside the Galaesus during his siege of Tarentum; while the Almo was historically famous as symbolizing Hannibal's eventual defeat — a symbolism whose meaning to Virgil must now be analysed.

The brook Almo, which flowed into the Tiber near the Ostian Way half a mile south of the walls of Rome, had long been celebrated for its share in the ritual of a Phrygian worship; that of Cybele, or Cybebe (A. X. 220), under her Troadic cult-title of 'The Great Idaean Mother of the Gods' (*Mater Deum Magna Idaea*).

Once every spring, to the accompaniment of wild oriental dancing and music performed by her Phrygian eunuchs (*galli*), the image of the Idaean Mother was drawn processionally by oxen in a wagon from her Palatine temple through the Capene Gate down to the Tiber's confluence with the Almo, in whose waters her Phrygian high-priest (*archigallus*) there solemnly bathed both the goddess and her paraphernalia. On the return journey her wagon and oxen were strewn with flowers.

Under the Empire, perhaps from the time of Claudius (A.D. 41-54), this Almo-rite, known as 'the washing' (*lavatio*), took place annually on March 27th; but during the Republic, as also under Augustus (29 B.C.-A.D. 14), it still formed the opening ceremony of Cybele's original festival on April 4th; the actual anniversary of her first arrival in Rome; under which date it is described by Ovid (43 B.C.-A.D. 17), whose life overlapped that of Virgil (70-19 B.C.), through the medium of a ritual myth (*Fasti* IV. 249-346).

April 4th is entered in the Republican calendars as sacred to 'the Great Mother' (*Matri Magnae*); while a note in the Praenestine version of the Republic calendar, after mentioning 'the games in honour of the Great Idaean Mother of the Gods' (*Ludi Matri Deum Magnae Idaeae*), recalls the fact that Cybele's transference from Phrygia to Rome was due to the insistence of the Sibylline Books (*quod Mater Magna ex Libris Sibullinis arcessita locum mutavit ex Phrygia Romam*).

Now the Sibylline Books, brought probably in the sixth century B.C. through Etruscan agency from Cumae to Rome, together with the Cumaean cult of Apollo, were until 82 B.C., twelve years before Virgil's birth, kept under strict religious custody in a vault beneath the Capitoline temple of Jupiter, Cybele's son and Venus' father, where their official interpretation was directed mainly towards the introduction of Greek cults and myths. In particular, their guardians encouraged a Roman adaptation of the Greek legend of Aeneas, which thus reciprocally influenced the interpretation of the Sibylline Books.

Consequently, by the time of the First Punic War (264-241 B.C.) both the legend of Aeneas, as modified in accordance with the Sibylline Books, and the Sibylline Books, as interpreted in accordance with the legend of Aeneas, had together won a twin authority at Rome, whose state-policy was appreciably influenced by their mutual interplay; with the result that Naevius (c. 264?-194 B.C.), who himself fought in that war, so linked it with the Trojan war in his metrical chronicle, the *Bellum Punicum*, as to bring Aeneas to Carthage on his way from Phrygia to Italy.

A generation later, Ennius (239-170 B.C.), who died just a century before Virgil's birth, did for the Second Punic War (218-201 B.C.) in his *Annales* what Naevius had recently done for the First; connecting the supposedly Trojan origins of Rome with the war in which he himself had fought.

Ennius was aged twenty-one when Hannibal invaded Italy;

and the following year, 217 B.C., which saw both Hannibal's victory at Lake Trasimene and his failure to penetrate the defences of Naples, witnessed Rome's alarmed recourse to the advice of the Sibylline Books. Their oracles were accordingly interpreted as recommending a temple on their own Capitoline hill for Aeneas' divine mother Venus (Aphrodite), as worshipped on Mount Eryx in Sicily; wherefore, in 216 B.C., the year of Hannibal's victory at Cannae, the Graeco-Sicilian cult of Venus *Erycina* was for the first time introduced at Rome.

Eleven years later, at the climax of the war, the Sibylline Books were yet further interpreted as predicting that the Carthaginians could be finally expelled from Italy only if the cult of Aeneas' divine compatriot, as worshipped on Mount Ida in the Troad, were transferred to Rome from Phrygia, as that of his divine mother had already been transferred to Rome from Sicily.

Therefore, in 204 B.C. — the very year in which Ennius left the army to begin his literary career in Rome—the small black, probably meteoric stone, encircled by a miniature mural crown, which was then Cybele's only emblem, was brought by sea with Delphic approval from Pessinus to Italy, and so up the Tiber to Rome, where it was temporarily and appropriately lodged in the Palatine temple of Victory on April 4th.

In the following year Hannibal was forced to evacuate Italy and to sue for peace, which was granted in 201 B.C. — a deliverance henceforth commemorated at Rome in the yearly rites of the Idaean Mother, whose own newly-built Palatine temple received her in 191 B.C., just forty-five years before Rome's final destruction of Carthage itself.

Thus, during the crisis of Rome's destiny as rival of Carthage for Mediterranean supremacy, a period of eighteen years, the Cumaean Sibylline Books in Rome were twice responsible for the introduction of a foreign cult whose rites would thenceforth symbolize the idea of victory against odds in Italy — first, on the Capitol, that of Venus under her Sicilian cult-title of *Erycina*; and then, on the Palatine, that of Cybele under her Troadic cult-title of *Idaea*.

Both these introductions, moreover, resulted directly from Roman belief in the legend of Aeneas, son of Venus by Anchises—Venus, the grand-daughter of Cybele; and Anchises, native of Cybele's own Mount Ida near Troy.

It is quite possible that Ennius, whose arrival in Rome coincided with that of Cybele, incorporated all these memories of the Second Punic War in his epic, which even more than Naevius' chronicle seems to have influenced the *Aeneid*; but any such incorporation will have preserved that strictly chronological order of events which had been recently followed by Naevius, and which was to be followed some two centuries later by Ovid in his metrical calendar.

The genius of Virgil alone achieved that imaginative telescoping of the centuries which so integrated the legendary coming of Aeneas with the historical coming of Cybele as to incorporate in one poetic synthesis all those memories of Carthage, of Sicily, and of Cumae, which belonged properly to the Second Punic War.

Ovid, however, is historically correct in distinguishing the two arrivals, while not forgetting their relationship: 'The Mother ever loved (the Phrygian mountains) Dindymus and Cybele and pleasant-fountained Ida, and the realm of Ilium. When Aeneas was carrying Troy to the Italian fields, the goddess almost followed his hallows-bearing ships; but she felt that fate did not as yet call for her divine intervention in Latium, and she remained behind in her accustomed place. But afterwards, when mighty Rome had already seen five centuries and had lifted up her head above the conquered world, the priest consulted the fateful words of the Euboean song (the Cumaean Sibylline Books) . . . Paean (Delphic Apollo) was consulted and said: "Fetch the Mother of the Gods; she is to be found on Mount Ida" . . . In her shrine thus spake the goddess: "It was my own will that they should send for me" . . . Attalus (the local king) replied: "Go forth! Thou wilt still be ours. Rome traces her origin to Phrygian ancestors". Straightway countless axes cut down those pinewoods (of Mount Ida) which once supplied the pious Phrygian (Aeneas) with timber in his flight . . . and the Mother of the Gods is lodged in a hollow ship' . . . (Then follows Cybele's voyage to Italy). . . 'She had now reached Ostia, where the Tiber divides to join the sea' . . . (Here Cybele works a miracle) . . . 'They came to a bend in the river, where the stream turns away to the left; men of old named it "the Halls of Tiber" ' . . . (Here Cybele spends the night of April 3rd-4th) . . . 'There is a place where the smooth Almo flows into the Tiber, and where the lesser river loses its name in the great one. Here a white-haired priest in purple robe washed the Mistress and her hallows in the waters of the Almo. Her attendants howled, the mad flute blew, and hands unmanly beat the leathern drums . . . The goddess herself, seated on a wagon, drove in through the Capene Gate; fresh flowers were scattered on the yoked oxen' (Ovid, *Fasti* IV. 249-346; translated by Sir J. G. Frazer, *The Fasti of Ovid*, London 1929).

Thus the ritual associations of the Almo, from the first inseparable from the Aeneas-legend, and familiar as such no less to Virgil than to Ovid who largely follows him, included all those historical memories of the Second Punic War which to Romans meant the fundamental conception of the *Aeneid* itself — that, namely, of a critical war against a formidable antagonist (Hannibal: Turnus) whose final defeat by a heroic leader (Scipio: Aeneas) coincided with the seaborne transference from Phrygia up the Tiber into Latium, under Cumaean-Sibylline patronage, of a Troadic goddess (Cybele: Vesta) with her hallows. Hence the undercurrents of Virgil's mind, whenever he crossed the Almo, are likely to have run along such lines as these:—

Mount Ida, in the Troad, as source both of Venus' Trojan motherhood and of Cybele's Roman cult-title; Carthage, whither Naevius and perhaps Ennius had already brought Aeneas, as the doomed Mediterranean rival of Rome; Mount Eryx, in Sicily, as source of Venus' Roman cult-title; Cumae, only twelve miles from Naples and reputedly its mother-city, as source of the Sibylline Books and of Apollo's Roman cult; the Tiber-mouth, as the arrival-point in Latium both of Aeneas and of Cybele with their respective ship-borne hallows; the Tiber-river, as carrying both of them onward to its Roman bank; and Rome, as receiving under Etruscan auspices from Cumae those Sibylline Books whose interpretation, in accordance with the Aeneas-legend, supposedly resulted in her final victory over Carthage through the divine intervention both of Aeneas' mother Venus on the Capitol and of Aeneas' compatriot Cybele on the Palatine.

Some such concatenation of ideas, already associated for Virgil's readers with the Almo-rite, appears indeed to be demanded by the explicit symbolism of the *Aeneid*, wherein the poetic fusion of recent history with ancient legend is effected mainly through the medium of Aeneas' ships, which are the very ships of Cybele herself (IX. 107-122; X. 219-231), built by Aeneas under her own Troadic Ida (III. 5-6) from her own Idaean pinewood (IX. 80-92) expressly provided by her for that purpose with the approval of her son, Idaean Jupiter (VII. 139; IX. 93-106).

Above all, Aeneas' own flagship, whereon are borne the symbols of Troadic Vesta (I. 68, 378-379; II. 293-297; III. 12; IV. 598), itself appropriately symbolizes both Venus' Idaean motherhood and Cybele's Idaean patronage; for its towering figure-head is so shaped as to represent Mount Ida, with the Idaean Mother's own lions thereunder (X. 156-158)—Mount Ida being elsewhere personified by Virgil as a 'huntress' (*Ida venatrix:* IX. 177-178), just as he personifies Mount Cybele as a 'worshipper' (*cultrix Cybele:* III. 111); since the Mountain Mother's worshippers were once also hunters of the Mountain Mother's lions.

It is, moreover, by implication, on the skin of one of Cybele's own Idaean lions that Anchises, as Venus' Idaean husband, is seated while carrying on Aeneas' shoulders the symbols of Troadic Vesta, herself Cybele's eldest daughter, out of burning Troy (II. 717-723, 747); just as it is Cybele, 'the Great Mother of the Gods' (*magna deum genetrix:* II. 788) who detains on her own Idaean shores Aeneas' wife Creusa, 'Venus' daughter-in-law' (*Veneris nurus:* II. 787), precisely in order that Aeneas' Idaean ship may carry, together with Iulus, 'Venus' most rightful care' (*Veneris iustissima cura:* X. 132), the symbols both of Cybele and of Vesta to the Tiber-country, where Lavinia will supplant Creusa because Lavinium must supplant Troy (II. 775-789).

The ships of Cybele, be it further noted, carry the household of Venus with the hallows of Vesta from the Troadic coastland of Mount Ida (II. 801-III. 12), whose cult of Cybele *Idaea* accompanies Aeneas' fleet (X. 252), to the Libyan coastland of Juno's Carthage, described at the very outset of the *Aeneid* in terms prophetic of the Punic Wars (I. 12-22; cf. IV. 622-629); from the future site of Hannibal's Carthage to the Sicilian coastland of Mount Eryx (X. 36), where Aeneas — as half-brother of its eponym, Venus' son Eryx (*litora . . . fraterna Erycis:* V. 23-24; *Erycis fines fraterni:* V. 630), slain there quite recently by Hercules in a boxing-match (V. 391-420, 483) — founds the cult of Venus *Erycina*, as the Sicilian counterpart of her Idalian cult in Cyprus, above Anchises' tomb (V. 759-761); and thence, by way of Apollo's Sibylline Cumae (VI. 1-12), to that Tiber-mouth (VII. 30-36) which in more than one sense stands 'over against' Carthage (I. 13-14) and where Aeneas upon landing at once invokes not only his ship-borne Vesta's symbols of Venus' household (VII. 120-123) but also both his two Idaean parents, Venus and Anchises (VII. 140; cf. 134) and his two Idaean patrons, Cybele and Jupiter (cf. 133) — 'Idaean Jupiter and the Phrygian Mother' (*Idaeumque Iovem Phrygiamque . . . Matrem:* VII. 139); that 'gracious Idaean Mother of the Gods' (*alma parens Idaea deum:* X. 252), with her mural crown and her yoked lions (X. 253), whom on his Ida-symbolizing ship (X. 156-158) Aeneas takes for his own martial leader in the Latin war (X. 254-255) precisely because that Roman cult-title meant to Virgil, as to his readers, the pledge of a victory whose divine personification (*Victoria:* XI. 436; XII. 187) had shared with Cybele her own Palatine temple on the very day of Rome's first Almo-rite so long ago.

It is further significant that Aeneas' fourfold Idaean invocation on the Tiber-bank should be uttered on the future site of Ostia, whose 'Tiber-mouths' (*Tiberina . . . ostia:* I. 13-14), confronting Carthage as in distant rivalry, are identical with those 'Tiber-halls' (*Tiberina . . . atria:* Ovid, F. IV. 329-330) where Cybele will pass her first night in Italy as talismanic in warfare against Carthage on behalf of Rome.

It is, indeed, upon this very spot that Aeneas not only passes his own first night in Italy, constructing there with morning his Roman camp-shaped headquarters in readiness for war (VII. 148-159) but also passes the night before his own first voyage up the Tiber to the future site of Rome (VIII. 26-101), Pallanteum being itself identical with the Palatine (IX. 9), after a ritual raising of Tiber-water in his hands (VIII. 66-78); just as Cybele will in her turn proceed thence with sunrise to the Palatine, after a ritual bathing in Almo-water where it joins the Tiber — while the Palatine temple of Victory, which will receive Cybele as a pledge of Rome's victory over Carthage, is remembered in the rites of recent Herculean victory over Cacus which receive Aeneas at Pallanteum (VIII. 102-305).

Nor, when Cybele on the Palatine is thus remembered, is Venus on the Capitol forgotten; since it is precisely during Aeneas' succession to victorious Hercules as a Palatine guest

(VIII. 362-369) that Venus persuades Vulcan — whose own cult below the Capitol was once the counterpart of Vesta's cult below the Palatine — to forge during the night those weapons of war (VIII. 370-453) which with morning Aeneas receives from Venus as her own pledge of victory over Turnus in the Trojan-Latin war (VIII. 608-731).

Nor, again, should it be overlooked with what emphasis Virgil correlates this same victory of Aeneas with the coming of Aeneas to Carthage (I. 263-264; IV. 229-236), to Sicily (V. 58-60, 728-731), and to Sibylline Cumae (VI. 86-96, 890-892); nor yet how he links Carthage with Rome's defeat of Hannibal (I. 12-22), while connecting both Sicily (V. 735-737) and Cumae (III. 441-460; VI. 69-74) with the Sibyl whose Books in Rome would not only foretell but ensure that defeat.

More than this: Dido in Carthage, when prophetically cursing Aeneas, actually conjoins the mythical war against Turnus with the historical war against Hannibal (IV. 622-629); while Aeneas at Cumae goes so far as to synchronize his own arrival at the site of Rome with the coming of the Sibylline Books to Rome itself, when promising to build upon the Palatine (as did Augustus in 28 B.C.) a temple of Apollo beneath whose statue the Sibyl's Books will be kept in a secret shrine constructed by himself for their priestly custody and prophetic interpretation (VI. 69-74).

CHAPTER II

IULUS AND JULIUS

in medio mihi Caesar erit templumque tenebit.
(*Georgics* III. 16)

THE environment of Virgil's childhood was the Mantuan countryside along the river Mincius.

Issuing from the southern shore of Italy's largest lake, the Alpine wind-swept 'Benacus with its roaring, surging swell as of a sea' (G. II. 160), 'Mincius, Benacus' child, crowned with grey sedge' (A. X. 205-206), meandered slowly southwards through rich farmlands — 'Hither your bullocks will of themselves come over the meadows to drink, here Mincius fringes his green banks with tender sedge, and from the hallowed oak swarm humming bees' (E. VII. 11-13) — until at length it broadened out into a sheet of water around 'Mantua, its plain affording food to snowy swans with its grassy river; there the flocks will lack neither limpid springs nor herbage, and all that the herds of cattle crop in the long days the chilly dew will restore in one short night' (G. II. 198-202); 'Mantua, rich in ancestry, yet not all of one stock — three races are there, and under each race four peoples; herself her peoples' head, her strength from Etruscan blood' (A. X. 201-203); founded by 'Ocnus, son of prophetic Manto and the Etruscan river (Tiber), who gave thee, O Mantua, thy walls and his mother's name' (A. X. 198-200).

So much, and no more, has Virgil consciously recorded about his childhood's environment — with one significant exception; the reference, at the opening of the *Georgics*' third book to his epic poem, so long projected (E. VI. 3) and originally planned to celebrate Octavian's personal exploits as an Iulus-descended Julius Caesar: 'I must essay a path whereby I too may rise from earth, and' (like Ennius, whose own self-epitaph is quoted here) ' "fly victorious on the lips of men". I first, if life but remain, will return to (Italy) the land of my fathers, bringing the Muses with me in triumph from their Aonian peak; I first will bring back to thee, Mantua, the palms of Idumaea (Palestine), and on thy green plain will set up a temple in marble beside the water, where great Mincius wanders in slow windings and fringes his banks with tender sedge. In the midst I will have Caesar, and he shall possess the shrine . . . Here, too, shall stand Parian marbles, statues that breathe — the descendants of Assaracus, and the great names of the race sprung from Jupiter, and (Apollo) the Cynthian founder of Troy' (G. III. 8-16, 34-36).

Here, then, we have Virgil associating the Julian myth, as propagated through the Roman interpretation of the Cumaean Sibylline Books and as appropriated in particular by Julius Caesar as claimant to direct descent from Jupiter through Venus, both with the memories of his own childhood and with those of the childhood of his race.

For Assaracus, son of Tros and father of Capys, was Anchises' grandfather, Aeneas' great-grandfather, and so great-great-grandfather of Alba Longa's founder Iulus, himself the eponym of that Julian clan into whose Caesarean family Julius Caesar adopted, as his own son and heir, Apollo's reputed son and lifelong client Octavian, the future Augustus, whom Virgil here chooses for the central figure of his epic poem.

In other words, under the consciously explicit symbol of a Julius-centred and Iulus-statued temple built in marble beside the Mincius at Mantua, Virgil subconsciously envisages his verbally constructed epic in its mentally reconstructed setting — the epic as reminiscent of the beginnings of the Italian poet's people, and the setting as reminiscent of the beginnings of the Italian people's poet. Nor is it more surprising that the boy Virgil should have learnt from his parents that Julian myth of Troy and Rome whose memory in after years he still continued to set in the very heart of his remembered homeland — itself Julius Caesar's personal recruiting-ground during the future poet's early life — than that any other sympathetically imaginative child, hearing his elders tell their tales of long ago, should henceforth associate the heroes of those tales with the surroundings in which he first shared their adventures.

Now the imagery of Virgil's *Eclogues*, while superficially that of Theocritus' *Idylls* (E. VI. 1), is none the less deeply reminiscent of a boyhood spent in a child's fairy-land, a veritable Italian 'Meliboea', or bee-and-cattle paradise of milk-and-honey, which must have meant to its native Virgil as a child much what it means to its eponym Meliboeus as a man: 'Here, amid familiar streams and sacred springs, you shall court the cooling shade. On this side, as aforetime, on your neighbour's border, the hedge whose willow-blossoms are sipped by Hybla's bees shall often with its gentle hum soothe you to slumber; on that, under the high rock, the woodman's song shall fill the air; while still your pets the cooing wood-pigeons and the turtle-dove shall cease not their murmuring from the skyey elm' (E. I. 51-58).

It is again Meliboeus who learns from the cattle-farmer Tityrus both of Octavian's far-reaching influence (6-10) and of Rome's distant majesty (19-25), as the boy Virgil must have heard of them from travellers to Mantua; and it is Meliboeus from whom all this idyllic 'Meliboean' peace is about to depart (64-78), as it departed from Virgil when he grew to manhood. Yet, in a truer sense, it never left him; for its memories, environmentally woven into the texture of his boyhood's day-dreams, were to be woven subconsciously into the texture of his manhood's poems under the Sibylline symbolism of Saturn's kingdom, the Italian Golden Age, about to be revived in all its peaceful earth-fertility beneath the sky-descending influence of Venus' Julian house.

As early as the first *Eclogue*, Octavian is already equivalent to a peace-granting and earth-restoring god (E. I. 1-10); while the fourth *Eclogue* associates the Cumaean Sibylline prophetic *carmen* (4) with the threefold thought of Saturn's Golden Age and Golden Race as returning to Italy (5-7), of its paradisally peaceful earth-fertility of plants and beasts as environmental to one particular Italian childhood (8-45, 60-63), and of Virgil's own poetic *carmina* (55) as integrating the two in harmony with their Sibylline counterpart (46-59); until, the sixth *Eclogue* having referred both to Virgil's projected epic (3) as disputing his devotion to the countryside (1-5) and to Silenus' rustic *carmina* (25) as including the theme of Saturn's earthly reign (41), the ninth *Eclogue* goes so far as to attribute idyllic earth-fertility to the starry influence of Julius Caesar as Venus' own son (46-50), here identified with that of the comet — Horace's *Iulium sidus* (*Carm.* I. xii. 47) — which appeared just after his death in 44 B.C.

Similarly the *Georgics*, whose theme is precisely man's environmental relationship to earth's fertility of beasts and plants, open with an invocation (G. I. 24-42) to Gaius Julius Caesar

Octavianus as Venus' own son, whose divinity is therefore able not only to increase earth-fertility and influence the farmer's seasonal round (24-28) but also to facilitate their transmutation into terms of poetry (40-42); this personal appeal being later followed by a detailed account of Saturn's Golden Age (125-146) in close connection with 'the glory of the divine countryside' of Virgil's Italy (168).

This same first book of the *Georgics* likewise ends with references both to the death and to the comet of Julius Caesar (466-488), followed by another invocation which concatenates, on behalf of the young Octavian as Julius Caesar's heir to Rome's Troy-inherited troubles, not only those *di patrii* among whom the *Aeneid* (II. 702, 717) will include Troy's own *Penates*, together with those *Indigetes* among whom the *Aeneid* (XII. 786, 794) will include Aeneas himself as Venus' sky-claimed son, but also both the Vestally-mothered Romulus and Vesta herself as mothering the Etruscan Tiber and the Roman Palatine — this fourfold entreaty then changing suddenly into a prayer to Octavian as a sky-claimed divinity able to restore to the Italian countryside its pristine fertility and peace (G. I. 498-508).

The second book of the *Georgics*, after including amongst 'Italy's glories' (G. II. 138) its 'eternal springtime' of seasonal earth-fertility (149-150), goes on to link the victories of Octavian as a Julius Caesar (170-172; cf. 163) both with those 'Roman hills' (*Romanis arcibus:* 172) which the *Aeneid* will give to Iulus (*Ascanione pater Romanas invidet arces?:* A. IV. 234) and with that 'land of Saturn (*Saturnia tellus*), great mother of earth's fertility, great mother of men' (G. II. 173-174) whose 'kingdom of Italy and land of Rome' the *Aeneid* will promise to Iulus too (*Iuli . . . cui regnum Italiae Romanaque tellus debentur:* A. IV. 274-276). Then Virgil, having elaborately likened the Italian rural springtime to that of the infant world during the Golden Age, with Mother Earth fertilized by Father Sky (G. II. 323-345), significantly makes his first explicit reference to the Julian myth, as adopted by the Sibylline Oracles, in calling the tillers of Italian soil 'a race sent from Troy' (*Ausonii, Troia gens missa, coloni:* 385); this adumbration of the *Aeneid*'s central theme being no less significantly followed, first by mentally visual reminiscences of Virgil's own boyhood spent beyond the Mincius-receiving river Padus (451-453) — 'O happy husbandmen! too happy, should they come to know their blessings! for whom, far from the clash of arms, most righteous Earth unbidden pours forth from her soil an easy sustenance (458-460) . . . Theirs is repose without care, and a life that knows not guile, being rich in treasures manifold. Yea, the ease of broad farmlands, caverns, and living lakes, and cool vales, the lowing of the kine, and soft slumbers beneath the trees — all are theirs. They have woodland glades and the haunts of game; a youth hardened to toil and inured to scanty fare; worship of gods and reverence for age; among them Justice, as she quitted the earth' (with Saturn's departing Golden Age; cf. *iam redit et Virgo, redeunt Saturnia regna:* E. IV. 6) 'planted her latest foot-steps' (467-474) — and then by a comparison of this idyllic country-life of Virgil's childhood both with that of the child-hood of Virgil's race and with that of Saturn's Golden Age:

'Such a life the old Sabines lived long ago, such Remus and his brother (Romulus). Thus, surely, Etruria waxed strong, thus Rome became of all things the most beautiful and with a single city's wall enclosed her seven hills. Nay, before (Jupiter) the Dictaean King held sceptre, and before a godless (Iron) race banqueted on slaughtered bullocks, such was the life Golden Saturn lived on earth' (532-538).

With such an ending to the *Georgics*' second book, so clearly reminiscent of the fourth *Eclogue*, it is no surprise to find the *Georgics*' third book beginning with a yet more definite adum-bration of the *Aeneid*'s central theme under that figure of Virgil's promised *templum de marmore* (G. III. 13) which itself foreshadows Aeneas' promised *de marmore templum* (A. VI. 69); since Aeneas will there be vowing to build, in his ancestrally native Italy (cf. A. III. 94-98), that 'temple in marble' to Apollo for his Sibylline Books (A. VI. 69-74) which in its turn foreshadows the Palatine temple in Carrara marble (Servius on A. VIII. 720) vowed to Apollo and built for his Sibylline Books (Suetonius, *Augustus* 31) beside the Tiber at his child-hood's native Rome by that same 'Caesar' (G. III. 16) to whom Virgil here vows to build his own 'temple in marble' beside the Mincius at his childhood's native Mantua — this implied parallel, between the Tiber and the Mincius, further fore-shadowing the *Aeneid*'s own juxtaposition of the two rivers in an ancestrally Mantuan context of oracular prophesy (A. X. 198-206).

For Mantua, whose name to its Etruscan citizens meant 'belonging to Mantus', the Etruscan Underworld deity (Servius on A. X. 199), to Virgil the Hellenist meant 'belonging to prophetic Manto' (*fatidicae Mantus:* A. X. 199); the Greek Manto being Apollo's oracular prophetess at Delphi. Hence Virgil, whose repeated emphasis upon Mantua's Etruscan origin suggests his awareness of its Etruscan god Mantus, will have associated his native Mantua with precisely that twofold idea — of the Underworld and of Apollo's own oracular prophetess — which the *Aeneid* attributes to Cumae with its Sibylline Books, themselves by Suetonius (*Aug.* 31) called *fatidici libri.*

Nor must it be forgotten how the *Aeneid* closely couples Aeneas' Cumaean vow (A. VI. 69-74) with his reference to the leaves (*'foliis tantum ne carmina manda':* 74) upon which the prophetic Sibyl wrote her oracles (*'fata canit foliisque notas et nomina mandat':* A. III. 444); and how on July 6th, 83 B.C., thirteen years before Virgil's birth, the old Sibylline Books finally perished in the fire which gutted Jupiter's Capitoline temple at Rome — their substitutes, newly manufactured in the East from old materials, and so reflecting that originally Hellenistic fusion of the Graeco-Roman poetic imagery of a Saturnian Golden Age with the Palestinian-Jewish prophetic imagery of a Messianic Paradise Regained which characterizes Virgil's fourth *Eclogue*, being written upon palm-leaves (Varro, *ap.* Lactant. *divin. instit.* I. 6), a primitive custom mentioned as such by Pliny (*Nat. Hist.* XIII. xi. 21, sect. 69).

Now the Palestinian (Virgil's 'Idumaean') palm, which then shared with the Mediterranean laurel its symbolism of victory throughout the Graeco-Roman world, was for every Jew throughout that world — including the many Jews of Virgil's Rome — a symbol of victory as won by obedience to that Palestinian oracular-palm prophetess Deborah (*Book of Judges*, IV. 4-V. 31) whose name, meaning in Hebrew 'Bee', belonged also under its Greek equivalent Melissa ('Bee') to Mantua's Virgilian eponym Manto, the seer Teiresias' daughter otherwise called Daphne, 'Laurel' (τῆς Τειρεσίου θυγατρὸς Δάφνης: Diodorus Siculus, IV. lxvi. 5); the specific designation 'Bee', given also to the divinely inspired priestesses of the fertility-goddesses Demeter, Persephone and the 'Great Mother' Rhea-Cybele, being the generic title of Apollo's oracular-laurel prophetess at Delphi (μελίσσας Δελφίδος: Pindar, *Pyth.* IV. 60=103); while the bee itself was a symbol not only of underworld-cult, of soothsaying divination, of poetic faculty, and of childhood's nourishment, but also of that naturally flowing honey which in connection with the leaves of trees meant to the Graeco-Roman mind the Saturnian Golden Age as remembered by the Sibylline Books (*et durae quercus sudabunt roscida mella:* E. IV. 30; cf. *mellaque decussit foliis:* G. I. 131) and which in connection with the date-palm meant to the Palestinian-Jewish mind, as influencing the new Sibylline Books, both the Mosaic Promised Land and the Messianic Paradise Regained (G. Robert-Tornow, *De apium mellisque apud veteres significatione et symbolica et mythologica*, Berlin 1893, pp. 74-150, 172-175) — a complex of mental associations verbally simplified into the one characteristically pregnant Virgilian line: 'I first will bring back to thee, Mantua, the palms of Palestine' (*primus Idumaeas referam tibi, Mantua, palmas:* G. III. 12).

Since, moreover, the old Sibylline Books themselves symbolized victory as won through obedience to their prophetic oracles, and since the new Sibylline Books not only inherited that ancestral symbolism but were written upon victory-symbolizing palm-leaves whose Graeco-Roman oracles conveyed a partly Palestinian-Jewish imagery, Virgil's declared ambition to signalize his own poetic victories (G. III. 8-12) by bringing back the palms of Palestine to his own native Mantua, and there triumphantly to build a temple symbolizing his own poetic celebration of the far-flung Trojan-Julian martial victories (13-48), must surely now be re-interpreted in the light of that fourth *Eclogue* whose style and material were both modelled upon those of the new Sibylline Books (Professor R. G. Austin, 'Virgil and the Sibyl', *Classical Quarterly*, XXI. 1927, pp. 100-105) with all their Levantine-Hellenistic and Palestinian-Jewish implications (Professor W. Y. Sellar, *Virgil*, Ed. 3, Oxford 1908, pp. 144-148; Mr. W. F. Jackson Knight, *Roman Vergil*, London 1944, pp. 184, 188).

Virgil, that is to say, while consciously remembering Zeus' marble temple built in the sixth-fifth centuries B.C. beside the river Alpheus (G. III. 19) at Olympia, whose victory-laurels were sometimes replaced by palms (*Olympiacae . . . palmae:* G. III. 49), at the same time subconsciously projects himself as building beside his native Mantuan river Mincius a 'marble temple' under whose statue of Apollo's reputed, and Julius Caesar's adopted, son Octavian he will deposit his own poetically symbolic counterpart of those new Palestinian-palm leaf-written and victory-betokening Sibylline Books for whose custody and interpretation under Apollo's statue this same Octavian has already, in 36 B.C., vowed to build beside his native Roman river Tiber his own Palatine 'marble temple', begun most probably in 31 B.C. and dedicated on October 9th, 28 B.C. in the presence of Augustus 'himself, seated at the snowy threshold of shining Phoebus' (A. VIII. 720).

So it is that eventually, but with legendary Trojan-Iulean origins substituted in place of contemporary Roman-Julian victories as its central theme, the *Aeneid*'s symbolism, evolved from that of the *Eclogues* and *Georgics* as fusing the poet's childhood with his people's, will verbally communicate Virgil's synthesis of Mediterranean traditions which, for centuries converging from all sides upon Italy and there cumulatively focused on the Sibylline books, linked Rome's own traditions of her early Latin, Sabine and Etruscan past, under the figure of Saturn's first Italian Golden Age, not with those only of its Cretan, Trojan and Greek counterpart, but with those also of that comparatively recent victory over Carthage which meant for her the prospect of an empire coinciding with the Mediterranean world but centring, under the figure of Saturn's second Golden Age, in an Italian world now Roman-Julian because once Trojan-Iulean.

The *Aeneid*'s symbolism is therefore largely based upon that of the two Roman hills which successively accommodated both the custody and the interpretation of the Sibylline Books — the Capitoline and the Palatine, facing each other across the Roman Forum.

On the Capitoline hill, shown to Aeneas by Evander (VIII. 347-354) and represented by Vulcan for Venus on Aeneas' shield (VIII. 652-653), will one day stand not only the cult-centres of Jupiter (with the old Sibylline Books therein) and his wife Juno, of their daughter Venus and (on the lower Capitoline ledge) her husband Vulcan, but also that 'House of Aeneas' (*domus Aeneae*) which shall be the Trojan-Roman people under its Iulean-Julian dynasty (IX. 448-449; cf. III. 97-98), together with that 'Palace' (*regia*) of Romulus which shall resemble both its own Palatine twin and the first 'House of

Vesta' (*aedes Vestae*) in being but a primitive thatched hut (VIII. 652-654).

On the corresponding Palatine hill, which is Evander's Pallanteum as visited by Aeneas (IX. 9), will stand not only the cult-centres of Cybele (adjoining Romulus' other hut) and (on the lower Palatine ledge) her eldest daughter Vesta, of Victory (XII. 187) and (VIII. 720) Apollo (with the new Sibylline Books therein: cf. VI. 69-74) but also that 'House of Augustus' (*aedes Augusti*) with its private Vestal shrine (cf. VIII. 678-681) whose occupation by Augustus in 29 B.C. (Sueton. *Aug.* 72) is foreshadowed in Evander's occupation of his 'Palace' (*regia*) with its private Vestal shrine (VIII. 363, 543) as Aeneas' host upon the same northern Palatine site (W. Warde Fowler, *Aeneas at the Site of Rome*, Oxford 1918, pp. 72-78).

Now Virgil, who already in the *Georgics* had coupled the Golden Age of Cybele's husband Saturn (G. II. 536-540) with Romulus' building of a wall enclosing all Rome's seven hills (*septemque una sibi muro circumdedit arces:* 535), now in the *Aeneid* not only makes Anchises' spirit in the Underworld conjoin an adaptation of this latter line (*septemque una sibi muro circumdabit arces:* A. VI. 783) both with the wall-symbolizing crown of Saturn's wife Cybele (784-787) and with the Iulean-Julian dynasty of the Trojan-Roman people as integrating under Augustus a revival in the heart of Italy of Saturn's Golden Age (788-794) with the expansion of a Mediterranean empire into the heart of Africa and Asia (794-807) but also, most significantly, makes him do so precisely when prophesying in the very presence of the Sibyl herself (*unaque Sibyllam:* 752; cf. 897) as Aeneas' guide into the Underworld.

Thus, since in fact Anchises here prophesies as the Underworld-mouthpiece of those same 'oracles of the gods' (*responsis . . . divom:* VI. 799) whose Cumaean mouthpiece is the Sibyl (*responsa Sibyllae:* VI. 44), his forecast both of Aeneas' Trojan-Roman destiny as Romulus' lineal ancestor (VI. 752-789) and of Augustus' Iulean-Julian destiny as Romulus' lineal descendant (789-805), with the one 'blood of Assaracus' (*Assaraci . . . sanguinis:* 778; cf. *Assaraci proles:* G. III. 35) linking all three together, must in part at least be quoted as profoundly relevant to any analysis of the *Aeneid*'s symbolism:

'"Lo! under Romulus' auspices, Aeneas my son, that glorious Rome shall bound her empire by earth, her pride by heaven, and with a single city's wall shall enclose her seven hills, blest in her brood of heroes: even as (Cybele) the Berecynthian Mother, turret-crowned, drives in her chariot through the Phrygian cities, glad in her offspring of gods, and clasping a hundred of her children's children, all denizens of heaven, all tenants of the heights above. Hither now turn thy two eyes: behold this people, thine own Romans. Here is Caesar and all Iulus' seed, destined to pass beneath the sky's mighty vault" (i.e. to be born on earth, in the upper world of living men). "This hero, this is he whom thou so oft hearest promised to thee, Augustus Caesar, son of a god" (i.e. of Julius Caesar, appointed priest of Capitoline Jupiter four years before the destruction of the old Sibylline Books, and deified after his death), "who shall again set up the Golden Age in Latium amid the fields where Saturn once reigned, and shall spread his empire past Garamant and Indian, to a land that lies beyond the stars, beyond the paths of the year and the sun, where sky-bearing Atlas turns on his shoulders the sphere, inset with gleaming stars. Against Augustus' coming even now the Caspian realms and Maeotian land shudder at the oracles of the gods" (i.e. at the Sibylline oracles, as prophesying from Jupiter's Capitoline temple the victories of his priest Julius Caesar and from Apollo's Palatine temple those of his reputed son Augustus), "and the mouths of sevenfold Nile are in tumult of terror. Nor, in truth, did (Hercules) Alcaeus' grandson range over such space of earth"' (VI. 781-801).

Now clearly, if the battlemented crown of Cybele here symbolizes the battlemented wall of Rome as built by Romulus, not only does the crowned image of Cybele symbolize the walled city of Rome, but Cybele herself actually symbolizes Rome. Each is a Mother; but, whereas Cybele's children are divine absolutely, as being the very gods of heaven, Rome's children are divine relatively, as being god-descended heroes, those 'sons of Romulus' (*Romulidis:* VIII. 638) who by descent are also 'sons of Aeneas' (*Aeneadae:* VIII. 648) as 'source of the Roman stock' (*Aeneas, Romanae stirpis origo:* XII. 166), himself both divinely descended (*genus ab Jove summo:* I. 380; *genus esse deorum:* IV. 12; *sate gente deorum:* VIII. 36; *deum gens, Aenea:* X. 228-229) and representing a divinely descended race (*gente deorum:* XI. 305).

In other words, Virgil here correlates both the motherhood

of Venus, Cybele's grand-daughter as worshipped on the Capitoline-Sibylline hill, and the motherhood of Cybele, Venus' grandmother as worshipped on the Palatine-Sibylline hill, with the motherhood of Rome herself as walled by Aeneas' descendant and Augustus' ancestor Romulus.

But he begins his genealogies with yet another motherhood—that of *Ilia mater* (VI. 778), who is not only Romulus' own mother by Mars (777-780) but also the sacerdotal representative of that *Vesta mater* (G. I. 498) whose motherhood is associated in the *Georgics* with the names explicitly of Romulus and Caesar (Augustus), and implicitly of Aeneas, in a Trojan-Roman context (G. I. 498-504); while Romulus, whose wall defends Rome's motherhood as symbolized by the threefold motherhood of Cybele and Venus and Vesta, resembles Augustus reputedly and Aeneas actually as being himself of divine-and-human parentage.

Hence Mars and Ilia are to Romulus and the Alban Mount what Venus and Anchises are to Aeneas and Mount Ida — Mars, moreover, as the Greek Ares, being Homerically mated with Venus' Greek counterpart Aphrodite, wife of Hephaistos, Virgil's Vulcan; while Ilia is herself descended from Venus' husband Anchises who, during Aeneas' flight with Iulus from Troy, carried to the foothills of Mount Ida those hallows of Vesta which Cybele's ship thence carried under Venus' guardianship to Italy for their eventual custody on the Alban Mount by Ilia, 'the Maid of Troy', as being both Venus' descendant and priestess of Cybele's first-born child Vesta.

For Virgil, who owes so much to Hesiod, cannot have overlooked the Hesiodic statement (*Theogony*, 453-454) that Hestia, Vesta's Greek equivalent as personifying the blazing hearth, was Rheia's first-born by Kronos; nor yet the Hesiodic description (*Works and Days* 109-120) of that Golden Age of Kronos, husband of Rheia, whence Latin imitators derived their own Italian Golden Age of Saturn, cult-partner of Ops. Ovid, indeed, merely follows the literary convention already established in Virgil's lifetime when (*Fasti* VI. 285, 384) he gives to Saturn and Ops, as Hesiod to Rheia and Kronos, three daughters — Vesta, Ceres, and Juno; the Hesiodic Hestia, Demeter, and Hera.

Since, therefore, Virgil further followed Greek mythology in identifying Rheia (or Rhea), as worshipped on Mount Ida in

Crete, with Cybele as worshipped on Mount Ida in the Troad, and since he puts this Cretan-Troadic Rheia-Cybele Idaean-Mother identification precisely into the prophetic mouth of that same Anchises (III. 104-113) who later elaborately compares Rome's wall with Cybele's crown (VI. 781-787), it follows that Virgil's Vesta — however purely Roman her symbolism both in the *Georgics* and in the *Aeneid* — will, genealogically regarded, have been the first-born of Cybele as worshipped on Vesta's own Palatine hill above Vesta's own Tiber river at Rome (*Vestaque mater, quae Tuscum Tiberim et Romana Palatia servas:* G. I. 498-499); under whose wall, as the architectural counterpart of Cybele's crown, the confluence of the Tiber with the Almo accommodated that same purely Phrygian rite of the Idaean Mother's *lavatio* which Virgil implicitly includes under the Phrygian rite of Cybele's drive in a chariot through Phrygian cities precisely when in a Romulean-Vestal context comparing Rome's wall with Cybele's crown.

This implication is indeed necessitated by the fact that the ritual custom of drawing Cybele's image in a vehicle through her city, and of strewing her path with springtime flowers, invariably — whether in Phrygia or elsewhere — involved as its grand climax, or rather as the very reason for her drive, the *lavatio* of her cult-image in running water, fresh or salt; whence the procession of drum-beating and flute-playing *galli* escorted her back again, now refreshed by her bath and by her flowers as symbolizing Mother Earth's renewed fertility from the showers of spring, to the temple where she reigned both as the guardian of her city and as the mother of its gods.

Now, at Virgil's Rome this springtide renewal on April 4th of the murally defensive symbolism of Cybele's crown was preceded by the springtide renewal on March 1st of the domestically defensive symbolism of Vesta's house (*aedes Vestae*); the yearly rekindling of whose hearth-fire, together with the hanging of fresh laurels, was thus the purely Roman counterpart of the yearly Phrygian rebathing of Cybele's meteorite-stone together with the throwing of fresh blossoms — both rites being alike directed towards renewing the vitality of a divine Mother whose guardianship, derived from that of Mother Earth herself, was believed to strengthen Rome against attack.

For Vesta's house, circularly encompassing the hearth-fire which was really Vesta herself, no less than Cybele's crown circularly encompassing the meteorite-stone which was really Cybele herself, was in Virgil's day regarded as symbolizing Venus' Rome, itself potentially coinciding with Earth (VI. 781-787); so that the springtide fire-and-laurel reinvigoration of Vesta's divine hearth within the ritually defensive round wall of her Rome-symbolizing house, no less than the springtide water-and-blossom reinvigoration of Cybele's divine meteorite within the ritually defensive round wall of her Rome-symbolizing crown, meant both for Virgil and for his readers the springtide blood-and-spirit reinvigoration of Venus' divine race within the wall of an Earth-equivalent Rome.

Thus Virgil in the *Aeneid* envisages a Rome whose divine motherhood, thrice personified by implication in that of Venus and Cybele and Vesta, will under the divine fatherhood of the Julian dynasty (*pater Romanus:* IX. 449) become identical with that of Earth herself; so that in Earth's refertilization by the Venus-descended and Vesta-worshipping Julian Caesar Augustus (VI. 792-794) shall be renewed that Golden Age of Cybele's own fertilizer Saturn (VIII. 319-325) which in the *Georgics* Virgil has correlated with Romulus' building of Rome's wall (G. II. 532-540) in terms significantly repeated when in the *Aeneid* comparing Romulus' wall with Cybele's crown (A. VI. 783-785).

Such a renewal of the fertility of Earth's divine motherhood, as is here symbolized under the Julian revival of Earth's Golden Age, therefore precisely corresponds to the renewal of the fertility of Rome's divine motherhood (VI. 784) as personified by Mother Venus and Mother Cybele and Mother Vesta, whose cults are renewed under Augustus as a Caesar who is Trojan because a Julius descended from Iulus (I. 257-296).

This fivefold renewal of a fivefold divine motherhood is, in fact, ritual throughout; but, being ritual, it is also mythical, since myth is the verbal equivalent of rite.[1]

Nor is it merely accidental that Virgil's younger contemporary Ovid, when describing Cybele's Roman rite in terms of Roman myth, both of them resulting from Roman interpretation of the Sibylline Books, correlates Cybele's ritual

[1] See S. H. Hooke, *Myth and Ritual* (Oxford, 1933), p. 3.

myth not only with Virgil's own version of the Sibylline Aeneas-legend (*Fasti*, IV. 248-276) but also with the cult of Venus (195, 286), the cult of Vesta (291-344), the fertility of Cybele as Mother (202, 319, 359), the identity of Cybele both with Ops as Saturn's wife and with Rhea as Kronos' wife (195-214), the fertility of Earth as connected with the cult of Cybele (249-250, 335-336, 346, 353-354, 367-372), the fertility of Earth as connected with the cult of Venus (195-196), the fertility of Earth as connected with the cult of Vesta (299-300), the sympathy of Earth with Cybele (267-268), the sympathy of Cybele with Rome (247-272), the cult of Cybele as renewed by Augustus in connection with the Almo-rite below the walls of Rome (345-348), Cybele's ritually mural-turreted crown as symbolizing her defence of city-walls (219-221), and Cybele's mythically lion-drawn chariot as symbolizing her victory over wild beasts (215-218); and with the Troadic Mount Ida, corresponding to the Cretan Mount Ida, as cult-centre of that Earth-Mother Cybele whose cult-title at Rome is *Idaea* (182, 207, 249, 264)—a complex of ideas neither Ovidian nor yet Virgilian in its origin, but traceable back to Roman interpretation of the Sibylline Books during the Second Punic War.

Hence it is precisely during Aeneas' visit to Carthage, Juno's claimant to Rome's potential Earth-equivalence (I. 12-22), that Venus claims from Jupiter — whose temple held the old Sibylline Books at Rome — that Roman Earth-equivalence (I. 234-237) which Jupiter prophesies as due to the 'House of Assaracus' (I. 278-285): ' "From this noble line shall be born the Trojan Caesar, who shall limit his empire with ocean, his glory with the stars, a Julius, name descended from the great Iulus" ' (286-288); himself the future builder of the walls of Romulus' birthplace Alba Longa from Aeneas' Lavinium (257-274).

CHAPTER III

TROY AND ROME

nec te Troia capit (*Aeneid* IX. 644)

THE word *ida* (ἴδη), in some early Mediterranean language once common both to the Troad and to Crete, originally meant a 'forest' or 'wood'[1]; being thus equivalent to the Latin *silva*.

Homer, indeed, repeatedly emphasizes the thickly forested or wooded character of the Troadic Mount Ida; while Virgil similarly emphasizes the *silvae* which prehistorically covered both the Alban and the Roman hills (VI. 765; VII. 659; VIII. 314-318, 342-352) as well as the site of Bovillae (IX. 381-393), from whose Alban *silva* is derived the name Silvia (VII. 487, 503) given to the daughter of Latinus' herdsman.

It would further appear that the early Latin kings (*Albani . . . reges:* XII. 826) who ruled over the wooded Alban hills with their Bovillan purlieus were for that very reason named the Silvii or 'Woodlanders' (Livy I. iii. 8); for Anchises in Elysium points out prophetically to Aeneas the figure of '"Silvius, an Alban name, thy last-born child, whom late in thy old age thy wife Lavinia shall bring up in the woods (*silvis*), a king and father of kings; from him shall our race have sway in Alba Longa"' (VI. 763-766). From this Aeneas-descended Alban king Silvius, moreover, shall eventually spring '"Silvius Aeneas, he who shall renew thy name, like thee peerless in piety or ever he win the Alban throne"' (768-770).

Similarly, the traditional name of the Trojan Vesta's Alban priestess, whom Virgil calls Ilia, 'the Maid of Troy', throughout the *Aeneid*, was Rea Silvia (Livy I. iii. 11); descended doubtless both from Silvius, Aeneas' son by Latinus' daughter Lavinia, and from Iulus, Aeneas' son by Priam's daughter Creusa, through later intermarriage between the Iulean and the Silvian royal families of Alba Longa (cf. *regina sacerdos . . . Ilia:* I. 273-274). Linguistically, therefore, since *Rea* and *silva* are the Latin equivalents respectively of *Rhea* and *ida*, the name *Rea Silvia* is the Latin equivalent of *Rhea Idaea*; so that, since Virgil himself by implication identifies Rhea with

[1] See A. B. Cook, *Zeus*, II. ii (Cambridge, 1925), p. 932.

Cybele on the ground that Rhea's cult on the Cretan Ida originated Cybele's cult on the Troadic Ida (III. 104-113), the Iulean-Silvian Alban priestess of Troy's own Vesta traditionally bore, as Romulus' mother by Mars, the very name of Cybele herself as later worshipped at Rome under the cult-title of *Idaea*.

Virgil's own recognition of this linguistic equivalence is in fact clearly suggested by his unique application of the name Rhea to another *sacerdos* who dwelt in another *silva*, not on an Alban but on a Roman hill, the Aventine; her divine lover being not Mars but Hercules, whose son by her is Aventinus, eponym of the same wooded hill: 'Him, in the wood of the Aventine hill, Rhea the priestess brought forth into the borders of light in secret birth, a woman mated with a god' —

> *collis Aventini silva quem Rhea sacerdos*
> *furtivum partu sub luminis edidit oras,*
> *mixta deo mulier* (VII. 659-661).

Now tradition told of an early King of Alba Longa named Aventinus, who was buried on the Aventine hill at Rome (Livy I. iii. 9); while modern research has found that the early cities of the Latin League (cf. *urbes Albanae ... Roma:* A. VII. 601-603) regarded the Alban Mount (cf. *qui nunc Albanus habetur; tum neque nomen erat neque honos aut gloria monti:* XII. 134-135) and the Aventine Mount at Rome (*Aventini montem:* VIII. 231) as the twin cult-centres of their political union.

Vulcan's fire-belching son Cacus, moreover, whom Virgil describes as slain by Aventinus' father Hercules, dwelt in a cave on the Roman Aventine (VIII. 190-267); and the early Virgilian commentator Servius records a tradition, known from other sources (Lactantius, *Divin. Instit.* I. 20), that this Aventine Cacus had a sister Caca who, having betrayed her brother to Hercules, was for that reason henceforth worshipped at Rome in a chapel where she received sacrifice like Vesta and had like Vesta a perpetually-burning fire — Cacus, in fact, being the Vulcan, and Caca being the Vesta, of Rome's earliest citizens (Frazer, *The Fasti of Ovid*, London 1929, Vol. II, pp. 207-208).

Thus Virgil's *Rhea sacerdos* on the wooded Aventine hill, corresponding to Livy's *Rea Silvia* who on the wooded Alban hill was priestess of Caca's counterpart Vesta, will by implication have been the prehistoric Roman priestess of Vesta's counterpart Caca; the two together traditionally representing the domestic aspect of the one Alban-Aventine cult which ritually united all the thirty cities of the Latin League.

Although the name 'Rea', traditionally given to Romulus' Alban mother Silvia, may perhaps originally have meant the 'guilty' (*rea*) Vestal Virgin who broke her vow of chastity by yielding to Mars, the more usual spelling 'Rhea' was unquestionably influenced, probably through the interpreters of the Sibylline oracles, by the name of Rhea-Cybele; and it is surely significant that Ovid, who perpetuates so many old traditions, associates Cybele's arrival at Rome both with a procession of Vestal Virgins and with her own miraculous acquittal of Claudia Quinta on a similar charge of unchastity (*Fasti* IV. 296-344).

In any case, the name 'Ilia', given explicitly by Virgil to the Alban *sacerdos* of the Trojan Vesta (I. 273-274; VI. 777-779), and the name 'Rhea', given implicitly by Virgil to the Aventine *sacerdos* of the Roman Caca (VII. 659-661), together reflect precisely that Sibylline appropriation both of the Aeneas-legend and of the Idaean Mother's worship which involved for Virgil's mind an imaginative coalescence between the cult of an Aventine-Alban Caca-Vesta and that of a Cretan-Troadic Rhea-Cybele. Virgil, in other words, recalling the Cretan-Troadic Rhea-Cybele's arrival at Rome under that cult-title of *Idaea* whose Latin equivalent he took to be *Silvia*, and imaginatively fusing it both with Hercules' arrival at the wooded Aventine Mount for union with the Roman Caca's priestess and with Mars' arrival at the wooded Alban Mount for union with the Trojan Vesta's priestess, characteristically transferred from the *sacerdos* in the Alban *silva* to the *sacerdos* in the Roman *silva* that name of 'Rhea' which, belonging properly to Cybele as *Idaea*, was borrowed later by Rea as *Silvia*.

Hence the Virgilian phrase *Idaea silva*, 'the wood of Ida' (II. 696), is of prime importance for analysing the largely unconscious processes of Virgil's mind at work upon the *Aeneid*; since the phrase will have carried, for his poetic imagination, all the mentally fused associations both of the Alban-Roman Vesta and of the Cretan-Troadic Cybele. Its context, in particular, will repay study.

Aeneas, remembering Hector's injunction to carry the

Trojan Vesta oversea and there to build walls for her Penates (II. 293-297), hastens homewards from his fruitless attempt to save burning Troy from the victorious Greeks, in order that he may at least save his own household, Anchises, Creusa and Iulus, together with their Vestal *sacra* as henceforth representing those of Troy itself.

His main purpose is to carry his now decrepit father into 'the high hills' (II. 634-636) of Mount Ida (801; cf. III. 6), as being the site not only of Anchises' early home but also of his union with Venus for the begetting of Aeneas himself — a union whose rashly boasted privilege incurred the blasting of Anchises' body by the lightning-bolt of Idaean Jupiter (II. 647-649).

Despite all Aeneas' appeals, however, Anchises prefers immediate death in his present Trojan house to prolongation of life in his early Idaean home; nor is he moved by supplementary appeals from Creusa, Iulus, and the rest of his household (637-654). Whereupon Aeneas, appealing from his Idaean father Anchises to his Idaean mother Venus, is on the point of again rushing forth into the doomed city (655-672) when Creusa reminds him of his first duty, the guardianship of their house ('*hanc primum tutare domum*': 677), by lifting up little Iulus — as the future founder and eponym of the Alban-Roman Julian house — to his father Aeneas, and imploring him not to abandon his son, his father, and his wife (673-678): 'So crying, she began to fill all the house with moaning; when on a sudden arises a portent, wondrous to tell. For, between the hands and faces of his sad parents, lo! from above Iulus' head a light tongue of flame seemed to shed a gleam and, harmless in its touch, to lick his soft locks and pasture round his temples. Trembling with alarm, we hastily shake out the blazing hair and quench with water the holy fires. But my father Anchises joyously raises his eyes to the stars and uplifts to heaven both hands and voice: "Almighty Jupiter, if by any prayers thou art moved, look upon us — this only do I ask — and, if our goodness earn it, grant thereon a sign, O Father, and ratify this omen."

'Scarcely had the aged man thus spoken when, with a sudden crash, it thundered on the left' (i.e. as a sign of Jupiter's favour) 'and a star shot from heaven, gliding through the shadows, and drawing a fiery trail amid a flood of light. We watch it glide over the topmost roofs of the house and then bury its brightness in the wood of Ida as it thus marked out the ways —

> *cernimus Idaea claram se condere silva*
> *signantemque vias* (696-697);

then the long-drawn furrow affords light, and all about reeks far and wide with sulphur. On this, indeed, my father is vanquished and, rising erect, salutes the gods and worships the holy star (*sanctum sidus*): "Now, now there is no delay; I follow and, where ye lead, there am I. O gods ancestral" (*di patrii*, including Troy's Vestal Penates), "save my house, save my grandson (*servate domum, servate nepotem*)! Yours is this omen, and under your divine protection Troy yet lives. Yea, I yield; and I refuse not, my son, to accompany thee" ' (679-704).

The symbolism of this episode is clear enough.

Jupiter, the Idaean Father (VII. 139), whose Idaean Mother is Cybele (VII. 139) and whose daughter Venus is Anchises' Idaean wife (II. 648-649), desires the fulfilment of Iulus' destiny as founder both of Rome's mother-city Alba Longa for the Penates of Troy's Vesta, Cybele's first-born, and of that Alban-Roman Julian house whose Trojan counterpart is Anchises' house — a fulfilment which depends upon the immediate rescue of Venus' grandson Iulus from the flames of Troy to the foothills of Mount Ida, together with Anchises as the *paterfamilias* now in charge of the Trojan Vesta's Penates and her perpetually burning fire (II. 289-297).

But Anchises, the human Idaean father, whose prophetic powers are emphasized throughout the *Aeneid* with particular reference to his grandson Iulus' destiny, obstructs the will of the divine Idaean Father, Jupiter, on the ground that, since Iulus' destiny results from his own intercourse with Venus on Mount Ida, the avenging fire of his divine counterpart has long since blasted not only Iulus' Idaean grandfather but also Iulus' Alban-Roman Julian destiny — a twofold punishment, of the innocent with the guilty, for which Anchises bitterly blames himself as both 'hated of heaven and useless' (II. 647).

Then, quite unexpectedly, his despairing regret for the past is turned into joyful hope for the future, as represented by the young Iulus; for the fire of Idaean Jupiter, no longer punitive but caressing, begins to play about Iulus' head — a sign that the guilty grandfather has all these years been wholly mistaken, as he will later be mistaken on a point of ancestral genealogy in Crete (III. 180-181), when supposing that the fiery blasting of his own body meant the blasting also of his innocent grandson's prospects as revealed by Venus.

This sign, whose meaning is at once clear to Anchises, requires only its ratification in another form to remove his lingering doubts; and the *sanctum sidus* — both recalling Horace's *Iulium sidus* (C. I. xii. 47) and anticipating Virgil's *patrium* . . . *sidus* (A. VIII. 681) — which descends from Jupiter over Anchises' house, only to descend thence into the *Idaea silva*, thus 'marking out the ways' and 'affording light', is immediately interpreted by Anchises' prophetic mind as illuminatively symbolizing the path of Iulus' destiny — not only in Iulus' own descent from Jupiter through Venus, the divine *materfamilias* of Anchises' house, but also in the descent through Iulus from Anchises' house of Rea *Silvia* as Virgil's Ilia, the counterpart of Rhea *Idaea* as Virgil's Cybele, and mother of Rome's founder as priestess in the Alban *silva* of that same Trojan Vesta whose Penates are now, precisely in consequence of the illuminating *sanctum sidus* which buried itself in the *Idaea silva*, to be carried by Aeneas on Anchises' lap to the foot of 'Phrygian Ida's hills' (III. 6) for transportation oversea 'with my comrades and son and with the great Penates-gods' —

cum sociis natoque, Penatibus et magnis dis (III. 12).

The typically Virgilian final integration of this twofold Iulean-Julian because Idaean-Silvian symbolism — that of the flame which happily pastured round the temples of Iulus' brow (*flamma . . . circum tempora pasci*) after appearing like a tongue of light from above Iulus' head (*summo de vertice visus Iuli fundere lumen apex:* II. 682-684), and that of the *sanctum sidus* which Anchises couples with the *di patrii* (or *di magni Penates*) when invoking their guardianship both of his Troy-representing house and of Iulus as eponymous founder of the Rome-representing Julian house (*adfaturque deos et sanctum sidus adorat . . . 'di patrii, servate domum, servate nepotem; vestrum hoc augurium, vestroque in numine Troia est':* (II. 700, 702-703) — occurs as central to the symbolism of Aeneas' shield (*in medio:* VIII. 675; cf. *in medio mihi Caesar erit:* G. III. 16), whereon 'Augustus Caesar, leading Italians into battle, with peers and people and with the great Penates-gods, stands on his ship's lofty stern; his joyous temples pour forth a twofold flame, and on his head dawns his father's star' —

> *hinc Augustus agens Italos in proelia Caesar*
> *cum patribus populoque, Penatibus et magnis dis,*
> *stans celsa in puppi, geminas cui tempora flammas*
> *laeta vomunt patriumque aperitur vertice sidus* (VIII. 678-681).

Nor is this all. For the twofold flame of Julius Caesar's star upon his adopted son Augustus' head symbolically corresponds, not only to the twofold sign of Iulus' destiny, but also to that twofold plume on Romulus' head which is interpreted by Anchises to Aeneas in Elysium as symbolizing Mars' fatherhood of Romulus by Ilia: ' "Nay more, a child of Mars shall join his grandsire (Numitor of Alba Longa), even Romulus, whom his mother Ilia shall bear of the blood of Assaracus. Seest thou how the twofold plume stands on his head (*geminae stant vertice cristae*) and how his father by his own token even now marks him out (*signat*) for the upper world?" ' (VI. 777-780)— a prophesy whose Alban-Vestal implications are immediately followed by their Idaean-Cybelene counterpart (781-787) in a Roman-Julian because Trojan-Iulean context (788-794).

Nor is this surprising, in view of the traditions partly followed and partly transfigured by Virgil. Dionysius of Halicarnassus, for example, Virgil's younger contemporary who came to Italy when the *Aeneid* was just being begun, relates how 'Idaeus, Dardanus' son, with part of their company, occupied the mountains which are now called after him "Idaean"; and there he built a temple to the Mother of the Gods (i.e. Idaean Cybele), and instituted mysteries and ceremonies which are observed to this day throughout all Phrygia. And Dardanus built a city named after himself (i.e. Dardania) in the region now called the Troad; the land being given to him by Teucer, the king, after whom the country was anciently called Teucris' (Dion. Halic. I. lxi. 4; translation by Dr. E. Cary in the Loeb Classical Library, London 1937) — a passage followed by an account of Aeneas' descent through Assaracus and Tros from Dardanus, husband of Teucer's daughter Bateia (I. lxii. 1-2); by an account of Aeneas' transportation of Troy's

Penates to Lavinium, whence his son Ascanius (i.e. Iulus) founded Alba Longa (I. lxiii-lxviii); and by an identification of these same Penates, as belonging to Vesta's temple, with the Samothracian 'Great Gods' which Dardanus took with him to the Troad (I. lxix; cf. II. lxvi).

To Virgil, therefore, as to his contemporaries, both the cult of Vesta and the cult of Cybele were traditionally of Troadic origin; the cult of Cybele being attributed to Dardanus' son Idaeus as eponym of Mount Ida in the Troad, and the cult of Vesta to Idaeus' father Dardanus as eponym of Dardania in the Troad. Hence, in the *Aeneid* as reflecting contemporary tradition, Troy's Vestal Penates originally belonged to Dardanus, Iasius' brother (III. 167-168), himself through Tros (G. III. 36) and his son Assaracus (G. III. 35; A. I. 284, VI. 650, 778, IX. 259, 643) the lineal ancestor of Iulus, whom for that reason Virgil calls Venus' own beloved *Dardanium caput* (X. 133); while Dardanus' first Vestal city was Idaean, being founded by him on those same foothills of Mount Ida where Cybele gave to Aeneas, precisely as *Dardanio juveni* (IX. 88) her own Idaean pines to carry Anchises and Iulus with Dardanus' Vestal Penates (III. 1-12) from Dardanus' second Vestal city of Troy (*Troiae Dardanus auctor:* VI. 650), called after him *Dardania* (III. 156), oversea to Italy, Dardanus' native land (III. 147-171).

But Virgil characteristically transfigured these traditions by implying a complementary equivalence between those two similarly wooded heights, in the east the Troadic-Idaean hills of Iulus' ancestor Dardanus and in the west the Alban-Silvian hills of Dardanus' descendant Iulus, whose Cybele-guarded Vestal foundations became the mother-cities respectively of Troy and of Rome.

For, though the symbols of Troy's Troadic-Idaean origins were traditionally those in the main of Cybele's cult as *Rhea Idaea*, while the symbols of Rome's Alban-Silvian origins were traditionally those in the main of Vesta's cult under *Rea Silvia*, Virgil so attributed to Troy the Alban-Silvian symbols of Vesta, and to Rome the Troadic-Idaean symbols of Cybele, as to transfer the Italian cult of Vesta in a legendary context to Troy, precisely as the Phrygian cult of Cybele had been transferred in a historical context to Rome.

This Virgilian transference was in fact facilitated, not only by the oracular influence of the Sibylline Books as the magnetic loadstone of Mediterranean traditions partly historical and partly legendary, but also by the traditional location of Dardanus' own birthplace in Italy, whence he was said to have migrated eastwards 'to the cities of Phrygian Ida and to Thracian Samos, now called Samothrace' (VII. 206-208); and it is significantly Dardanus' own Vestal Penates, as identified with the Samothracian *di magni* or 'Great Gods' (III. 12) who became also 'Phrygian' (III. 148), whose 'sacred images' identify Italy with their 'own proper home' precisely as being Dardanus' birthplace, urging Aeneas to build in Italy those 'great walls' for themselves as 'the great gods' ('*tu moenia magnis magna para*': III. 159-160) which Hector earlier demanded for them oversea ('*his moenia quaere magna pererrato statues quae denique ponto*': II. 294-295).

Nor is it merely accidental that Virgil should bring Dardanus' cult of Vesta under Aeneas precisely to Crete as the Idaean source of Teucer's cult of Cybele (III. 104-178), nor yet that this symbolical coincidence should result precisely from Anchises' prophetic misinterpretation (III. 102-103, 178-188) of Delian Apollo's oracular reply to Aeneas as representing Dardanus' descendants: ' "Ye enduring sons of Dardanus, the land which first bare you from your parent stock shall welcome you back again upon her fruitful breast. Seek out your ancient mother. There the House of Aeneas shall lord it over all lands, even his children's children and they who shall be born of them" ' —

> *Dardanidae duri, quae vos a stirpe parentum*
> *prima tulit tellus, eadem vos ubere laeto*
> *accipiet reduces. antiquam exquirite matrem.*
> *hic domus Aeneae cunctis dominabitur oris,*
> *et nati natorum et qui nascentur ab illis* (III. 94-98).

Thus Virgil explicitly personifies as a Mother that same *tellus* which as *Romana tellus* will belong to the *regnum Italiae* of Iulus (IV. 274-276), himself 'the second hope of mighty Rome' (*magnae spes altera Romae:* XII. 168); this Dardan-Iulean Motherland being here promised to that same *domus Aeneae* which, as representing the Roman people, is later coupled by Virgil with the *pater Romanus* as representing the Iulean-Julian dynasty (IX. 448-449).

The preliminary fulfilment of Apollo's Delian prophecy (III. 94-98), as interpreted by the Cretan prophecy of Dardanus' Vestal Penates (III. 147-171), comes therefore at the point where 'Aeneas and his chief captains and fair Iulus' (VII. 107), precisely as 'Dardanus' sons' (VII. 195) returning to Dardanus' Italian motherland (VII. 205-211; VIII. 36-39, 134-142), at last land upon the Tiber-bank (VII. 25-36) for their first meal upon Italian-Dardan soil (VII. 107-115); whereupon Iulus himself unwittingly identifies for Aeneas the very site (VII. 116-134) where he is to build the archetypal equivalent of his 'great walls' for Dardanus' 'great gods', the Samothracian-Phrygian Penates of Troy, in their 'own proper home': 'Straightway Aeneas cries "Hail, O thou motherland (*tellus*), destined as my due! and hail, O ye Penates, faithful to Troy! Here is our house-and-home (*domus*), this is the land of (Dardanus) our father (*patria*)!" ' —

> *continuo 'salve fatis mihi debita tellus*
> *vosque', ait, 'o fidi Troiae, salvete Penates:*
> *hic domus, haec patria est'* (VII. 120-122).

What follows is of deep significance.

For Aeneas, having thus coupled Dardanus' motherland with Dardanus' cult of Vesta in terms recalling those both of Apollo in Delos (III. 94-98) and of the Penates in Crete (III. 156-168), proceeds to couple the Idaean cults of Cybele and Jupiter with those of Venus and Anchises (*Idaeumque Iovem Phrygiamque ex ordine Matrem invocat, et duplicis caeloque Ereboque parentis:* VII. 139-140); this fourfold invocation being followed by Idaean Jupiter's thunder-and-lightning ratification of Aeneas' decision, resulting from Iulus' jesting cry, to found his first Italian settlement on that very spot (141-145): 'Aeneas himself outlines the groundplan of his walls with a shallow trench, laboriously prepares the site, and with mound and battlements after the fashion of a (Roman) camp encircles his first settlement on the coast' (157-159).

Thus, at long last, in Dardanus' own motherland, 'the sons of Dardanus' are provided with 'those walls' (III. 94, 100) which are 'the due' (VII. 145) no less of Troy's Penates (II. 294; III. 159) than of themselves; walls, moreover, whose typically Roman castrametation (VII. 159) archetypically foreshadows that of the walls of Rome herself (I. 7) as founded from Lavinium-founded Alba Longa.

The name, too, of Aeneas' camp-city — not only founded from Dardanus' Phrygian Troy, and adumbrating the successive Italian foundations of Aeneas' Lavinium, Iulus' Alba Longa and Romulus' Rome, but actually founded, by Virgilian implication (VIII. 36-37), on the very site of what was once Dardanus' own Italian Troy until removed by him to Phrygia — is itself *Troia* (IX. 644; X. 27, 74, 214); a name carrying for Virgil's mind not only all the Troadic-Idaean associations of Dardanus' Phrygian 'Troy-town', but also all the Alban-Silvian associations (VI. 756-770) of Iulus' Sicilian 'Troy-game', whose Cretan-Idaean labyrinthine symbolism belongs both to the Iulean-foundation ritual[1] of Lavinium's daughter-city Alba Longa and to the Julian-revival ritual of Alba Longa's daughter-city Rome (V. 545-602).

For it is precisely when dreaming by night in his newly-founded Italian Troy, on the eve of his first visit to the site of Rome (VIII. 18-65), that Aeneas is welcomed by 'Tiberinus, the very god of the place' (31) as actually bringing back to its original site a 'Troy-town' whose symbol as a mother-city is a mother-sow — ' "O seed of a race of gods!" (Dardanus being son of Aeneas' grandfather Jupiter; cf. "*Italiam quaero patriam et genus ab Jove summo*": I. 380); "thou who from foeman's hands bringest back to us our Troy-town (*Troianam . . . urbem qui revehis nobis*) and preservest her Pergama (Troy's citadel) for ever! O thou long looked-for on Laurentine ground and Latin fields!" (cf. "*Dardanidae duri, quae vos a stirpe parentum prima tulit tellus, eadem vos ubere laeto accipiet reduces*": III. 94-96). "Here is fixed thy house-and-home (*hic tibi certa domus*; cf. '*hic domus Aeneae*': III. 97), fixed — draw not back! — thy Penates. Nor be scared by threats of war; all the swelling wrath of Heaven has abated" (cf. "*cunctis dominabitur oris, et nati natorum et qui nascentur ab illis*": III. 97-98). "Even now, lest thou deem these words the idle feigning of sleep, thou shalt find a huge sow" (cf. "*antiquam exquirite matrem*": III. 96) "lying under the holm-oaks on the shore, just delivered of a litter of thirty young, the mother reclining on the ground white (*alba*); white, too, the young about her breasts (*ubera*; cf. '*ubere*': III. 95). By this token shall Ascanius (Iulus) found a

[1] See W. F. Jackson Knight, *Cumaean Gates* (Oxford, 1936), pp. 76-90, 107-131.

city" (to the accompaniment of his "Troy-game": V. 596-597), "Alba ('White') of glorious name. Not doubtful is my prophecy" ' (VIII. 36-49).

Aeneas, awakening from his prophetic dream and finding the mother-sow (81-85), thereupon passes symbolically from the site of Troy to the site of Rome (86-101); this Tiberine voyage of Aeneas thus itself symbolizing his Trojan-Roman destiny as the prototype of an Augustus who, being a Julius descended from Iulus, is at once both 'the Trojan Caesar' as belonging to 'the House of Assaracus' (I. 283-288) and 'the Roman Father' as belonging to 'the House of Aeneas' (IX. 448-449).

It will be remembered how in the *Georgics*' third book 'the seed of Assaracus' is linked both with 'father Tros' as eponym of Apollo's Troy and with 'Caesar', putative son of Apollo and adopted son of Julius Caesar, as central to the theme of Virgil's projected epic, originally planned to celebrate Roman-Julian victories by poetically symbolizing Mediterranean traditions prophetically symbolized in Apollo's Sibylline oracles (G. III. 8-48); while this victory-celebrating epic (cf. E. VI. 3-4), in its eventually Trojan-Iulean *Aeneid*-form, perpetuates the centrality of this same theme by emphasizing not only Apollo's prophetic guidance, as mediated through his Delian and Cumaean-Sibylline oracles, the latter through Anchises prophetically emphasizing Roman-Julian victories (VI. 791-800), but also Assaracus' ancestral presence as manifested in three ways — spiritually, in his sharing of his grandson Anchises' Elysium both with Ilus as the Trojan Ilium's eponym and with Dardanus as the Ilian Troy's founder (VI. 650); lineally, in his 'House of Assaracus' (I. 284), his 'blood of Assaracus' (VI. 778), his 'kin of Assaracus' (XII. 127); and ritually, in his 'Lar of Assaracus' as invoked, together with Vesta's hearth and her Penates, by Iulus himself (IX. 258-260) for the purpose of victoriously linking Aeneas' Italian Troy with the site of Rome (IX. 192-196) during Aeneas' visit thereto (IX. 8-9).

It is therefore of particular interest to find the *Aeneid* putting into Apollo's mouth a prophecy, enigmatically worded like his own Sibylline oracles, which symbolically celebrates Julian victories won on behalf of Augustus' Rome under the figure of Iulean victories won on behalf of Aeneas' Troy, with 'the race of Assaracus' as their one connecting link.

The context of this prophecy, moreover, is significant.

For 'Iulus, sorely weeping' (*multum lacrimantis Iuli:* IX. 501) in childlike sympathy with his slain friend Euryalus' mother — that same young Euryalus who, with Nisus, was to have fetched Aeneas back from the site of Augustus' Rome to that of his beleaguered Troy under the Iulus-invoked guarantee of Assaracus' household-spirit or 'Lar' (176-502) — is suddenly roused from his grief by the trumpet's call to a battle (503-589) during which Iulus, with the young manliness of a boy, victoriously conquers his first foe (590-637); whereupon Apollo, looking down upon (638-640) Iulus' defence of Aeneas' Troy-town (*urbem:* cf. *Troianam . . . urbem qui revehis nobis:* VIII. 36-37), 'thus addresses victorious Iulus: "A blessing, boy on thy young manliness! So man scales the stars, thou son of gods and sire of gods to be! Rightly shall all wars, that destiny may bring, sink beneath the race of Assaracus; nor can Troy contain thee" ' —

> *. . . his victorem adfatur Iulum:*
> *'macte nova virtute, puer: sic itur ad astra,*
> *dis genite et geniture deos. iure omnia bella*
> *gente sub Assaraci fato ventura resident;*
> *nec te Troia capit'* (IX. 640-644).

Thus Apollo here not only foretells, in terms of oracularly riddling implication, that closing of Janus' temple by Augustus in 29 B.C. which was earlier foretold explicitly by Jupiter as symbolizing a world-peace won by the victories of Iulus' deified descendant Augustus as the Trojan Julius Caesar of 'the House of Assaracus' (I. 283-296) — this earlier prophecy of Jupiter bearing the same equivalent relationship to the earlier Sibylline oracles, delivered from Jupiter's old Capitoline temple, as Apollo's later prophecy bears to the later Sibylline oracles delivered from Apollo's new Palatine temple — but further symbolizes under 'the race of Assaracus' that one genealogically continuous line which, running from Iulus' divine ancestors to his deified descendants, renders this Iulean defence of Aeneas' Troy prophetically equivalent to a Julian defence of Augustus' Rome.

Indeed, the very keynote of the *Aeneid*, as struck by Virgil himself in its first seven lines, is the idea of continuity, as of a single thread persisting throughout some complicated pattern over far distances of time and space — Troy at the one end of the long series, Rome at the other; with Rome inheriting from the Alban-Silvian height that same racial and religious life which Troy inherited from the Troadic-Idaean height.

This racial life is that of 'the Trojan blood' (I. 19) of that 'Ilian race' (VI. 875) whose identity with 'the Roman race' (I. 33) as founded by Aeneas (XII. 166) is derived from the Troadic-Idaean intercourse in Phrygia of Aeneas' human father, Assaracus' grandson Anchises, with Aeneas' divine mother, Cybele's granddaughter Venus; while the complementary religious life is that of the Roman-Julian because Trojan-Iulean Caesar Augustus, himself at once both a god (I. 289) and a god's son (VI. 792), whose victories abroad enable him at home to restore the peaceful earth-fertility of the Golden Age in accordance with those Sibylline oracles which derive his own adoptive ancestry from the Alban-Silvian intercourse in Italy of Romulus' divine father, Cybele's grandson Mars, with Romulus' human mother, Assaracus' descendant Ilia (I. 223-296; VI. 752-807).

The symbolism of the *Aeneid* is therefore axial, revolving as it were spherically about one central line between two poles — the one pole being a Troy whose symbols are Roman, the other pole a Rome whose symbols are Trojan; and the subjectively Roman thought of the poet travels from Rome to Troy, while the objectively Trojan theme of the poem travels from Troy to Rome:

'Arms I sing and the man who first from the coasts of Troy, exiled by destiny, came to Italy and Lavinian shores; much buffeted he on both land and sea by violence from above, on account of cruel Juno's unforgetful wrath, and much enduring in war also, till he should found his city and bring his gods into Latium; whence the Latin line, the lords of Alba, and the walls of lofty Rome' (I. 1-7).

CHAPTER IV

TEUCER AND DARDANUS

> hic genus antiquum Teucri, pulcherrima proles,
> magnanimi heroes, nati melioribus annis,
> Ilusque Assaracusque et Troiae Dardanus auctor.
> (*Aeneid* VI. 648-650)

THE centrality of Juno's anger in the *Aeneid*'s seven-line prelude (*saevae memorem Iunonis ob iram:* I. 4) corresponds to the centrality of Teucer's descendants in the *Aeneid*'s twelve-book narrative as summarized therein. For it is Juno who first describes the Trojan ancestors of the Romans as 'Teucrians' (I. 38), and it is as 'Teucrians' (I. 89) that she first tries to destroy them utterly.

Her rival Venus, moreover, employs Juno's terminology when appealing to Jupiter against his wife's persecution of the Trojans: ' "Surely it was thy promise that from them some day, as the years rolled on, the Romans were to arise; and that from them, even from the restored blood of Teucer, should come rulers, to hold the sea and all lands under their sway" ' (I. 234-237).

Jupiter himself repeats Venus' phrase (*a sanguine Teucri*) when sending Mercury to remind Aeneas of his Trojan-Roman destiny: ' "He it was should rule Italy, a land pregnant with empire and clamorous with war, should hand on a stock from Teucer's noble blood, and should bring the whole world beneath his laws" ' (IV. 229-231); while Aeneas, who in Elysium applies Jupiter's own phrase (*genus alto a sanguine Teucri*) to his cousin Deiphobus, son of Priam (VI. 500), also in Elysium sees 'Teucer's olden stock, offspring most fair, high-souled heroes born in happier years, Ilus and Assaracus and Dardanus, Troy's founder' (VI. 648-650); just as in Carthage, after calling his country 'Teucria' (II. 26), Aeneas had appealed to Dido not to thwart the Italian destiny of those 'Teucrians' (IV. 349) who as 'Teucrians' (IV. 397) quit Carthage for Italy.

Above all, when Apollo's Delian oracle darkly hints at the

Roman destiny of 'Dardanus' sons', with instructions to seek out their ancestral motherland (III. 94-98), Anchises unhesitatingly interprets the oracle as referring to Teucer's Cretan motherland: ' "In mid-ocean lies Crete, the island of great Jupiter, where is Mount Ida, the cradle of our race. There men dwell in a hundred great cities, a realm most fertile, whence our earliest ancestor Teucer, if I recall aright what I have heard, first sailed to the Rhoetean (i.e Troadic) shores, and chose a site for his kingdom. Not yet had Ilium and its Pergamean citadels been reared; men dwelt then in the valley-depths. Hence (i.e. from the Cretan to the Troadic Ida) came the Mother whose cult-name Cybele is that of her other mountain-haunt (*hinc Mater cultrix Cybele*), the Corybantian cymbals and the Idaean grove; hence came the faithful silence of her mysteries, and yoked lions passed under their Mistress' chariot. Come, then, and let us follow where the gods' bidding leads!" ' (III. 104-114).

But when, after reaching Crete, Anchises learns that the oracle's reference was to Dardanus' Italy and not to Teucer's Crete at all (147-179), he now 'at once recognizes the twofold descent and double parentage, and his own deception by a new mistake about old places' (180-181) — a perplexity of mind, both topographical and genealogical, reflecting that of 'the memorials of the men of old' (102); those classical mythographers, in fact, from whose variant traditions Virgil conflated the following version.

Electra, Atlas' daughter, bore to Jupiter two sons, Dardanus and Iasius, their Italian birthplace being Corythus (Cortona) in Etruria (III. 167-171; VII. 205-209; VIII. 134-136); both brothers eventually migrating from Italy eastwards, with different but correlative destinies — Dardanus, by marriage with Teucer's daughter, becoming the father of Teucer's grandchildren; and Iasius becoming the father of the Penates (*Iasiusque pater, genus a quo principe nostrum:* III. 168).

Now the Penates, as their name implies, were the gods of the *penus Vestae*, 'Vesta's inmost shrine', by Virgil called *penetralia Vestae* (V. 744; IX. 259); but the word *penus* originally meant the 'provision-cupboard' or 'store-room' containing the household victuals, and earlier still the 'provender' itself (I. 704). Thus the Penates, who in every private home were the gods of its larder, in Vesta's public home (*aedes Vestae*) guarded those 'gifts of Ceres' (*dona . . . Cereris:* VIII. 181), personified by Ceres herself *Cererem:* I. 177), which were the ears of corn to be crushed by Vesta's virgins and cooked by them into cakes upon Vesta's hearth-fire as symbolizing the sustenance of the state (W. Warde Fowler, *The Roman Festivals*, London 1899, reprinted 1933, pp. 149-150).

Dionysius of Halicarnassus, moreover, who gives the name 'Bateia' to the daughter of Teucer whom Dardanus married (I. l. 3; I. lxii. 1), gives the name 'Iasus' to Dardanus' brother (I. lxi. 1-2), adding that this Iasus 'was struck with a thunderbolt for desiring to lie with Demeter' (4), herself the Greek equivalent of the Latin Ceres.

Thus Dardanus' brother, the Dionysian Iasus and the Virgilian Iasius, is identical both with the Homeric Iasion, who likewise was struck with a thunderbolt for daring to lie with Demeter in a fallow ploughland (*Odyssey* V. 125-128), and with the Hesiodic Iasion who lay with Demeter in a fallow ploughland 'in the rich land of Crete' (*Theogony* 969-971) — that very Crete, 'a realm most fertile' (*uberrima regna:* III. 106), amidst whose ploughlands (*arvis:* III. 136, 171) the Virgilian Penates describe Iasius as 'the father from whom first sprang our kind' (III. 168).

Nor is this all. For the Hesiodic Iasion resembles the Virgilian Iasius in being a father — the father, by Demeter in the fertile Cretan harvest-field, of Ploutos, whose name means 'Wealth', primarily the farmer's wealth derived from earth-fertility as resulting in abundant corn-crops (H. J. Rose, *A Handbook of Greek Mythology*, Ed. 2, London 1933, pp. 78, 94); while Diodorus Siculus, Virgil's elder contemporary, actually describes Ploutos, Iasion's son by Demeter, as a guardian — like the Italian Penates — of stores, particularly of the stored grains of corn (*Historical Library* V. lxxvii. 1-2).

Hence the Virgilian Penates, who amongst the fertile Cretan farmlands not only claim to be Iasius' own children but also identify their proper home with the fertile Italian farmlands (*ubere glaebae:* III. 164) as native to their uncle Dardanus, Iasius' brother (167-168), are the multiple Virgilian counterpart of the single Hesiodic Ploutos, Iasion's child, whose mother Demeter corresponds to Ceres in personifying the cornland; Ceres herself, accordingly, by Virgilian implication, being by Iasius the mother of Dardanus' Penates as domestically guarding Vesta's store of corn-ears in the Virgilian *penetralia Vestae*.

This interpretation of Iasius' paternity is perhaps supported by the authority of Hellanicus himself (fifth century B.C.) as quoted by the mythographer known under the name of Apollodorus:

'Electra, Atlas' daughter, had two sons by Zeus — Iasion and Dardanus. Now Iasion loved Demeter, and in an attempt to violate the goddess he was killed by a thunderbolt. Grieved by his brother's death, Dardanus left Samothrace and came to the opposite (Troadic) mainland. That country was ruled by a king, Teucer, son of the river Scamander and a nymph Idaea; and the inhabitants of the country were called Teucrians after Teucer. Being welcomed by the king, and having received a share of the land and the king's daughter Bateia, he built a city Dardanus; and on the death of Teucer he called the whole country Dardania. And Dardanus had two sons born to him (by Bateia, Teucer's daughter) — Ilus and Erichthonius; of whom Ilus died childless, while Erichthonius succeeded to the kingdom and . . . begat Tros. On succeeding to the kingdom, Tros called the country Troy after himself, and . . . begat . . . sons — Ilus, Assaracus, and Ganymede . . . And Assaracus had . . . a son Capys; and Capys had . . . a son Anchises, whom (Venus) Aphrodite met in love's dalliance, and to whom she bore Aeneas' (Apollodorus, *Library* III. 1-2; translated by Sir J. G. Frazer in the Loeb Classical Library Edition, London 1921).

Thus Anchises was in point of fact both Teucrian and Dardan: Teucrian, as descended from Bateia's Cretan-Troadic father Teucer; and Dardan, as descended from Bateia's Italian-Troadic father Dardanus — a 'twofold descent and double parentage' (III. 180) implied in Dido's first welcome to Aeneas at Carthage: ' "Art thou that Aeneas whom gracious Venus bore to Dardan Anchises . . .? Yea, I myself remember Teucer's coming to Sidon" ' (I. 617-619).

Bateia, therefore, although never verbally named in the *Aeneid*, was mentally important to Virgil as representing the maternally Teucrian descent of the Dardanians; and it is clear that, like the learned Byzantine scholar Eustathius (*ad Hom.* p. 351), Virgil himself followed an ancient tradition which identified Bateia, as Teucer's daughter and Dardanus' wife, with the Homeric Myrine whose tomb outside Troy was commonly called 'Batieia':

'Now there is before the city a certain steep mound apart in the plain, with a clear way about it on this side and on that; and men' (i.e. the pre-Hellenic natives) 'indeed call this "Batieia", but the immortals' (i.e. the Hellenic invaders) 'call it "The Tomb of lithe Myrine". There did the Trojans and their allies divide their companies . . . And the Dardanians were led of the princely son of Anchises, Aineias, whom bright Aphrodite conceived to Anchises amid the spurs of Ida . . . And godlike Askanios led the Phrygians . . .' (*Iliad* II. 811-815, 819-821, 862-863; translated by A. Lang, W. Leaf and E. Myers, London 1882).

Virgil's appropriation of this Homeric scene is typically transformative.

For, identifying the Homeric 'Batieia' with the ancestral mound of Bateia, mother of Teucer's grandchildren by Iasius' brother Dardanus, he not only conflates this human Bateia with her divine sister-in-law Ceres, mother of Vesta's Penates by Dardanus' brother Iasius, but also — through the sudden magic of a mentally kaleidoscopic twist — transfers Bateia's mound to Ceres, bestows the name of Bateia's Teucrians upon Ceres' Penates, and musters the Penates as 'Teucrian' at Ceres' ancestral mound, together with Ascanius and Anchises and their household, under Aeneas' leadership: ' "Ye household-servants, take heed to what I say. As one leaves the city, there is a mound and olden temple of forlorn Ceres, with an ancient cypress hard by, preserved through many years by the reverence of our ancestors. To this one goal from various directions we will wend. Do thou, my father, take in thy hand the (Vestal) hallows and our ancestral Penates . . ." So I spoke . . . and we passed on amid the shadows . . . until we reached the mound of ancient Ceres and her hallowed home. Here at last, when all were mustered, Creusa alone was missing and failed the company, her son and her husband . . . Ascanius, my father Anchises, and the Teucrian Penates, I entrust to my fellows . . .' (II. 712-717, 721, 725, 742-748).

Aeneas, having concealed his charges, now returns in search of Creusa; whose phantasmally enlarged apparition, suggesting her quasi-deification as already an ancestral presence (II. 771-773), accounts for her mysterious absence from Ceres' mound by the revelation that Aeneas' Hesperian destiny involves her own Troadic detention by 'the great Mother of the gods' (788) — and so by that same Cybele whose cult, together with its symbols, long ago came from Crete with Teucer to the Troad (III. 107-113).

Creusa, in other words, is thus detained — not temporarily, like the rest of her family, at that ancestral cult-symbol of Ceres to which Aeneas brings the domestic cult-symbols of her sister Vesta — but permanently, by Vesta's and Ceres' common mother Cybele; whose own orgiastic cult-symbolism was inherited from Teucer by Bateia in the Troad.

Now Virgil, by his earlier insistence, no less unprecedented than emphatic (I. 267-268), that Ascanius' original *cognomen* in the Troad was not 'Iulus' at all but 'Ilus', a name otherwise peculiar to the eldest sons of Tros and his grandfather Dardanus, unconsciously betrays his own sense of a genealogical parallelism, amounting to a symbolical equivalence, not merely between Aeneas' son Iulus and Tros' son Ilus, but yet further between both of them and Dardanus' son Ilus.

Hence the Virgilian transference of Bateia's mound to Ceres, as being both the sister of Dardanus' Vesta and the mother of Iasius' Penates, involves the absence from that mound of Iulus' Cybele-detained mother Creusa as being in Virgil's mind equivalent symbolically to Ilus' Cybele-worshipping mother Bateia.

It is at this point that Diodorus Siculus becomes important as recording late mythographical conflations which, regarded by Virgil's immediate predecessors as genuinely old traditions, gave Virgil himself some precedent for so fusing the cult of Vesta's sister Ceres with that of their mother Cybele in connection with Dardanus and Iasius, Electra's sons by Cybele's son Jupiter, as to substitute Iasius' fatherhood by Ceres of Dardanus' Vestal Penates for Iasion's fatherhood both of Ploutos by Demeter and of Corybas by Cybele:

'Demeter, becoming enamoured of Iasion, presented him with the fruit of the corn . . . and Electra (presented her son Iasion) with the sacred rites of (Cybele) the Great Mother of the Gods, as she is called, together with cymbals and kettle-drums and the instruments of her ritual . . . And Iasion married Cybele, and begat Corybas. And then, after Iasion had been removed into the circle of the gods, Dardanus and Cybele and

Corybas conveyed (from Samothrace) to Asia the sacred rites of the Mother of the Gods, and removed with them to Phrygia . . . And Corybas (Iasion's son by Cybele) gave the name Corybantes to all who, in celebrating the rites of his mother, acted like men possessed . . . To Iasion and Demeter, according to the story the myths relate, was born Ploutos or Wealth; but the reference is, as a matter of fact, to the wealth of the corn, which was presented to Iasion because of Demeter's association with him . . .' (Diod. Sic. V. xlix. 1-4; translated by C. H. Oldfather in the Loeb Classical Library Edition, London 1939).

Strabo, moreover, contemporary both with Virgil and with Ovid, agrees with Diodorus Siculus in connecting Dardanus and Iasion with Samothrace and Cybele's Corybantes:

'Iasion and Dardanus, two brothers, used to live in Samothrace. But, when Iasion was struck by a thunderbolt because of his sin against Demeter, Dardanus sailed away from Samothrace, went and took up his abode at the foot of Mount Ida, calling the city Dardania, and taught the Trojans the Samothracian Mysteries. In earlier times, however, Samothrace was called Samos' (Strabo, *Geography* VII, fragment 49=50) — an exact parallel to the *Aeneid*'s statement, put into the mouth of Latinus as recalling dimly remembered tales told by Auruncan elders, that Dardanus ' "won his way to the Idaean cities of Phrygia and to Thracian Samos, now called Samothrace" ' (VII. 205-208).

Strabo adds that 'many writers have identified the gods that are worshipped in Samothrace with the Cabeiri, though they cannot say who the Cabeiri themselves are; just as the Cyrbantes and Corybantes, and likewise the Curetes and the Idaean Dactyli, are identified with them' (Strabo VII, fr. 50=51, trans. H. L. Jones in Loeb Edition, London 1924) — a passage recalling both Anchises' mention of Cybele's 'Corybantian cymbals and Idaean grove' (III. 111-112) and Aeneas' reference to Crete as 'the shores of the Curetes' (III. 131); the context in either case being concerned, moreover, with the maternally Teucrian descent of the Dardanians, whose paternal descent from Dardanus is regarded as inseparable from the paternal descent of Dardanus' Penates from his brother Iasius (III. 167-168).

The historical explanation of all this legendary *contaminatio* is twofold.

In the first place, the Greeks themselves quite early identified the Troadic-Idaean Cybele, whose ritual dancers were the orgiastic Corybantes, with the Cretan-Idaean Rhea, whose ritual dancers were the orgiastic Curetes (cf. G. IV. 149-152); both the Cretan Curetes and the Troadic Corybantes being later identified by the Greeks with the Samothracian Cabeiri, whom they called 'The Great Gods' (οἱ μεγάλοι θεόι).

In the second place, the Romans — doubtless influenced by early Etruscan interpretations of the Sibylline Books — yet further identified the Samothracian Cabeiri with their own Penates, whom accordingly they too called 'The Great Gods' (*di magnii:* cf. A. III. 12; VIII. 679), and whom they represented as taken from Samothrace to the Troad by an Etruscan-born Dardanus after the death of his Etruscan-born brother Iasius, Iasus, or Iasion, only to be brought by Aeneas, Dardanus' descendant, from the Troad to Italy as Dardanus' and Iasius' motherland.

Servius (on *Aen.* II. 325), supported by Arnobius (*Adv. Nat.* iii. 40), actually includes Ceres herself among the Etruscan Penates; an inclusion all the more significant as contained in a comment upon the one passage in the *Aeneid* which, within the compass of only two lines, groups together all the four proper-names (*Dardania*, *Troes*, *Ilium*, *Teucri*) most relevant to the genealogical aspect of Virgilian symbolism:

> '*venit summa dies et ineluctabile tempus*
> *Dardaniae. fuimus Troes, fuit Ilium et ingens*
> *gloria Teucrorum*' (II. 324-326).

This fourfold name-group, moreover, is placed in the mouth of one who, from Apollo's temple to Anchises' house, 'himself bears along in his hand the hallows and vanquished gods, together with his little grandson' (*sacra manu victosque deos parvumque nepotem ipse trahit:* II. 320-321); phraseology at once recalling not only Juno's description of the Teucrian-Dardan Ilian-Trojan race as 'carrying into Italy Ilium and its vanquished Penates' (*Ilium in Italiam portans victosque Penates:* I. 68) but also both Aeneas' instructions to Anchises: ' "Do thou, father, take in thy hand the hallows and ancestral Penates" ' (*tu, genitor, cape sacra manu patriosque Penates:* II. 717) and his description of Anchises' grandson, 'little Iulus' (*parvus Iulus:* II. 723; *nepotem:* 702), as following his Penates-bearing grandfather to an 'olden temple' (713), 'the mound of ancient Ceres and her hallowed home' (742).

Nor is it merely accidental that this name-group, so relevant both topographically and genealogically to Anchises' confusion of his twofold origin (III. 180) should be placed in the mouth of Panthus, priest of Apollo (II. 318-319) — the Trojan counterpart of that Delian Apollo who, having directed 'the sons of Dardanus' to seek out their 'ancient mother' (III. 94-96), places in the mouth of Dardania's Penates in Crete (III. 148-156) the correct identification of this 'mother' with Italy (166), whose Etruscan city Corythus (170) was the birthplace both of Dardanus, father by Teucer's daughter Bateia of the human Dardanidae, and of his brother Iasius, father by Cybele's daughter Ceres of the divine Penates (167-168), themselves the Virgilian equivalent both of Demeter's Ploutos and of Cybele's Corybantes as identified with the Curetes and Cabeiri.

An exact parallel to the inclusion of Ceres among the Etruscan Penates is the inclusion of Demeter among the Samothracian Cabeiri by a scholiast commenting on Apollonius Rhodius' reference to Samothrace as 'the island of Atlas' daughter Electra' (*Argonautica* I. 916); while another commentator on the same passage, whose context is the Samothracian mysteries, records a Greek mention of only two Cabeiri, Dardanus and Iasion, Electra's sons, whose birthplace seems originally to have been located in Samothrace itself.

The early Etruscan appropriation of Greek mythology, as interpreted through the medium of the Sibylline Books brought by Etruscan influence from Cumae to Rome, is doubtless responsible for the later location in Etruscan Corythus (Cortona) of Dardanus' and Iasius' birthplace; and it is suggestive that Servius, commenting on the relevant Virgilian passages, preserves a variant of this Etruscan version of the legend, whereby Atlas' daughter Electra was wife of the Etruscan king Corythus (IX. 10), founder of the Etruscan city Corythus (III. 170; VII. 209; X. 719), by whom she had only one son, Iasion; Dardanus being her only son by Zeus — the probability being that, as so often in folklore (J. Rendell Harris, *The Cult of the Heavenly Twins*, Cambridge 1906, pp. 4-9), the two brothers were originally twins: Iasius mortal, as son of Electra's human consort Corythus, but mated with the divine Ceres

(Demeter); and Dardanus immortal, as son of Electra's divine consort Jupiter (Zeus), but mated with the human Bateia (Myrine).

Virgil in any case had sufficient authority for connecting the Penates, not only with Ceres, Iasius and Dardanus, but also with the Dardanidae, themselves through Bateia Teucrians, whose companionship with the Penates during their common migration from east to west symbolically repeats the companionship of Dardanus with Iasius on their common migration from west to east.

Nowhere in the *Aeneid* is this twin-brotherly companionship, of the mortal with the immortal, more clearly stressed than by Hector himself in Troy, whom Aeneas significantly hails as 'Light of Dardania, surest hope of the Teucrians' (II. 281), and who in his turn — precisely as a son of Dardanus who by Bateia is also a grandson of Teucer — transfers to Aeneas by collaterally inherited right his own hereditary companionship with the Penates:

' "Troy commits to thee (as being Priam's ancestrally-related son-in-law) her hallows and Penates; take them as the companions (*comites*) of thy destiny; seek for them those mighty walls which, when thou hast wandered over the deep, thou shalt at last establish" ' (II. 293-295) — Donatus explaining that these 'great walls' (*moenia . . . magna*) are for the 'great gods' (*di magni*); an idea repeated by the Penates themselves when, appearing to Aeneas during sleep in Crete just as Hector appeared to him during sleep in Troy, they spoke oracularly in Apollo's name: ' "Do thou prepare walls mighty for the mighty!" ' (*tu moenia magnis magna para:* III. 159-160), as answering Aeneas' own appeal in Delos: ' "Grant us a home of our own! In our weariness grant us walls (*moenia*) and a race and an abiding city!" ' (III. 85-86).

Thus the brotherly companionship of Iasius with Dardanus is to be perpetuated in the brotherly companionship of Iasius' children, the Penates, with Dardanus' children, the Dardanidae, within that abiding because archetypal city (*urbem:* IX. 639), Aeneas' Italian Troy (*Troia:* IX. 644) whose walls (*moenia:* VII. 157; IX. 160), as foreshadowing those of Aeneas' Lavinium (*urbem et promissa Lavini moenia:* I. 258-259) and Iulus' Alba Longa (*longam multa vi muniet Albam:* I. 271) and Romulus' Rome (*altae moenia Romae:* I. 7; *Mavortia condet moenia:* I. 276-277), will defend the home of their one race (*genus ab Iove summo:* I. 380) as restored once more to its ancestral motherland.

So it is that Latinus, addressing the Trojans as maternally Teucrian (*Teucros:* VII. 193), recalls their paternally Dardan descent (*Dardanidae:* 195) from that Etruscan Dardanus who migrated from Italy by way of Samothrace to Phrygia (205-209); while Aeneas' ambassador, recalling that intercourse of Jupiter with Electra which made all sons of Dardanus the grandsons of Jupiter himself (*ab Iove principium generis:* 219), bases the claim of 'the Dardan menfolk' (*Dardana pubes:* 219) to an Italian home for their ancestral Penates (*dis sedem exiguam patriis:* 229) on the ground that 'hence Dardanus sprang and hither he returns' (*hinc Dardanus ortus, huc repetit:* 240-241)—a statement definitely implying Aeneas' symbolical equivalence to Dardanus, with the corollary-implication that Creusa and Iulus are symbolically equivalent to Bateia and Ilus.

So it is also that Tiberinus, appearing (like Hector and the Penates) to Aeneas during sleep, not only welcomes him in terms which imply his equivalence to a returning Dardanus (VIII. 36-38) but couples his House with his Penates as together sharing Dardanus' original homeland (*hic tibi certa domus, certi . . . Penates:* 39) — a welcome clearly echoing the terms both of Aeneas' coupling of the two ideas: 'Hail, O Penates faithful to Troy! Here is our house-and-home, this is our father's land' (*o fidi Troiae, salvete, Penates; hic domus, haec patria est*'*:* VII. 121-122), and Delian Apollo's identification of the *domus Aeneae* with those Dardanidae whose greatness when restored to their 'ancient mother' (III. 94-98) shall correspond to the greatness both of their Penates and of their walls (III. 158-160).

But the phraseology of Aeneas and Tiberinus is reminiscent no less clearly of Virgil's description in the *Georgics* of the brotherly companionship and immortal race of the bees — those very bees which in the *Aeneid* will explicitly symbolize the Dardanidae as seeking an Italian home for their Penates (VII. 64-101, 195, 229): 'The bees alone have children in common, hold the dwellings of their city (*urbis*) jointly, and pass their life under great laws. They alone know a fatherland (*patriam*) and fixed (*certos*) Penates . . . Their race (*genus*) abides immortal; through many years (*multosque per annos*) stands firm the fortune of their House (*domus*); and grandsires' grandsires (*avi . . . avorum*) are numbered on its roll' (*Georgics* IV. 153-155, 208-209).

This unforgettable word-picture of the bees' House, whose identity both material and immaterial is thus unbrokenly perpetuated, was surely present as a thought-picture to Virgil's own memory when in the *Aeneid* he came to describe the unbrokenly perpetuated identity (VII. 45-49, 160-194) of Latinus' House (*domum:* 52), with its materially long row of statues representing the immaterially long line of his grandsires (*avorum:* 177), and with its sacred laurel-tree preserved 'through many years' (*multosque . . . per annos:* 60); Latinus' daughter Lavinia — the eponym of his city (*urbe:* 171) as later refounded by his son-in-law Aeneas for Troy's Vestal hallows and Penates (XII. 187-194) — herself already personifying that fortune of Latinus' House (VII. 50-58, 71-80) whose central symbol is the laurel-tree whereon, under the figure of swarming bees (59-70), are explicitly symbolized both Aeneas, as Lavinia's destined bridegroom (313-314), and Aeneas' Trojans, as the grandsires' grandsires of Augustus' Romans (81-106, 195-285) descended partly from Lavinia (VI. 756-807).

Now Aeneas' marriage with Lavinia undoubtedly corresponds, upon one level of Virgilian symbolism, to Augustus' marriage with Livia in 38 B.C.; a marriage immediately followed by portents comparable with those (*portenta deum:* VII. 58, *monstris:* 81) which in Latinus' House connect its laurel with Lavinia as personifying its fortune (D. L. Drew, *The Allegory of the Aeneid*, Oxford 1927, pp. 84-85).

For an eagle dropped into the newly-wedded Livia's lap a sprig of berried laurel (cf. *lauri bacas:* G. I. 306); and this berried laurel-sprig, planted by Livia as portending good luck to her marriage with Augustus in the matter of progeny (cf. *laurus parva sub ingenti matris se subicit umbra:* G. II. 18-19), grew up so quickly as soon to furnish the Julian emperors with their victory-symbolizing laurel-wreath (cf. *victrices . . . laurus:* E. VIII. 13) as Roman *triumphatores* (Pliny, *Nat. Hist.* XV. 136-137; Dio Cassius, XLVIII. 52; Suetonius, *Galba* I: see Frazer, *The Fasti of Ovid*, Vol. II, pp. 403-404).

Thus, already for some years before Virgil's completion of the *Aeneid*, a laurel-tree had been recognized as symbolizing the fortune of Augustus' House as belonging to that *gens Iulia* into which Livia was later to be adopted as Iulia by Augustus' will; while Servius (on *Aen.* VI. 230) records the tradition that a laurel-tree sprang up on the Palatine hill at the moment of Augustus' birth.

It is therefore deeply significant that Virgil, who in the *Georgics* had described his future epic a *templum* with Augustus 'in its midst' (G. III. 16), should in the *Aeneid* describe Latinus' palace as a *templum* with a laurel-tree 'in its midst' (A. VII. 59, 192); and further that, just as the Augustus-centred temple-epic contains both the statues of Augustus' Trojan ancestors and the symbols of Augustus' Roman victories (G. III. 22-36, 46-48), so too the laurel-centred temple-palace contains both the statues of Latinus' Italian ancestors and the symbols of their Italian victories (A. VII. 170-193).

Virgil, moreover, no less significantly integrates this twofold temple-symbolism under the figure of those bees which, swarming on Latinus' laurel-tree as itself symbolizing the fortune of Latinus' House in regard to Lavinia's marriage as decided by Aeneas' victory over his rival Turnus (VII. 52-80), themselves represent those living Trojan ancestors whose unborn Roman descendants (VI. 717), within their Elysian *domos* (VI. 705), resemble bees (VI. 707-709).

Nor does this Virgilian bee-and-laurel symbolism end here. For the Elysian bee-resemblance of Aeneas' descendants by Lavinia (VI. 756-807) is mentally associated by Virgil both with that 'sequestered grove' (*seclusum nemus:* VI. 704) whose recent verbal counterpart was Elysium's centrally situated 'fragrant laurel-grove' (*odoratum lauri nemus:* VI. 658) and with those 'crackling forest-thickets' (*virgulta sonantia silvae:* VI. 704) whose later verbal counterpart will be the 'forest and laurel-crackling thickets' (*silvam et virgulta sonantia lauro:* XII. 522) of Virgil's conflagration-simile as applied precisely to the decision of Lavinia's marriage by Aeneas' victory over Turnus — this fire-and-laurel comparison itself recalling that symbolic self-conflagration of Lavinia under Latinus' bee-swarming laurel (VII. 59-80) whose counterpart is Virgil's conflagration-comparison with smoked-out bees of Latinus' Lavinians under Aeneas' victory for Lavinia's hand in marriage (XII. 587-592).

It is in laurel-centred Elysium, too, that Aeneas is instructed by Anchises (VI. 891) both about that 'city of Latinus' which is not 'Laurentum' but Lavinium (Frazer, *The Fasti of Ovid*, Vol. II, pp. 492-496) and about those 'Laurentine peoples' whose name Virgil derives (VII. 63) from Latinus' *laurus*, in accordance with the contemporary popular derivation of the term *ager Laurens* from that territory's many laurels (Varro, *de lingua Latina* V. 152); so that, by the 'mighty forest' (*ingentem . . . lucum:* VII. 29) through which the Tiber flows, is probably implied that extensive *silva Laurentina* whose name was misinterpreted as meaning the 'laurel-forest'.

Virgil, that is to say, mentally visualizes Lavinia's territorial dowry, as Latinus' heiress wooed by many suitors from near and far (VII. 50-55), under the figure of a thickly laurelled kingdom whose dynastic emblem is accordingly one of its laurel trees, found by Latinus himself during his building of Lavinium and dedicated by him to laurel-loving Apollo (VII. 61-62; cf. E. III. 62-63; E. VI. 82-83; A. III. 91); this laurel, growing 'in the midst' of King Latinus' palace as the symbol of his royal House's dynastic fortune, being therefore the western counterpart of that eastern laurel which, 'overhanging the altar and clasping the Penates in its shade', grew 'in the midst' of King Priam's palace as the symbol likewise of his royal House's dynastic fortune (II. 512-514).

In other words, Latinus' laurel bears for Virgil's mind the same symbolical relationship to the issue of Aeneas' marriage with Latinus' daughter Lavinia, namely Silvius (VI. 763), as that borne by Priam's laurel to the issue of Aeneas' marriage with Priam's daughter Creusa, namely Iulus (II. 563); so that those 'forests' wherein Lavinia 'will bring up' her son Silvius as 'a king and father of kings' (*educet silvis regem regumque parentem:* VI. 765) will by Virgilian implication be those of the *silva Laurentina*, itself belonging to Iulus' own 'kingdom of Italy and Roman land' (IV. 274-276).

CHAPTER V

LAOMEDON AND TIBERINUS

> ... Laomedontia pubes
> gramineo ripae religavit ab aggere classem.
> Aeneas primique duces et pulcher Iulus
> corpora sub ramis deponunt arboris altae
> instituuntque dapes. . . .
> (*Aeneid* VII. 105-109)

OUR conclusions up to this point may now be briefly summarized.

The *Aeneid*, whose secondary theme is Iulus' founding of the Julian clan, has for its primary theme Aeneas' founding of the Roman race; both themes, derived mainly from traditions mediated through the Sibylline oracles, finally merging into that of the walls of Rome as superseding the walls of Troy.

But the walls of Troy are those of the Dardanidae as sharing them with the Penates in their common fatherland: ' "O fatherland! O Ilium, home of gods, and ye war-famous walls of Dardanus' sons!" ' —

> *o patria, o divum domus Ilium et incluta bello*
> *moenia Dardanidum!* (II. 241-242);

so that, since the mother of Dardanus' sons is Teucer's daughter Bateia, Ilium's divine citizens are primarily Teucer's Cybele and Dardanus' Vesta.

Hence the fulfilment both of Aeneas' Roman destiny and of Iulus' Julian destiny involves the transference on shipboard of Ilium's divine and human citizens, as both Teucrian and Dardan, from the neighbourhood of the destruction of Troy's walls to that of the construction of Rome's walls; a transference, assisted throughout by Venus but obstructed by Juno, itself involving a long sea-voyage from the country of Creusa to that of Lavinia, for whose hand a fierce land-warfare follows against Turnus.

The voyage ends where the warfare begins — at the site of a token-Troy near the site of a token-Rome, with the Tiber-river linking the two sites into one integrally Trojan-Roman neighbourhood which symbolizes Aeneas' and Iulus' destinies as further involving both Aeneas' foundation of his Lavinium from his Troy and Iulus' foundation from Lavinium of his Alba Longa, mother-city of Romulus' Rome.

Aeneas' own flagship, built like the rest of his fleet from Cybele-provided Idaean pine-wood, and representing Cybele's Mount Ida with her Phrygian lions, thus constructionally carries those emblems of Venus' grandmother and Jupiter's mother whose companions on shipboard are the hallows of Vesta, Cybele's daughter and Ceres' sister, as there represented by her perpetually burning hearth-fire, her Pergamean *Lar* of Assaracus, and her *Penates*, children of Ceres by Iasius, brother of Dardanus, himself father of all the *Dardanidae* by Bateia, daughter of Teucer, eponym of the *Teucri*.

Thus Aeneas' fleet, led by his flagship, carries from east to west under the patronage of laurel-loving Apollo — from the laurel-centred Kingdom of Priam to the laurel-centred Kingdom of Latinus — not only the paternally Dardan and maternally Teucrian Trojans of Venus' Ilium, but also their divine counterparts as represented by the symbols both of Dardanus' Vesta and of Teucer's Cybele.

So it is that Aeneas' landing in Latium with Vesta's Penates on Cybele's ship is announced to Diomede, then founding Arpi (X. 28; XI. 250, 428) or Argyripa (XI. 246), in these comprehensive terms: 'that Teucrians are setting foot in Latium; that Aeneas, arriving on shipboard, is not only bringing thereto his vanquished Penates but is proclaiming himself its fate-destined king; and that many tribes are joining the Dardan hero, whose name spreads far and wide in Latium' (VIII. 10-14).

Now Aeneas proclaims himself a king by right of his two successive marriages, the one past and the other future, with kings' daughters who embody the dynastic heritage of their respective fathers — first Creusa, daughter of Laomedon's son Priam (*Laomedontiaden Priamum:* VIII. 158), and then Lavinia, daughter of Faunus' son Latinus (*Fauno . . . genitum:* VII. 47); so that, while Aeneas' Troadic kingship (*Teucrorum . . . regem:* I. 38; *rex erat Aeneas nobis:* I. 544; *rex ipse . . . Troius Aeneas:* VII. 220-221) is derived from that of Ilus' son and Tros' grandson Laomedon, his Italian kingship (*Latio regnantem:* I. 265; *qui . . . Italiam regeret:* IV. 229-230; *regnique coronam cum sceptro:* VIII. 505-506) is derived from that of

Picus' son and Saturn's grandson Faunus (*Fauno Picus pater, isque parentem te, Saturne, refert, tu sanguinis ultimus auctor:* VII. 48-49).

Aeneas, therefore, inherits two kingships over two kingdoms — that of Laomedon's grandfather Tros over his 'Trojan' kingdom, and that of Faunus' grandfather Saturn over his 'Saturnian' kingdom; the statue of 'aged Saturn' in Latinus' palace representing him as the source of Latinus' own kingship (VII. 180-181) over the Latins as 'Saturn's race, righteous not by bond or laws, but self-controlled of their own free will and by the custom of their ancient god' (VII. 202-204).

It is clearly for this reason that Evander, who has already learnt Aeneas' royal destiny from his prophetic mother Carmentis (VIII. 337-341), welcomes Aeneas to his Saturnian kingdom with the words: ' "First from heavenly Olympus (to Italy) came Saturn . . . (who) chose that the land be called Latium, since in these borders he had found a safe hiding-place (from Jupiter). Under his kingship were the Golden Ages men tell of; in such perfect peace he ruled the peoples" ' (VIII. 319-325) — the implication being that Aeneas, like Augustus in Virgil's own day (VI. 791-794), is destined through victory in war to revive the peace of Saturn's Golden Age as Saturn's heir through Lavinia to Saturn's Italian kingship over Latium.

Nor is it accidental that Virgil, immediately after describing Latinus' consultation of 'the oracles of Faunus, his prophetic sire' (VII. 81-82) and 'the reply of his father Faunus' (102) in regard to Latinus' own descendants by Lavinia's husband Aeneas (96-101), goes on to describe the landing of 'the Laomedontian menfolk' (*Laomedontia pubes:* 105), including 'Aeneas and his chief captains and fair Iulus' (107) on that same Tiber-bank (*ripae:* VII. 106; *ripa:* VIII. 28) whereon Aeneas will soon be unhappily pondering the probable issues of his destiny precisely as 'the Laomedontian hero' (*Laomedontius heros:* VIII. 18) until reassured by Tiberinus (VIII 18-80); since Laomedon bears the same ancestral relationship to the unhappy associations of Aeneas' 'Trojan' kingship as that borne to the happy associations of Aeneas' 'Saturnian' kingship by Faunus.

Laomedon, Priam's father, was first-cousin to Capys, Anchises' father; Capys being the son of Assaracus, whose brother Ilus was father of Laomedon — both Ilus and Assaracus being sons of Tros (cf. G. III. 35-36) and so grandsons of Erichthonius, great-grandsons of Dardanus, and great-great-grandsons of Teucer (VI. 648-650).

Thus the one original Teucrian-Dardan line branches off into the two distinct lines of common descent from Troy's eponym Tros — that of Ilus, Laomedon, Priam, Creusa; and that of Assaracus, Capys, Anchises, Aeneas — with Ascanius or Iulus, as Creusa's son by Aeneas, reuniting in his own person the two Tros-descended lines of Dardan-Teucrian descent.

Aeneas himself, already Saturn's great-grandson as Venus' son by Anchises, thus not only carries to Italy in his own person the cults both of his own great-grandmother Cybele and of his own mother Venus, Jupiter's daughter by Juno and Vulcan's wife, but also carries to Italy in Cybele's ship, under the patronage of Apollo, both the cult of Dardanus' Vesta as entrusted to him by Laomedon's own grandson Hector (II. 281-297) and the cult of Teucer's Cybele as represented by Laomedon's own grand-daughter Creusa (II. 788).

Hence the *Troes* (VII. 21) who land on Tiberinus' bank as *Laomedontia pubes* (105) are sent by 'Anchises' son' (*satus Anchisa:* 152) as *Teucri* (155) to Latinus' palace of 'Laurentian Picus' (171) with its statue of Saturn (180); where, greeted by Latinus as 'the sons of Dardanus' (*Dardanidae:* 195), they announce themselves to 'the son of Faunus' (213) as '*Dardana pubes*' (219) seeking a home for their *di patrii* (229) — Anchises' own name for the *Penates* (II. 702; cf. *patrios Penates:* II. 717).

It is at this point important to note that the landing of 'the Laomedontian menfolk' on the Tiber-bank (VII. 105-108) is immediately followed by that eating of their tables which through Iulus' unwitting reminder (109-119) leads both to Aeneas' salutation of the Penates as 'faithful to Troy' (121) and to his building of the walls (145, 157-159) of that 'Troy-town' (VIII. 36) which as 'the Laomedontian hero' (VIII. 18) Aeneas has brought back to Tiberinus' country (65) for refoundation there as the home of Troy's Penates (39).

For it was precisely as 'Laomedon's sons' (*Laomedontiadae:* III. 248) that Aeneas' Trojans were warned in the Strophades by Celaeno: ' "Italy is the goal of your voyage; wooing the winds, ye shall go to Italy and freely enter her harbours" ' (i.e.

the Tiber-mouth, Ostia, site of Aeneas' Troy; cf. *Tiberinaque longe ostia:* I. 13-14); '"but ye shall not gird with walls your promised city until dread hunger . . . force you . . . to eat your tables"' (III. 253-257).

The connection of ideas is obvious — being one between Laomedon and the building of the walls of a Troy; with an implied contrast between the faithfulness of the Penates and the faithlessness of Laomedon in regard to the building of that Troy's walls.

Now Virgil, who in the *Georgics* attributes the founding of Troy to Apollo (*Troiae Cynthius auctor:* G. III. 36), in the *Aeneid* attributes it to Dardanus (*Troiae Dardanus auctor:* A. VI. 650; *Dardanus Iliacae primus pater urbis et auctor:* VIII. 134); the reason, of course, being that Apollo helped Neptune to rebuild Dardanus' Troy for Laomedon (cf. *Iliad* VII. 452-453). Laomedon's faithlessness, moreover, lay in his refusal to pay Neptune and Apollo the price he had promised them (*Iliad* XXI. 441-457) for their rebuilding in Phrygia of Dardanus' Troy, which thus became both 'Neptune's Troy' (*Neptunia Troia:* A. III. 3) and 'Laomedon's Troy' (*Laomedonteae . . . Troiae:* G. I. 502); while the Penates' faithfulness lies in the loyal fulfilment of their promise to guide Aeneas safely to the site of his rebuilding in Italy of *Dardania*, Dardanus' Troy (A. III. 156-168).

The same complementary contrast, implied already in the *Georgics* (I. 498-502), appears also in Dido's ironical coupling of 'the perjury of the Laomedontean race' (*Laomedonteae . . . periuria gentis:* A. IV. 542) with 'the pledge and faith of (Aeneas) who, they say, carries about with him his ancestral Penates' (*en dextra fidesque, quem secum patrios aiunt portare Penates:* IV. 597-598), precisely when reproaching Aeneas for continuing his interrupted voyage from Phrygia to Italy.

Neptune himself refers to 'the walls of perjured Troy built by my own hands' (*structa meis manibus periurae moenia Troiae:* V. 811), and swears by Troy's rivers 'Xanthus and Simois' (V. 803), precisely when reassuring Venus as to Aeneas' safe continuance of that same voyage; while it is Apollo himself who, as Troy's joint-rebuilder for Laomedon, warns the *Laomedontiadae* through Celaeno about the building-site of their Italian walls (III. 245-257), just as it is Apollo himself who warns the Dardanidae (III. 94) through Troy's faithful Penates about their building of 'great walls for the great' in Dardanus' motherland (III. 154-160) — that same *tellus* (III. 95) which Aeneas salutes in Italy (*tellus:* VII. 120) when saluting the Penates' faithfulness to Troy (VII. 121).

Above all, it is Apollo himself who through his priest-king Helenus, Laomedon's grandson ruling in Buthrotum, itself a miniature Laomedon's Troy as rebuilt by Apollo (III. 349) with miniature rivers Xanthus (350, 497) and Simois (302), oracularly clarifies his own earlier warning to 'Laomedon's sons' (245-257) by telling Aeneas to continue his voyage to Italy (381) in order to 'exalt Troy' there by his deeds (462).

Aeneas' farewell to Laomedon's grandson is correspondingly pregnant with meaning: ' "Fare ye well, ye whose own destiny is already fulfilled; we are still summoned from fate to fate. Your rest is won. No ocean plains need ye plough, no ever-retreating Ausonian (Italian) fields need ye seek. A copy of Xanthus (=Scamander river) ye see and a Troy, which your own hands have built under omens happier, I pray" ' (i.e. than those under which Apollo helped Neptune to build Laomedon's Troy), ' "and more beyond the reach of the Greeks" ' (i.e. the agents of divine vengeance on Laomedon's 'perjured Troy'). ' "If ever I enter the Tiber and Tiber's neighbouring fields, and there look upon the walls promised to my race, then hereafter, of our sister cities and allied peoples, in Epirus, in Hesperia (Italy) — who have the same Dardanus for founder (*idem Dardanus auctor*) and the same unhappy history" ' (i.e. Laomedon's as inherited by Priam's Troy; cf. G. I. 501-502) ' "— of these twain we shall make one Troy in spirit. May that charge await our children's children!" ' (III. 493-505).

Although Virgil here probably refers to Augustus' founding of Nicopolis in Epirus in 24 B.C. on the site of his final defeat of Marcus Antonius, and in commemoration of the surrender of Alexandria, the underlying symbolism of Aeneas' farewell to Helenus goes far deeper. For Aeneas' Italian Troy on the Tiber-bank is to resemble Helenus' Epirote Troy in its minutely detailed correspondence on a tiny scale to Dardanus' Phrygian Troy on the Xanthus-bank, but without (so Aeneas prays) its unhappy Laomedontian associations of bad faith and consequent defeat in war — the implication, as gradually unfolded throughout the *Aeneid*, being that the faithfulness of Troy's Penates, themselves belonging to Dardanus' Vesta and sharing her hearthfire with Assaracus' Lar, will so cancel the faithlessness of Laomedon, son of Assaracus' brother Ilus, as to supplant his elder branch of Tros' dynasty by the younger branch of Capys, son of Ilus' brother Assaracus; Priam and Hector and Astyanax (III. 472-491) thus respectively forfeiting their own representative Trojan royalty to their cousins Anchises and Aeneas and Iulus as representing that 'House of Assaracus' under whose Ilian-Iulean-Julian dynasty (I. 283-290) 'wars shall cease, and the rough ages (i.e. the Iron Age) shall soften (into Saturn's Golden Age restored); hoary Faith and Vesta, Quirinus (Romulus) and his brother Remus, shall give laws. The gates of war (i.e. Janus' temple) shall be closed' (I. 291-294).

The epithet *canus*, 'hoary', here given to Faith as coupled with Vesta (*cana Fides et Vesta:* I. 292) in connection with 'Assaracus' House' (I. 284), belongs elsewhere in the *Aeneid* to Vesta (*canae . . . Vestae*) as twice coupled with Assaracus' own Pergamean Lar or household-spirit (V. 744; IX. 259).

Iulus, moreover, precisely when about to employ Nisus and Euryalus as links between a token-Troy and a token-Rome already linked together by Aeneas' Tiberine voyage, not only adjures them 'by the great Penates, by Assaracus' Lar, by hoary Vesta's shrine' but in the same breath entrusts to their keeping his 'fortune' and his 'faith' (IX. 258-261); so that Iulus' *fides*, here coupled in a Trojan-Roman context with Iulus' *cana Vesta*, symbolically anticipates Julius' *cana Fides* as earlier coupled in a Trojan-Roman context with Julius' *Vesta* (I. 286-293).

Now the cognate epithet *incanus*, 'quite-hoary', given in the *Georgics* to the white-bearded 'chin of the Cinyphian he-goat' (*incanaque menta Cinyphii . . . hirci:* G. III. 311-312), belongs in the *Aeneid* to the white-bearded 'chin of the Roman king' (*incanaque menta regis Romani:* VI. 809-810), Romulus' immediate successor, the Sabine-born Numa Pompilius; pupil in ritual observance of Picus and Faunus (Plutarch, *Numa* XV), and founder at Rome of the cults of Fides and Vesta, Quirinus and Janus (Livy I. xviii-xxi) — and so precisely of the four Roman cults attributed by Virgil to Assaracus' House under Iulus' descendant Julius (I. 292-294).

Virgil, that is to say, kaleidoscopically transfers from Numa both to his Fides and to his Vesta that quality of 'hoariness' which, as Iulus' Vesta and Julius' Fides, they share with Latinus (*canitiem:* XII. 611)—Latinus, be it noted; whose resemblance to Numa, as a white-haired Italian king of early times, is enhanced by his Sabine ancestry (VII. 177-179), by his cults of Quirinus (VII. 187, 612) and of Janus (VII. 601-619; XII. 195-198), and by his descent from Picus and Faunus (VII. 45-48), Faunus being his instructor in prophetic interpretation after ritual observance (VII. 81-103).

This entire train of thought, hitherto detected analytically from widely scattered and deeply buried hints, is in fact demonstrably traceable within the compass of some sixty lines in the *Aeneid*'s sixth book, that mine of Virgilian symbolism:

Latinus' daughter Lavinia, as mother of Aeneas' Dardan-Italian descendants (VI. 756-776); Numa's immediate predecessor Romulus, both as Vestally mothered 'of Assaracus' blood' and as founder of a Rome whose walls are explicitly comparable with that crown of Cybele whose walls are implicitly comparable with the walls of Troy (777-787); Aeneas' Roman destiny and Iulus' Julian destiny as together culminating in an Augustus Caesar who, as divine, is destined to restore the Golden Age of Saturn's kingship in a Latium peacefully central to a Mediterranean empire in accordance with the Sibylline oracles (788-805); Aeneas' landing in Latium as Augustus' ancestral prototype of peace through victory in war (806-807); and Numa, with his easily recognizable 'locks and quite-hoary chin', as 'the Roman king' of Sabine birth and imperial fortune (808-812).

Nor must it be forgotten that Virgil, who early couples Aeneas' 'pledge and faith' (*dextra fidesque*) with those same *patrii Penates* (IV. 597-598) which Aeneas rescued together with Iulus from Troy (II. 717-724), later couples Iulus' 'fortune and faith' (*fortuna fidesque*) with those same *magni Penates* (IX. 258-260) which Aeneas (III. 12) and Augustus (VIII. 679) both carry on shipboard, themselves both alike 'standing on the lofty stern' (*stans celsa in puppi:* VIII. 680; X. 261); that Aeneas after death will be honoured as *Indiges* (XII. 794); that Aeneas' Lavinian kingship will be transferred by Iulus (*regnumque ab sede Lavini transferet:* I. 270-271) to an Alba Longa whose kingship will belong to 'Hector's race' (*regnabitur . . . gente sub Hectorea:* I. 272-273) until Vesta's 'queen-priestess' (*regina sacerdos*) bears to Mars the royal builder of

Rome's walls (I. 273-277); that Hector's race, to which Romulus' kingship belongs, is 'Laomedon's race' (*Laomedonteae ... gentis:* IV. 542); that Virgil, when supplanting the walls of Laomedon's Troy by the walls of Romulus' Rome, at the same time supplants 'Hector's rivers, Xanthus and Simois' (*Hectoreos amnis, Xanthum et Simoenta:* V. 634) by Latinus' rivers, Tiber and Numicus or Numicius (VII. 150-151); and that Virgil's contempories knew this latter river as the site of Aeneas' cult as *Indiges* (Livy I. ii; Dion. Halic. I. lxiv).

Virgil thrice mentions the Numicus, each time in close connection with the Tiber. Thus Aeneas' 'Laomedontian menfolk' (VII. 105), on their first morning in Latium (130-132, 148-149), 'search out the city (Latinus' Lavinium) and boundaries and coasts of the (Latin) race. This, they learn, is the pool of the Numicus' spring; this the Tiber river; here dwell the brave Latins' (VII. 149-151); those same Latins who later, as supporting Turnus against Aeneas' claim to Lavinia's hand and heritage, are described as 'they who till thy glades, O Tiberinus, and Numicus' sacred shore' (VII. 797-798)—sacred in anticipation of Aeneas' cult thereon as the locally-worshipped 'Laomedontian hero' (VIII. 18) or *Indiges* (*indigetem Aenean:* XII. 794).

So too, when the spokesman of the Dardanidae asks Latinus to grant them a home for their Penates (VII. 229) he justifies his request on the ground that 'Hence sprang Dardanus and hither he returns; while with high decrees Apollo urges us to Etruscan Tiber and the sacred shallows of the Numicus' spring' (VII. 240-242)—in other words, to that Etruscan-Latin riverine system, called by Tiberinus his 'great house-and-home' (*hic mihi magna domus:* VIII. 65), the site of Aeneas' own House with its Penates (*hic tibi certa domus, certi ... Penates:* VIII. 39), which extends from the neighbourhood of Dardanus' Etruscan Corythus (III. 170) past the neighbourhood of Evander's token-Rome to that of Aeneas' token-Troy, and whose 'greatness' is the topographical counterpart of the 'greatness' both of the Penates and of their walls as demanded not only by Apollo (III. 159-160), as joint-builder for Laomedon of the walls of Troy, but also by Laomedon's grandson Hector (II. 293-295), as inseparably connected with the walls of Troy (II. 270-279; cf. I. 483-484).

Virgil, in fact, postulates two symbolically parallel riverine systems — an eastern, that of Troy, with its Xanthus and its Simois; and a western, that of Rome, with its Tiber and its Numicus — both of which, while linked together by the wall-builders Apollo and Dardanus, are associated with the idea of building mighty walls for citizens, both divine and human, who are themselves as mighty as their walls.

At Cumae, for example, Aeneas' prayer implies Apollo's pity for the Troy he built (VI. 56, 62); while Aeneas' appeal, as the Trojan king (*Tros . . . rex:* 52, 55) to whom is destined an Italian kingdom (*non indebita posco regna meis fatis:* 66-67), ' "that the Teucrians may settle down in Latium with Troy's wandering gods and storm-tossed powers" ' (67-68), is answered by Apollo's Sibyl thus: ' "Into Lavinium's kingdom shall come the Dardanidae — relieve thy heart of this care — yet they shall not also joy in their coming. Wars, grim wars I see, and Tiber foaming with streams of blood. A Simois thou shalt not lack, nor a Xanthus, nor a Doric camp" ' (84-89).

Earlier than this, in Sicily, it is 'to the mothers of Dardanus' sons' (*Dardanidum . . . matribus:* V. 622), and so to the multiple equivalent of Teucer's daughter Bateia, that Juno's messenger appeals: ' "Who forbids us to cast up walls and to give a city to our citizens? O fatherland, O Penates in vain rescued from the foe! shall no walls any more be called the walls of Troy? Shall I nowhere see a Xanthus and a Simois, Hector's rivers?" ' (V. 631-634) — an appeal eventually resulting in that Sicilian compromise whereby 'Aeneas marks out the city with a plough and allots homes; this he bids be Ilium, and these places Troy' (755-757).

Still earlier, at Buthrotum, where the Dardanus-descended and Laomedon-descended representative of Troy's own rebuilder Apollo has himself upon a miniature scale rebuilt Troy, together with tiny reproductions of Hector's rivers Xanthus and Simois for the consolation of Hector's widow, Virgil crystallizes the multiplicity of his symbolism into one facet of illuminating brilliance. For, just as elsewhere Aeneas' birth is connected explicitly with 'the water of the Phrygian Simois' (*Phrygii . . . Simoentis ad undam:* I. 618) and Aeneas' death implicitly with its western counterpart, the water of the Italian Numicus (VII. 242, 797; XII. 794), so here Hector's death is connected symbolically with their half-way equivalent in Epirus, 'the water of a mimic Simois' (*falsi Simoentis ad undam:*

III. 302), whose fruitless quasi-Phrygian hero-cult of an always-absent Hector (301-312) is thus implicitly contrasted with the fruitful Italian hero-cult of an always-present Aeneas.

A corresponding contrast, this time wholly explicit, is that between the birth of Aeneas' Italian Troy (*nascentis Troiae:* X. 27; *Troiam . . . nascentem:* X. 74-75), with its Tiber and Numicus (VII. 150-151), and the death of Hector's Phrygian Troy (*at non viderunt moenia Troiae Neptuni fabricata manu considere in ignis? . . . quos distulit Hector in annum:* IX. 144-155; *eversae . . . fumantia Troiae excidia:* X. 45-46; cf. II. 290, 325, 624-625; III. 3; XI. 288-290), with its 'Xanthus and Simois' (X. 60) — this contrast, between the death of the old order in the east and the birth of the new order in the west (*maior rerum mihi nascitur ordo:* VII. 44), being resolved by Virgil into the one integral idea of a Phoenix-like rebirth or resurrection of the old eastern order (*recidiva . . . Pergama:* VII. 321-322; X. 58) in its original western birthplace (*tendimus in Latium . . . illic fas regna resurgere Troiae:* I. 205-206).

For Dardanus' Italian Troy, rebuilt in Phrygia first by Dardanus himself and then for Laomedon by Neptune with Apollo's help, is to be rebuilt a third time by Aeneas once more in Italy, where Tiberinus accordingly welcomes him not only as 'awaited on Laurentine ground and Latin fields' but also as actually 'bringing back' the city of Troy (VIII. 36-38).

The Tiber, then, personified in 'the very god of the place, Tiberinus of the pleasant river', his 'aged head' hair-crowned with 'shady sedge' and his body mantled in thin grey lawn under the poplar-leaves (VIII. 31-34) — a memory, surely, of Virgil's own 'Mincius, crowned with grey sedge' (X. 205-206) — has been longing for Aeneas in that same Dardan-Laomedontian context wherein Aeneas simultaneously has been longing for the Tiber; as Juno herself implies when, espying 'the joyful Aeneas and his Dardan fleet' (VII. 288-289), she bitterly complains how 'they find shelter in the Tiber's longed-for channel' (303) but comforts herself with the prospect of a second Trojan war resulting in a second fiery destruction of Troy upon Italian soil (295-298, 313-322).

Aeneas' interest in the Tiber began, according to the *Aeneid* as we have it, with the prophecy of Laomedon's granddaughter in Troy: ' "Thou shalt come to the land of Hesperia (i.e. the 'Western' or 'Sunset Land'), where amid the rich fields of husbandmen the Lydian (Etruscan) Tiber flows with gentle sweep; there in store for thee are happy days, a kingdom, and a royal wife" ' (II. 781-784)—Faunus' grand-daughter in Lavinium.

But Aeneas' yearning for the Tiber began only with his arrival at Buthrotum, where for the first time he found one who as Laomedon's grandson already enjoyed happy days, a kingdom, and a royal wife; the sight of whose already built Troy beside his already reproduced Xanthus (III. 349-351) recalled to Aeneas' mind the thought of his own as yet unbuilt Troy beside his own as yet undiscovered Tiber: ' "If ever I enter the Tiber and Tiber's neighbouring fields, and look upon the walls granted to my race" ' (500-501)—a thought and a sight together integrated under the figure of two Troys in one (*unam faciemus utramque Troiam animis:* 504-505) beside two rivers in one.

In Sicily, again, Aeneas' longing for the Tiber is clouded both with uncertainty as to its nature and with disappointment that Anchises cannot share his building of its Troy: ' "Not with thee was I suffered to seek Italy's bounds and destined fields, nor yet Ausonian Tiber, whate'er it be" ' (V. 82-83); while Anchises' wife Venus, reminding Neptune of his own rebuilding for Laomedon of Dardanus' eastern Troy beside the Xanthus (V. 803-811; cf. *Neptunus muros . . . quatit:* II. 610-611; *fumat Neptunia Troia:* III. 3; *moenia Troiae Neptuni fabricata manu:* IX. 144-145), prays him to conduct Aeneas' fleet in safety to the site of their western counterpart: ' "Grant them to gain Laurentine Tiber . . . if those walls are granted by the Fates" ' (V. 796-797).

Neptune's reply to Venus, recalling the Xanthus as choked with blood during the Trojan war in Phrygia (V. 806-808; cf. I. 473), is paralleled by Apollo's reply to Aeneas, through the Cumaean Sibyl, foretelling the Tiber as streaming with blood during the Trojan war in Italy (VI. 86-87); the two replies being fused in Turnus' reply to Drances, describing the Tiber as swollen with Ilian blood (XI. 393-394).

When, at long last, Aeneas enters the Tiber-mouth, it is appropriately at the dawn of a new day (VII. 25-26): 'Then lo! Aeneas, gazing forth from the flood, looks upon a mighty forest. Through its midst Tiberinus with his pleasant stream leaps out to sea in swirling eddies and yellow with plenteous sand' (29-32)—the phrase *multa flavus harena* (31) clearly echoing the sense of the corresponding Greek name *Xanthus*, meaning 'the Yellow river', given to Troy's Scamander because of its sandy floor.

But, whereas the sandy-yellow Xanthus was the symbol of Troy's bloody eastern defeat, the sandy-yellow Tiber is the symbol of Troy's bloody western victory (VIII. 49-65): '"Alas! What carnage awaits the hapless Laurentines! What a price, Turnus, shalt thou pay me! How many shields and helms and bodies of the brave shalt thou, O father Tiber, sweep beneath thy waves!" ' (VIII. 537-540).

So concerned is Venus at the Trojan blood shed beside the Tiber and Numicus around the walls of Aeneas' Italian Troy (X. 22-29) that she desperately implores Jupiter to restore the Teucrians in safety to the ruins of Hector's Phrygian Troy beside the Xanthus and Simois: ' "If there is no country for thy relentless consort (Juno) to bestow upon the Teucrians, then, by the smoking ruins of overturned Troy, I beseech thee, O Father, let me dismiss Ascanius (Iulus) from arms unscathed — let my grandson still live! (44-47) . . . What has it availed (Aeneas) to escape the plague of war, to have fled through the midst of Argive fires, to have exhausted all the perils of sea and desolate lands, while his Teucrians seek Latium and reborn Pergama (Troy's citadel)? Were it not better for them to have settled down on their fatherland's last ashes, and on the ground where once was Troy? Restore, I pray, Xanthus and Simois to an unhappy people, and let the Teucrians retrace once more the woes of Ilium!" ' (55-62).

It is to be noted, finally, that Aeneas' invocation of 'father Tiber' (*Thybri pater:* VIII. 540) in the neighbourhood of Evander's Pallanteum on receiving Vulcan's arms from Venus (535) is verbally echoed by Pallas' invocation of 'father Tiber' (*Thybri pater:* X. 421) while fighting on behalf of Aeneas' Italian Troy (X. 378) as being himself both the eponym of Pallanteum and the son of Evander (VIII. 104), 'king' and 'founder of Rome's citadel' (*rex Evandrus, Romanae conditor arcis:* VIII. 313) — that Roman citadel which, in the last analysis, shall be the Trojan 'citadel reborn' beside the Tiber as the Xanthus' counterpart.

Thus the *Aeneid*'s symbolism is identically developed from that of the *Georgics*; wherein Virgil not only linked Augustus, in a Trojan-Roman context of victory in war, both with

'Assaracus' seed' as descended from Tros and with Apollo as joint-builder of Laomedon's Troy (G. III. 16-36), but earlier still linked 'the perjury of Laomedon's Troy' with the warfare of Augustus' Rome, and both of them with 'Etruscan Tiber and the Roman Palatine' as mothered by Vesta, with Vestally mothered Romulus as builder of Rome's walls, with the *Indigetes*, and with the *Penates* as *di patrii* (G. I. 498-502).

CHAPTER VI

ATLAS AND HERCULES

> . . . super et Garamantas et Indos
> proferet imperium: iacet extra sidera tellus,
> extra anni solisque vias, ubi caelifer Atlas
> axem umero torquet stellis ardentibus aptum: . . .
>
> nec vero Alcides tantum telluris obivit. . . .
> (*Aeneid* VI. 794-801)

VIRGIL, as we have seen, mentally visualizes the Tiber-country — what Aeneas, recalling Creusa's prophetic description of it (II. 781-782), calls 'the Tiber's neighbouring fields' (III. 500) — as topographically linking together into one riverine neighbourhood, along the central line of Italy, Dardanus' token-Cortona and Evander's token-Rome and Aeneas' token-Troy.

But Aeneas and Evander and Dardanus are themselves lineally linked together, as Virgil particularly emphasizes (VIII, 134-142), by their common descent from both Atlas and Jupiter: since one of Atlas' daughters, Electra, bore to Jupiter Aeneas' ancestor Dardanus; while another of Atlas' daughters, Maia, bore to Jupiter Evander's father Mercury.

It is precisely for this reason that Mercury, when sent by Jupiter to remind Aeneas of his Roman destiny (IV. 222-237) alights upon 'the peak and steep sides of enduring Atlas, who props the sky upon his summit — Atlas, whose pine-wreathed head is ever girt with black clouds, and beaten with wind and rain; fallen snow mantles his shoulders, while rivers plunge down the aged chin and his rough beard is stiff with ice' (246-251) — before descending therefrom to Dido's Carthage, where Aeneas is prematurely founding his city (252-276) instead of founding it in the neighbourhood of Rome at that Tiber-mouth whose distant rivalry with Carthage is emphasized at the very outset of the *Aeneid* (*Karthago, Italiam contra Tiberinaque longe ostia:* I. 13-14).

For Jupiter personifies the sky whose burden is borne on the shoulders of his father-in-law Atlas as personifying his mountain; so that Mercury's spatial descent, from the sky as resting on the mountain, appropriately symbolizes Mercury's lineal descent from Jupiter as Atlas' son-in-law — a relationship collaterally shared with Mercury by Aeneas himself, who is thus no less appropriately recalled to the fulfilment of his Roman destiny in the Tiber-country by a divine cousin who is also both Evander's own father and Dardanus' own half-brother, as well as half-brother of Aeneas' own mother Venus.

But Aeneas' lineal descent from Jupiter as Atlas' son-in-law is likewise shared by all the *Dardanidae* (VII. 195-221; cf. I. 380, 560); while the name *Atlas* is but the Greek ἄτλας, 'enduring', whose Latin equivalent is *durus*.

Hence the characteristically pregnant phrase *Atlantis duri*, 'enduring Atlas' (IV. 247), occurring as it does precisely in connection with the visit of Atlas' grandson Mercury to the descendant of Atlas' grandson Dardanus, is not to be interpreted apart from the phrase *Dardanidae duri*, 'enduring sons of Dardanus' (III. 94) — Aeneas himself, as *Dardanides* (XII. 775), being the most enduring of them all (I. 3-6) — nor yet apart from the verb *durate*, 'endure!' (I. 207), as applied to 'the wearied sons of Aeneas' (*defessi Aeneadae:* I. 157) precisely with reference to the resurrection in Dardanus' Italy of his Troy (I. 204-206).

In all three cases the idea is fundamentally the same — that of the vast effort involved in fulfilling a burdensome and wearisome task from which there can be no lawful relief; the idea, in short, which underlies the entire *Aeneid*: 'So vast was the effort involved in founding the Roman race' —

tantae molis erat Romanam condere gentem (I. 33).

Indeed, the noun *moles*, here applied to Aeneas' heroic fulfilment of his Trojan-Roman destiny, implies just that conception of a heavy burden shouldered enduringly upon a massive frame, but only at the cost of immense and tedious exertion, whose mythologically familiar example is Atlas' sky-supporting mountain-mass (*Atlantis duri, caelum qui vertice fulcit:* IV. 247); while the verb *moliri*, corresponding to the noun *moles* as *durare* to *durus*, is significantly twice applied in this same Atlantean context to Aeneas' shouldering of this same Roman burden (*molitur . . . laborem:* IV. 233; *moliris . . . laborem:* 273).

By typically Virgilian implication, therefore, the starry burden of Aeneas' ancestor 'mightiest Atlas, who on his shoulder sustains the heavenly spheres' (*maximus Atlas . . . aetherios umero qui sustinet orbis:* VIII. 136-137), is symbolically inherited by Atlas' descendant Aeneas, whose own starry destiny (I. 259-260), inherited in turn both by Iulus (IX. 641) and by Augustus (I. 287), is also the starry destiny of his Roman race (III. 158; VIII. 98-100) as founded by an 'Atlantean' effort (I. 33), and as descended partly from Latinus: ' "Seek not, O my son," ' replies 'the oracle of Faunus, his prophetic sire' (VII. 81-82), ' "to ally thy daughter in Latin wedlock, and put no faith in the bridal-chamber prepared (for Turnus). Strangers shall come, to be thy sons-in-law, whose blood shall exalt our name to the stars, and the descendants of whose stock shall behold, where the circling sun looks on either Ocean (east and west), the whole world rolling as their kingdom under their feet" ' (VII. 96-101) — a prophecy immediately followed by mention of the 'Laomedontian men-folk' as landing, already rumoured, upon the Tiber-bank (102-106).

Aeneas' own starry burden, so far implicit, is explicitly symbolized by that 'starry shield' which symbolizes his Roman destiny — 'father Aeneas, source of the Roman stock, ablaze with starry shield' (*pater Aeneas*, *Romanae stirpis origo*, *sidereo flagrans clipeo* (XII. 166-167): 'There the story of Italy and the triumphs of Rome had (Vulcan) the Lord of Fire fashioned, not unversed in prophecy, or unknowing of the age to come; there every generation of the stock to spring from Ascanius (i.e. the Julian clan), and the wars they fought one by one' (VIII. 626-629).

For it is precisely as one descendant of sky-shouldering Atlas visiting another on the site of Rome (VIII. 134-151) that Aeneas shoulders his destiny as portrayed upon his shield: 'Such sights he marvels at on the shield of Vulcan, his mother's gift; and, though he knows not the deeds, he rejoices in their portraiture, uplifting on his shoulder (*attollens umero*) the fame and destinies of his descendants' (VIII. 729-731) — the fame and destiny, in particular, of that Augustus Caesar (VIII. 675-728) who, as foreseen by Aeneas himself in Elysium under Anchises' prophetic guidance, ' "shall spread his empire past Garamant and Indian, to a land that lies beyond the constellations, beyond the paths of the year and of the sun, where sky-bearing Atlas turns on his shoulder the globe inset with gleaming stars . . . Nor, in truth, did (Hercules) the grandson of Alcaeus range over such space of earth, though he pierced the bronze-footed deer (of Arcadia), or brought peace to the woods of Erymanthus, and made Lerna tremble at his bow" ' (VI. 794-797, 801-803).

Now this prophetic coupling of Augustus' victories both with Atlas' starry burden and with Hercules' earthly labours is paralleled precisely during Aeneas' visit to Evander on the site of Augustus' Rome, where the victory-celebrating rites of Hercules are temporarily interrupted while the two kings swear mutual fidelity in warfare on the basis of that common descent from sky-shouldering Atlas which alone entitles Aeneas — recently hailed by Tiberinus as a destined *victor* in that warfare (VIII. 61) — to participate on equal terms in the festival of victorious Hercules (VIII. 97-183) as preliminary to the shouldering of his victory-symbolizing shield.

Nor is this twofold Virgilian coupling of Hercules with Atlas in an Augustan-Roman context merely accidental.

For Alcaeus' grandson Hercules, ritually remembered at Augustan Rome as *Victor* (cf. *victor Alcides:* VIII. 362-363), was also mythically remembered at Augustan Rome as having temporarily shouldered Atlas' own starry burden (Ovid, *Fasti* I. 565-568) during his visit to those Atlantides or Hesperides whose dragon-guarded apple-tree (Dicdorus Siculus IV. xxvii), referred to by Virgil in the sixth *Eclogue* (61), is in the *Aeneid* mentioned by Dido precisely as the result of Mercury's descent from Atlas to Aeneas in connection with his Roman destiny as Augustus' ancestor: ' "Near Ocean's bound and the setting sun lies Aethiopia (Morocco), farthest of lands, where mightiest Atlas (*maximus Atlas:* cf. VIII. 136) turns on his shoulder the globe inset with gleaming stars (*axem umero torquet stellis ardentibus aptum:* cf. VI. 797). Thence a priestess of Massylian race has been shown me, warden of the fane of the Hesperides, who gave dainties to the dragon and guarded the sacred boughs on the tree" ' (IV. 480-485) — these words of Dido in regard to Atlas being significantly echoed both by Anchises in regard to Augustus' Herculean exploits (VI. 794-803) and by Aeneas during Evander's Herculean festival (VIII. 102-137).

It is further significant that Ovid, after echoing Virgil's own emphasis on the massiveness of Cacus' mountain-barricade against Hercules' attack (*Fasti* I. 543-564; *Aeneid* VIII. 190-235), goes on to relate how Hercules 'shoves it with his shoulders — the shoulders on which the sky itself had once rested — and by the shock he loosens its vast weight; its overthrow was accompanied by a crash that startled even the upper air, and the battered ground sank under the burden of its bulk' (*Fasti* I. 565-568) — a description so manifestly reminiscent of the corresponding passage in the *Aeneid* (VIII. 233-246), as to suggest that Ovid, who understands so much of the *Aeneid's* underlying symbolism, here understood Virgil to imply just that mythical association of Hercules with Atlas as a sky-bearer which was so familiar to the readers of both Augustan poets.

Consequently Virgil's readers will themselves have understood his implication that Aeneas' Roman task, being organically Atlantean by right of mythically inherited destiny, is also functionally Herculean by right of mythically recounted example.

But also by right of ritually mediated identification.

For the Atlas-descended Trojan king Aeneas is solemnly enthroned by the Atlas-descended Roman king Evander 'on a shaggy lion's skin' (*villosi pelle leonis:* VIII. 177), and so upon the very 'garb of Hercules' himself (*Herculeo . . . amictu:* VII. 669; with context) as worn for panoply by Hercules' own victory-winning son Aventinus, eponym of the recent scene of Hercules' victory in his lion-skin over Cacus; and Aeneas, thus royally enthroned, joins Evander in ritually eating and drinking the sacrificial elements of Hercules' own quasi-sacramental meal (VIII. 172-184) in celebration of that Herculean victory wherein Aeneas himself participates not only thus ritually but also through the medium of Evander's quasi-initiatory myth (185-272), followed both by a ritual wine-drinking (273-279) and by a ritual celebration of Hercules' mythical labours on man's behalf (280-305).

Thus it is as Hercules' own duly accredited successor that Aeneas, after surveying the site of Augustus' Rome under Evander's guidance (306-361), as 'founder of Rome's citadel' (313), is welcomed by Rome's earliest founder to his humble guest-house: ' "These portals," quoth he, "Alcaeus' grandson stooped to enter as victor; this palace (*regia*) welcomed him. Dare, my son, to scorn riches; fashion thyself also to be worthy of deity, and come not disdainful of our poverty". So saying, beneath the sloped roof of his cramped lodging he led large Aeneas' (362-367).

Thus Aeneas spends his first night in future Rome upon the very bed (367-369) whereon quite recently slept his predecessor Hercules as victor on that same Aventine hill whose wood Virgil associates both with 'the priestess Rhea' (VII. 659) and with her son by Hercules, Aventinus, who 'displays on the sward his palm-crowned chariot and victorious steeds, and on his shield bears his father's device, a hundred snakes and the Hydra girt with serpents' (655-658); 'Himself he went on foot, swinging a huge lion-skin, unkempt with terrifying mane, its white teeth crowning his head; in such guise he stooped to enter (Latinus') royal palace, shaggy-rough, his shoulders enveloped in the garb of Hercules' (666-669).

But the lion-skin which envelopes the shoulders of Hercules' son by Rhea, whose name is that of Cybele herself, is by Virgilian implication the skin of one of Cybele's own lions as described by Anchises: 'And yoked lions have learnt to bear the burden of their Mistress' chariot' (III. 113); while Aeneas' own burden was first personified by Anchises, himself burdened with the Trojan-Roman Vesta's hallows, and borne with them upon a lion-skin by implication belonging to one of Rhea-Cybele's lions:

' "Come, then, dear father, mount upon my neck; on my shoulders I will carry thee, nor will such a task (*labor*) overburden me . . . Do thou, father, take in thy hand the (Vestal) hallows and ancestral Penates" . . . So I spoke; and over my broad shoulders and bowed neck I spread the cover of a tawny lion's skin (*fulvi . . . pelle leonis*), and stoop to the burden' (II. 707-708, 717, 721-723).

Hence Atlas-descended and Hercules-succeeding Aeneas is to Dido, as to Virgil himself, primarily a burden-bearer; one ' "whom men describe as carrying about with him his ancestral Penates, even as he bore on his shoulders a father outworn with age" ' (IV. 598-599) — shoulders which, lineally derived from those of Atlas and resembling those of Hercules when he bore Atlas' own burden on their lion-skin covering, carried the very symbol of Aeneas' Trojan-Roman destiny.

Thus Virgil's Atlantean-Herculean symbolism, already implicit during Aeneas' departure from the site of Troy's destruction, appropriately becomes explicit during Aeneas' visit to the site of Rome's construction; his visit to, and departure from, Elysium linking the two sites together in a prophetically

Augustan context both of Trojan-Roman destiny and of Atlantean-Herculean effort (VI. 752-807).

From the very outset of his Pallantean visit, moreover, Aeneas has in fact stepped suddenly forward into the future, with its Potitian-Pinarian cult of the Roman Hercules at the *ara maxima* in the *forum boarium* or Roman cattle-market (VIII. 102-104, 185-188, 268-272); his subsequent perambulation through Augustan Rome bringing him to 'the Carmental Gate, as the Romans call it; a tribute of old to (Evander's mother) the nymph Carmentis, soothsaying prophetess, who first foretold the greatness of Aeneas' sons and the glory of Pallanteum' (337-341): 'So talking, each with each, they drew nigh to the lodging of poor Evander, and saw cattle all about, lowing in the Roman Forum and the brilliant Carinae' (359-361).

This Virgilian contrast, of course, means that Aeneas, dazzled by the revelation of his destiny, is rudely awakened from his daydream by a sudden stepping back again from that remote future into the actual present of mere 'walls and a citadel and scattered house-roofs, which to-day Rome's empire has exalted to heaven, but then Evander ruled, a scant domain' (98-100); a present so humble and unpretentious that only its recent share in Hercules' victory can redeem it from insignificance.

Evander, therefore, having warned Aeneas that, however great his destiny, he must learn from Hercules not to despise the lowliness of Rome's beginnings, conducted his guest into his tiny room (362-367) 'and laid him upon bedding of strewn leaves and the skin of a Libyan she-bear; night rushes down, and clasps the earth with dusky wings' —

> . . . *stratisque locavit*
> *effultum foliis et pelle Libystidis ursae.*
> *nox ruit et fuscis tellurem amplectitur alis* (367-369).

Seldom is even Virgil's symbolism so subtle as here. For Aeneas not only spends his first night on the site of Rome — that very night, moreover, during which his victory-symbolizing starry shield is forged by Cacus' father Vulcan (198, 370-453) — in the same room where Hercules himself so recently slept as victor over Vulcan's son Cacus (362-363), but he spends it lying on a bear-skin emblematic of Evander's own racial ancestress Callisto, mother of Arcas (cf. *Arcas:* 102, 129) the eponymous ancestor of those 'Arcadians, a race sprung from Pallas, who were the company of king Evander and followed his banner' (51-52) from Arcadia to Pallanteum (53-54); itself, accordingly, 'a Greek city' (VI. 97) with Arcadian traditions.

The story went that Jupiter (Zeus), having changed Callisto into a she-bear for his begetting thereon of Arcas, whose Greek name suggested 'bear' (ἄρκτος, ἄρκος), later uplifted her to the sky, where she now shines by night as the constellation of 'The She-Bear (*Ursa*, Ἄρκτος); meanwhile entrusting Callisto's son Arcas to Evander's grandmother Maia — that same Maia who is the daughter of that same Atlas who uplifts the constellations of the sky' (*idem Atlas generat, caeli qui sidera tollit:* VIII. 141), as well as the mother of that same Mercury (138-139) without whose agency Aeneas would never have slept upon Evander's bear-skin, the emblem of Evander's Arcadian hospitality.

Now Virgil's readers, familiar as they were with all that concerned the Delphic oracle, will not have failed to hear talk of that famous Delphic painting by Polygnotus (c. 470-440 B.C.) in which Callisto was symbolically depicted as lying on 'a bear-skin by way of bedding' (τῇ Καλλιστοῖ δὲ ἀντὶ μὲν στρωμνῆς ἐστιν αὐτῇ δέρμα ἄρκτου: Pausanias X. xxxi. 10); so that the symbolism of Aeneas' own bedding, as the skin of a she-bear spread over a mattress of leaves, will not have escaped them.

No less clear, too, will have been their recollection of the sheep-skins on which Latinus himself, as Aeneas' future father-in-law, lay by way of bedding — sheep-skins no less emblematic of Latinus' father Faunus, the shepherds' own particular god, than Evander's bear-skin is emblematic of his ancestress Callisto; and of how it was precisely while lying on those sheep-skins that Latinus learnt from Faunus (VII. 81-106) the Roman destiny of Aeneas' descendants, 'whose blood shall exalt our name to the stars' (98-99).

Now Latinus' sheep-skin bedding belongs, as Virgil himself implies, to that oracular rite of 'incubation' which in Greece sometimes involved the consultant's sleeping all night upon a beast's skin wrapped round his body. Pausanias (I. xxxiv. 5), for example, records how inquirers at Amphiaraus' sanctuary, near Oropus, slept on a ram's skin, 'awaiting a revelation in a dream' — a Greek custom which spread with Greek colonization to southern Italy where, in Apulia, consultants of Calchas' oracle slept in the folds of a ram's skin (Strabo VI. iii. 10 = 284).

It follows that Latinus' future son-in-law, sleeping all night in the folds of a bear-skin emblematic of his host's ancestral She-Bear — herself now a constellation of the night-sky, Aeneas' own figurative destination (I. 259-260), as shouldered both by their common ancestor Atlas, whose daughter (Evander's grandmother) foster-mothered the She-Bear's son, and once by victorious but humble Hercules, who passed the night upon her bear-skin as Aeneas' exemplar — is at least placed most appropriately for receiving some kind of incubatory revelation in a dream; his position being paralleled in that of the man, traditional amongst the Algonquin Indians, who by dreaming on a bear-skin could divine things otherwise hidden from him (C. G. Leland, *The Algonquin Indians of New England*, p. 344; quoted by Sir J. G. Frazer, *Pausanias' Description of Greece*, London 1898, Vol. II, p. 476).

There are, in point of fact, unmistakable indications that Virgil, had he lived to complete his final revision of the *Aeneid*, would have told how Venus, having first persuaded Vulcan to make Aeneas' war-equipment during the night of Aeneas' sleep upon the bear-skin (VIII. 366-415), appeared to Aeneas in a dream with the promise of its celestial apparition in token of the imminence of his war, together with an outline of his own celestial destiny as achieved through ultimate victory.

For Aeneas next morning is early astir; and Evander, who has risen no less early, goes to greet his guest with a reminder that, though war is imminent, his victorious destiny is assured (VIII. 454-519); when suddenly there is a flash of lightning with a peal of thunder from a cloudless sky, a sign from Venus (520-527) that Vulcan's Cyclopean manufacturers of thunder and lightning (VIII. 416-432) and of war-equipment (433-438) had finished making Aeneas' own war-equipment (439-453) while he slept upon the bear-skin (366-464):

'In the serene expanse of sky they see, amidst a cloud, arms gleaming red in an otherwise clear sky, and clashing thunderously. The others stood aghast; but the Trojan hero recognized (*adgnovit*) the sound and his goddess-mother's promises. Then he cries' (*memorat*; suggesting the translation of something remembered into something spoken): '"Ask not, my host, ask not, I pray, what fortune the portents forbode; it is I who am summoned of Heaven. This sign (*signum:* 534; cf. 523) my goddess-mother foretold (*cecinit*; suggesting an oracular prophecy) she would send if war were at hand, and to my help would bring through the air arms wrought by Vulcan. Alas, what carnage awaits the hapless Laurentians! What a price, Turnus, shalt thou pay me!"' (VIII. 528-537)—this promise of Venus being nowhere else even hinted at in the *Aeneid* as we have it.

Aeneas' reaction to its fulfilment, moreover, is significant.

For not only has he obviously been expecting it as a call to arms against Turnus, and so as a sign that he must leave Pallanteum at once, but his unhesitating recognition of it when it comes is immediately in his mind connected with the place where he has just been sleeping on the bear-skin as Hercules' successor to Evander's homely hospitality: 'With these words he rises from his lofty throne; and then, before all else, he quickens the slumbering altars with Hercules' fires, and joyfully visits yesterday's Lar and little Penates' (541-544)—an allusion to the fact that Aeneas' *Volcania arma* appeared in the air while he was seated in talk with Evander out of doors 'in the midst of the dwellings', one of which is 'the lodging and seclusion of his guest Aeneas' (463-468).

Nor does Virgil here forget Latinus' oracular sheep-skin incubation, with its preparatory sacrifice of ewes (*mactabat rite bidentis:* VII. 93); since, in nearly identical terms, he at once goes on to tell how Aeneas' Trojan company join Evander in sacrificing 'duly chosen ewes' (*mactant lectas de more bidentis:* VIII. 544)—a sacrifice, preparatory to Aeneas' departure for battle, described in terms (*Evandrus pariter, pariter Troiana iuventus:* VIII. 545) verbally reminiscent of that Hercules-meal (*vescitur Aeneas simul et Troiana inventus:* VIII. 182) which quasi-sacramentally initiated Aeneas into his Herculean destiny as Victor in the coming war with Turnus.

That destiny, already ratified under the figure of his enthronement on 'the skin of a shaggy lion' (*villosi pelle leonis:* VIII. 177), now draws nearer to its fulfilment; for Evander forthwith mounts Aeneas as a quasi-Hercules on a horse which, besides being 'specially chosen' for him (*ducunt exsortem Aeneae:* 552) resembles Hercules himself in being 'wholly covered with a tawny lion-skin' (*quem fulva leonis pellis obit totum:* 552-553); itself verbally reminiscent of that 'tawny lion's skin' (*fulvique insternor pelle leonis:* II. 722) which wholly covered Aeneas' own neck and shoulders when carrying Anchises thereon out of Troy.

Virgil, in other words, implies a parallel, clear enough to his own imagination, between Aeneas' 'Anchisean' burden, as borne symbolically from the site of Troy's destruction in a context of recent defeat, and Aeneas' 'Herculean' burden, as borne symbolically from the site of Rome's construction in a context of recent victory; a parallel, in fact, between the contrasted fates of Anchises and of Hercules respectively as Aeneas' two predecessors and exemplars in regard to a burden both Trojan and Roman.

Now not only the phrase *ducere exsortem*, here applied to Aeneas' horse as covered with a lion-skin (VIII. 552), but also the phrase *pelle Libystidis ursae*, recently applied to Aeneas' bed as covered with a bear-skin (VIII. 368), have earlier been employed by Virgil in reference to Acestes (V. 37, 534); so that the poet's repetition of both these phrases, the former rare in Latin literature and the latter unique, betrays some corresponding mental association between Aeneas' Pallantean welcome by the recently immigrant Arcadian king Evander, for the glad celebration of the anniversary rites of his recent visitor Hercules, and Aeneas' Sicilian welcome by the recently immigrant Trojan king Acestes, for the sad celebration of the anniversary rites of his recent visitor Anchises (III. 707-714; V. 28-63) — the connecting link in Virgil's mind being Hercules, as a recent visitor to Sicily, where he slew Venus' son and Aeneas' half-brother Eryx in a boxing-match (V. 410-414) just as he slew Venus' stepson and Aeneas' step-brother Cacus at Pallanteum.

Acestes' Sicilian welcome, moreover, resembles Evander's Pallantean welcome in being associated by Virgil with the idea, not only of humble hospitality in a newly-founded foreign colony, but also both of war-equipment and of a Libyan bear-skin (precisely the threefold thought underlying Virgil's account of Aeneas' night on the site of Rome: VIII. 359-465); since Acestes, on sighting Aeneas' fleet arriving from Libya, hastens to greet him 'bristling with weapons and the skin of a Libyan she-bear' (*horridus in iaculis et pelle Libystidis ursae:* V.

37) — a phrase further resembling that applied to Hercules' son Aventinus, 'bristling and with shoulders enveloped in the garb of Hercules' (*horridus Herculeoque umeros innexus amictu:* VII. 669), a huge lion-skin.

Similarly, the sudden fiery apparition of Aeneas' weapons in the Pallantean sky, followed by Evander's singling out of Aeneas for the honour of a specially chosen gift-horse (*ducunt exsortem:* VIII. 552), is closely paralleled by the sudden fiery apparition of Acestes' arrow in the Sicilian sky, followed by Aeneas' singling out of Acestes for the honour of a specially chosen gift-bowl (*exsortem ducere:* V. 534); the bowl belonging to Anchises in virtue of its history (V. 535-538), just as the horse belongs to Hercules in virtue of its covering (VIII. 552-553).

The verbally betrayed mental symbolism in either case is, though but implicit, clear enough. For on the one hand, in connection with the Sicilian commemoratory rites of Anchises, the local but not indigenous king Acestes is presented by his temporary but ancestrally related guest Aeneas with a bowl which, as being Anchises' own peculiar property, betokens the locally mediated goodwill of Anchises himself towards Acestes' future armed defence of his allotted kingship over that Trojan-Sicilian colony, founded shortly afterwards by Aeneas (V. 711-771), whose city is to be named Acesta (718) and whose divine patroness will be Venus *Erycina* (759-760); while on the other hand, in connection with the Pallantean commemoratory rites of Hercules, the local but not indigenous king Evander presents his temporary but ancestrally related guest Aeneas with a horse which, as wearing Hercules' own peculiar apparel, betokens the locally mediated goodwill of Hercules himself towards Aeneas' future armed defence of his allotted kingship over that Arcadian-Pallantean colony, founded rather earlier by Evander (VIII. 51-54, 337-341), whose city is to be named Rome (VIII. 98-100, 313, 337-341) and whose divine patroness will be Venus *Erycina* too — the connecting links in Virgil's mind, therefore, being not only Hercules but Venus. Nor does this implicitly contrasted parallelism between the *Aeneid*'s fifth and eighth books, themselves significantly equidistant from the poem's centre, end even here.

For, just as the Pallantean episode of the gift-horse, symbolically pledging Hercules' patronage of Rome in time of war, is followed by that of the grimly martial cavalry-parade wherein Aeneas, for once without Iulus (VIII. 546-550), concludes the glad solemnities of victorious Hercules' immortality by riding royally forth at the head of his Trojan compeers, to the sadly voiced admiration of many onlookers (585-596) into those all-too-long manœuvres of serious battle and of real warfare (597-625) wherewith he will eventually found his long-promised walled city at Lavinium (I. 257-266); so too the Sicilian episode of the gift-bowl, symbolically pledging Anchises' patronage of Acesta in time of war, is followed by that of the gaily martial cavalry-parade wherein Iulus, for once without Aeneas (V. 545-552), concludes the sad solemnities of frustrated Anchises' mortality by riding royally forth at the head of his Trojan compeers, to the gladly voiced admiration of many onlookers (553-579), into those all-too-short manœuvres of sportive battle and of mimic warfare (580-595) wherewith he will eventually found his long-promised walled city at Alba Longa (I. 267-274; V. 596-600) — whence, under its name of 'Troy', Iulus' initially Sicilian mimicry of warfare will eventually pass to Rome (V. 600-602), and so to the very starting-point of Aeneas' initially Pallantean reality of warfare in defence of his archetypal 'Troy' (*subsidio Troiae:* X. 214).

It is, moreover, precisely at the point when Aeneas' cavalry-parade has halted for rest outside Pallanteum (VIII. 597-607) that Venus, herself the main connecting link between Pallantean Rome and Sicilian Acesta, presents Aeneas with his equipment for the coming war (608-625); including that 'vast' and 'starry' burden, 'Vulcan's shield' (447, 729; XII. 167), whose 'ineffable fabric' (VIII. 625), expressly designed for Aeneas' future armed defence of his Roman destiny (381-386, 400-404, 441-453), portrays not only the general outlines of that destiny as already surveyed by Aeneas topographically inside Pallanteum (306-361) and as subsequently defended by his own descendants (626-728) the *Aeneadae* (648) and *Romulidae* (638) but also the particular details of 'every generation of the stock to spring from Ascanius (Iulus) and the wars they fought one after another' (628-629) especially under Augustus Caesar (675-728), himself no less central to the pattern of Aeneas' shield (*in medio:* 675) than to that of Virgil's temple-epic (*in medio:* G. III. 16) — this shield-portraiture, as lingeringly surveyed under his mother Venus' guidance outside

Pallanteum (617-625, 729-731), being in fact the glyptic equivalent of the soul-portraiture lingeringly surveyed by Aeneas under his father Anchises' guidance inside Elysium (VI. 752-892); the two surveys being linked together by that one Atlantean-Herculean symbolism which belongs both to Augustus and to Aeneas as the bearers of that burden which is Rome.

CHAPTER VII

SHIELD AND MAZE

> Talia per clipeum Volcani, dona parentis,
> miratur rerumque ignarus imagine gaudet,
> attollens umero famamque et fata nepotum.
> (*Aeneid* VIII. 729-731)

VIRGIL applies identically the same terms, 'they entangle circles with circles' (*orbibus orbis impediunt*) to the process of dynamically shaping both Aeneas' 'Roman' shield (VIII. 448-449) and Iulus' 'Trojan' game (V. 584-585) — a verbal repetition betraying some mental association between both of them and that entangling or weaving process (*impediunt texuntque:* V. 593) which results in the one convolutionary pattern (*textum:* VIII. 625; cf. V. 589).

Now the pattern of Iulus' game resembles that of the Cretan labyrinth or maze (V. 588-593); while the underlying significance of all labyrinths or mazes, whether curvilinear or rectilinear, whether static or dynamic, is that of a shield or defence against unauthorized penetration material or spiritual (W. F. Jackson Knight, *Cumaean Gates*, Oxford 1936, *passim*).

There is thus an *a priori* probability that Virgil's poetic mind, hereditarily aware of this significance, unconsciously appropriated the labyrinthine pattern in its dynamically curvilinear form as its symbol for the material and spiritual defence of that Trojan-Roman destiny whose fulfilment involves the preliminary foundation both of Aeneas' Lavinium and of Iulius Alba Longa as the successively rising twin steps towards the one finally supreme foundation of Romulus' Rome (I. 1-7); this maze-pattern, as a gradually woven entanglement of one circle with another, being accordingly shared as their common symbol for Virgil's mind no less by Aeneas' 'Roman' shield, as later employed by him defensively on the material plane (VIII. 447-448; XII. 697-741) for his thereby spiritually safe construction of the walls of Lavinium (I. 257-266); XII. 791-886) than by Iulus' 'Trojan' game, as later employed by him defensively on the material plane (V. 596-600) for his thereby spiritually safe construction of the walls of Alba Longa (I. 267-274; VIII. 47-49) — both these foundations in their turn being superseded by that of a Rome whose defensive symbol is still that maze-pattern which in the *Aeneid* belongs both to the shaping of Aeneas' shield as representing Rome's triumphs (VIII. 626-629) and to the playing of Iulus' game as perpetuated in Augustus' Rome (V. 600-602).

This probability, already strong, is further strengthened by comparison of the circumstances attending Aeneas' visits, with all their complementary contrasts, to Elysium and to Pallanteum.

For Aeneas' topographical survey of Pallanteum, including a view of the Tarpeian or Capitoline citadel (VIII. 347-348) and concluding with Evander's detailed advice for Aeneas' defence of his destiny in the coming war (470-519), is appropriately succeeded by his lingering survey outside Pallanteum of a defensive picture (629) whose Roman story, detailed in relief upon the fabric of Vulcan's shield (626-731), includes that of the Tarpeian or Capitoline citadel in its specifically defensive context (652-653) — the long delay, resulting from Aeneas' mental absorption therein, being outspokenly encouraged by his patroness Venus in person, both as Vulcan's wife and as guardian of Vulcan's shield (606-625), precisely because the particular relevance of the shield's defensive picture to the fulfilment of Aeneas' destiny has been manifested to him already during his Pallantean tour; this same defensive relevance being personified in Evander himself, as 'founder of the Roman citadel' (313).

Conversely, Aeneas' phantasmagoric survey of Elysium, including a view of Minos, the destiny-allotting urn, Pasiphae, and Theseus (VI. 432, 447, 618), and concluding with Anchises' detailed advice for Aeneas' defence of his destiny in the coming war (888-901), is appropriately preceded by his lingering survey outside Elysium of a labyrinthine pattern (27) whose Cretan story, detailed in relief upon the entrance of Apollo's temple (14-33), includes that of Minos, the destiny-allotting urn, Pasiphae, and Theseus in their specifically labyrinthine context (14, 22, 24-26, 28-30) — the long delay, resulting from Aeneas' mental absorption therein, being outspokenly discouraged by his patroness the Cumaean Sibyl in person, both as Apollo's priestess and as guardian of Apollo's temple (33-41), precisely because the particular relevance of the temple's labyrinthine pattern to the fulfilment of Aeneas' destiny will be manifested to him only during his Elysian tour; this same labyrinthine relevance being personified in Anchises himself as invoked, both as spirit and as ashes, by Aeneas in Sicily (‘*salvete . . . cineres animaeque*’: V. 80-81).

For it was in honour (V. 550, 603) no less of Anchises' spirit than of his ashes that the pattern of the same Cretan labyrinth (588-593) as that which Aeneas studies so thoughtfully at Cumae was by his express command in Sicily (545-552) delineated at Anchises' tomb (605, 664); nor was it until Anchises had thus been irrevocably associated with this pattern of the Cretan labyrinth that he called Aeneas by way of Cumae to Elysium for the revelation therein, not merely of his destiny in general, but in particular of its necessary defence in war (721-740).

Consequently in Elysium, ‘when Anchises has led his son through every detail and has fired his soul with love of fame to come, he then straightway recounts the wars to be waged hereafter by the hero, and instructs him of the Laurentine peoples and Latinus' city, and in what manner he is to flee or face each toil’ (VI. 888-892) — Anchises' final instructions (*et quo quemque modo fugiatque feratque laborem*) thus verbally echoing that twofold idea of backward-and-forward movement, of ‘to-and-fro’, which earlier characterized Virgil's description of the pattern of the Cretan labyrinth as traced round about Anchises' Sicilian tomb (*et nunc terga fuga nudant, nunc spicula vertunt infensi:* V. 586-587; *texuntque fugas et proelia:* 593) by those who as ‘Teucrians' sons’ thereby associate with the idea of Crete (*ut quondam in Creta . . . hand alio Teucrum nati:* 588-592) that same Anchises who himself associated the idea of Crete both with Teucer's descendants and with the destiny of an Aeneas (III. 102-120) who in Elysium is addressed by the Sibyl as ‘famed leader of the Teucrians’ precisely when referring to Minos' Cretan brother, ‘Rhadamanthus of Knossos’ (VI. 562-566).

In other words, while Aeneas' descent from Dardanus connects his destiny with the past both of Dardanus' Italy and of Dardanus' Troy, Aeneas' descent from Teucer connects his destiny with the past both of Teucer's Troy and of Teucer's Crete; that ‘kingdom of Knossos’ (*Gnosia regna:* III. 115) which is identical with the ‘Minos' kingdom’ (*Minoia regna:* VI. 14) in the ‘land of Knossos’ (*Gnosia tellus:* VI. 23) surveyed pictorially, together with the Cretan labyrinth (*hic labor ille domus et inextricabilis error:* VI. 27), by Aeneas at Cumae before receiving his detailed instructions from Anchises in Elysium on the manner of his fighting in Italy—Anchises' word *laborem* (VI. 892) echoing the *labor* (VI. 27) of the labyrinth.

Thus, since the connecting link in Virgil's mind between Crete and Troy and Italy is that Italian 'game of Troy' (*Troiae lusus*) whose manner of fighting is the pattern of Crete's labyrinth, it is no surprise to find that the material result of Anchises' spiritual directions in Elysium is Aeneas' employment in Italy of that manner of fighting which, as the maze-pattern studied by him at Cumae, is associated in Virgil's mind both consciously with Iulus' game and unconsciously with Aeneas' shield.

Indeed, at the very point where the fulfilment of Aeneas' destiny, as Lavinia's bridegroom and Lavinium's refounder, depends mainly on the defensive use of his shield against Turnus' attacks in their finally decisive duel (XII. 464-765), Virgil describes the foot-manœuvres of Aeneas' real combat in terms unmistakably reminiscent of those describing the horse-manœuvres of Iulus' mimic combat as employed during Iulus' foundation of his Alba Longa from Lavinium: 'This manner of horsemanship, these contests Ascanius first revived when he was surrounding Alba Longa with walls and taught the Early Latins, even as he himself solemnized them as a boy, and with him the Trojan youth. The Albans taught their children; from them in turn mighty Rome received them, and kept as an ancestral observance; and to-day the boys are called "Troy" and the troop "Trojan" ' (V. 596-602).

Now Virgil describes Iulus' mimic combat thus: 'They galloped apart in equal ranks, and the three companies, parting their bands, broke up the columns; then, recalled, they wheeled about and charged with level lances. Next they enter on other courses and other counter-courses (*cursus . . . recursus*) in opposing groups, and they entangle alternate circles with circles (*orbibus orbis impediunt*), and awaken mimicries of battle under arms (*pugnaeque cient simulacra sub armis:* cf. *ludo . . . belli simulacra ciebat:* V. 674). And now they bare their backs in flight (*fuga*), now turn their spears in charge, now make peace and ride on side by side. As of old in high Crete the labyrinth is said to have held a path woven (*textum*) with blind walls and a bewildering device (*ancipitemque . . . dolum;* cf. *dolos tecti ambagesque:* VI. 29) with a thousand ways (*mille viis*), where the tokens of the trail were continually being broken off by the undiscoverable and irretraceable maze (*indeprehensus et irremeabilis error;* cf. *inextricabilis error:* VI. 27): even in such a course (*cursu*) do the Teucrians' sons entangle their tracks (*vestigia*) and weave their flights and fights in sport (*texuntque fugas et proelia ludo*); like unto dolphins that . . . sport (*ludunt*) amid the waves' (V. 580-595).

Similarly labyrinthine in pattern is the manner of Aeneas' and Turnus' foot-manœuvres in real combat as contrasted explicitly with mimic combat: 'And now here, and now there (Juturna) displays her triumphant brother (Turnus); yet she suffers him not to close in fight, but flits far away. None the less Aeneas threads the winding maze' (literally, 'twisted circles': *tortos . . . orbis*) 'to meet him, and tracks down (*vestigat*) his man' (XII. 479-482). . . . 'And (Turnus) now hither, now thither, entwines baffling circles (*incertos implicat orbis:* XII. 743) . . . (as when a hunted stag) takes flight to and fro a thousand ways (*mille fugit refugitque vias:* 753) . . . Five circles they cover in their course, and they unweave as many circles to and fro; since it is no trifling or sportive prizes that are at stake, but it is for the life and blood of Turnus that they strive':

> *quinque orbis explent cursu totidemque retexunt*
> *huc illuc; neque enim levia aut ludicra petuntur*
> *praemia, sed Turni de vita et sanguine certant* (XII. 763-765).

This last quotation is of particular interest.

For *ludicrum Troiae*, the 'sport of Troy' (Tacitus, *Annales* XI. xi), was an alternative name for that *Troiae lusus*, the 'game of Troy' (Suetonius, *Claudius* xxi), whose performance was termed *Troiam ludere*, 'playing Troy' (Suetonius, *Caesar* xxxix); while the word *ludibria*, 'sports' or 'mockeries' (Lucretius II. 47), applied to Roman cavalry-manœuvres as contrasted with actual warfare, is used by Lucretius (II. 41, 324) in connection with those phrases *belli simulcra cientis* and *belli simulacra cientes* whose Virgilian echoes are the phrases *pugnaeque cient simulacra* and *ludo . . . belli simulacra ciebat* (V. 585, 674) applied to Iulus' Sicilian performance of sportive cavalry-manœuvres in the *Troiae lusus*.

Thus Virgil's use of the adjective *ludicrus*, 'sportive' (XII. 764), in this circle-weaving and circle-unweaving martial context, unwittingly betrays his own sense of a complementary contrast between Aeneas' real foot-combat, with two lives at stake, and Iulus' mimic horse-combat, the *ludicrum Troiae* with its *ludicra praemia*, involving but small risk to life.

Virgil, in short, not only employs the same labyrinthine phraseology for the defensive symbolism of the Trojan-Roman destinies both of Aeneas (XII. 826-828) and of Iulus (V. 600-602) but significantly links the defence of both destinies with the symbolism of that shield (XII. 166-168) whose Cyclopean shaping he describes in similarly labyrinthine phraseology: 'A giant shield they shape, to confront all the weapons of the Latins, and they entangle sevenfold circles with circles' (VIII. 447-449) — this sevenfold convolutionary patterning of Vulcan's giant shield (*ingentem clipeum informant . . . septenosque orbibus orbis impediunt*), as manifested during Aeneas' Pallantean visit, at once recalling the sevenfold convolutionary patterning of Anchises' giant snake, itself a symbol of defensive guardianship, as manifested during Aeneas' Sicilian visit (*septem ingens gyros, septena volumina traxit:* V. 85) before the manifold convolutionary patterning of Iulus' game (*alternosque orbibus orbis impediunt:* V. 584-585); the connecting links in Virgil's mind being once again not only Venus, as the wife both of Vulcan and of Anchises, but also Hercules as associated both with Sicily and with Pallanteum, both with the seven-headed giant snake of Lerna (VI. 287, 803; VIII. 299-300; cf. XII. 518) and with his own Hesiodic giant shield (*Aspis* 139-321), made by Vulcan's Greek counterpart Hephaistos.

Nor does Virgil's defensive symbolism end here; since the 'five circles' of Aeneas' foot-manœuvres against those of Turnus (*quinque orbis:* XII. 763) are unquestionably echoed in Virgil's poetic memory from the 'five folds' of Achilles' Homeric giant shield (πέντε . . . πτύχες: *Iliad* XVIII. 481); the shields of Aeneas and Turnus having only just recently been described as clashing together in the crisis of those same labyrinthine manoeuvres (*concurrunt clipeis:* XII. 724).

For Aeneas' sevenfold shield, made for his mother Venus by Vulcan with circles whose impenetrability is contrasted in Virgil's thought with the penetrability of 'the circles of the sevenfold shield' of Turnus (*clipei . . . septemplicis orbis:* XII. 925), is by Turnus himself expressly compared (XI. 438-440) with Achilles' fivefold shield, made for his mother Thetis by Hephaistos (*Iliad* XVIII. 369-617); so that, since Achilles' shield contained a glyptic representation of Ariadne's labyrinthine dance as performed on Daidalos' dancing-floor at Knossos in Crete (590-606), the labyrinthine pattern of Ariadne's Cretan dance must from the first have been associated in Virgil's mind with the admittedly Homeric prototype of Aeneas' shield.

Virgil's Vulcan and Venus, moreover, are Homer's Hephaistos and Aphrodite (or Charis; the Latin *venus*, *venerari*, being precisely equivalent in meaning to the Greek χάρις, χαρίξεσθαι: F. Altheim, *A History of Roman Religion*, trans. H. Mattingly, London 1938, p. 143); while Hephaistos has been identified with Daidalos (A. C. Pearson, *The Fragments of Sophocles*, Cambridge 1917, vol. I, p. 110) no less convincingly than Aphrodite with Ariadne (L. R. Farnell, *The Cults of the Greek States*, Oxford 1896-1909, vol. II, pp. 631-635, 748-749).

But the traditional link between Daidalos (Daedalus) and Ariadne, and so perhaps also originally between Hephaistos (Vulcan) and Aphrodite or Charis (Venus) is the maze-pattern; whether that pattern be rendered statically as in Daedalus' Cretan labyrinth, or dynamically as in Ariadne's Cretan dance.

For certain scholia on the Homeric description of Ariadne's Cretan dance (Schol. A.B. *ad Iliad* XVIII. 590) explain that Theseus, having rescued the Athenian boys and girls from Daedalus' Cretan labyrinth by means of Ariadne's clew (cf. *Aeneid* VI. 27-30), together with them 'wove a circling dance for the gods that resembled his own entrance into and exit from the labyrinth, Daedalus showing them how to dance it' (see A. B. Cook, *Zeus*, I (Cambridge, 1914), p. 481).

It follows that Virgil, inevitably associating the idea of Achilles' Greek shield with that of Ariadne's Cretan dance, thereby no less inevitably associated the idea of Aeneas' 'Roman' shield with that of Daedalus' Cretan labyrinth, to whose pattern he elaborately likens that of Iulus' 'Trojan' game; this fourfold mental association unconsciously finding its verbal utterance in the one term *orbibus orbis impediunt*, as applied both to the game and to the shield, in contexts referring respectively to Venus' passively-concerned man-partner Anchises (V. 584-585) and to Venus' actively-concerned god-partner Vulcan (VIII. 448-449) — Venus and Vulcan being ultimately, not merely Aphrodite and Hephaistos, but Ariadne and Daedalus themselves.

Why, then, did Virgil mentally visualize the shaping-process of Aeneas' shield as involving a sevenfold entanglement of circles (*septenosque orbibus orbis impediunt:* VIII. 448-449), whereas Achilles' shield was shaped in only five folds?

The probable explanation is illuminating.

For this sevenfold convolutionary pattern, resembling that of a coiling and uncoiling snake (cf. V. 84-85), appears identically not only upon coins of Knossos, as conventionally symbolizing the Cretan labyrinth, but also upon an early Etruscan wine-pourer, as conventionally symbolizing the 'Trojan game', whose name in its Etruscan form TRUIA is actually inscribed upon the pattern itself (A. B. Cook, *Zeus*, vol. I, pp. 476-477, figs. 332, 343; W. H. Matthews, *Mazes and Labyrinths*, London 1922, pp. 44-46, 156-159, figs. 30, 133-135; W. F. Jackson Knight, *Cumaean Gates*, pp. 76-79, fig. 11).

'The same cunning artist Daedalus who planned the labyrinth', writes Sir J. G. Frazer, 'was said to have made a dance for Ariadne, daughter of Minos . . . Moreover, when Theseus landed with Ariadne in Delos on his return from Crete, he and the young companions whom he had rescued from the Minotaur are said to have danced a mazy dance in imitation of the intricate windings of the labyrinth; on account of its sinuous turns the dance was called "the Crane" (Plutarch, *Theseus* 21; Julius Pollux, iv. 101) . . . There are good grounds for thinking that there was a famous dance which the ancients regularly associated with the Cretan labyrinth. Among the Romans that dance appears to have been known from the earliest times by the name of Troy or the Game of Troy. Tradition ran that it was imported into Italy by Aeneas, who transmitted it through his son Ascanius to the Alban kings, who in their turn handed it down to the Romans. It was performed by bands of armed youths on horseback. Virgil compares their complicated evolutions to the windings of the Cretan labyrinth; and that the comparison is more than a mere poetical flourish appears from a drawing on a very ancient Etruscan vase found at Tragliatella. The drawing represents a procession of seven beardless warriors dancing, accompanied by two armed riders on horseback, who are also beardless. An inscription proves that the scene depicted is the Game of Troy; and attached to the procession is a figure of the Cretan labyrinth, the pattern of which is well known from coins of Cnossus, on which it is often represented' (Frazer, 'The Dying God', vol. IV of *The Golden Bough*, London 1911, pp. 76-77).

Now this particular pattern, whose sevenfold convolutions significantly correspond to the dance performed by the seven fully-armed warriors on the Etruscan vase, themselves each carrying a large round shield, strikingly resembles the roughly-drawn outlines of a still larger round shield — itself, like the maze-pattern as circularly delineated both on the Knossian coins and on the Etruscan vase, a symbol of defence against penetration by an unauthorized intruder, and so of that guardianship which at Troy was symbolized by the 'Palladium', or shield of Athena, the Latin Minerva (Knight, *op. cit.*, pp. 97, 101); Virgil not only emphasizing the symbolism of Minerva's Palladium as Troy's own magically defensive shield-guardian (II. 162-194) but making Turnus himself refer to it in a context coupling the idea of Aeneas' own magically defensive shield-guardian with that of Etruria as Aeneas' ally in war (IX. 148-152).

Consequently Virgil, who was clearly familiar with the maze-pattern as common both to the Cretan labyrinth and to the Trojan game (V. 588-602), seems to have unconsciously visualized Aeneas' Roman shield under the likeness of a defensive symbol at once Cretan and Etruscan, Trojan and Roman; so that Virgil's explicitly Trojan-Roman symbolism must now be correlated with his implicitly Cretan-Etruscan symbolism.

No sooner has Aeneas shouldered his shield as symbolizing the burden of his own Trojan-Roman destiny (VIII. 513, 729-731) than he visits the Etruscan king Tarchon, encamped with his Etruscan army close to the Pallantean site of Rome (VIII. 603-605), with whom he agrees to join his Trojan forces (X. 148-154), 'mustering the Etruscan country-folk in armed bands' (IX. 11) both as their military leader (VIII. 494-503; X. 155-156) and as their future king in place of the outlawed Etruscan tyrant Mezentius (VIII. 470-495, 503-513); thereby, through his Etruscan recruitments as the Trojan commander in a Roman neighbourhood, even 'winning his way to the farthest cities of Corythus' (*extremas Corythi penetravit ad urbes:* IX. 10), the eponymous founder of Corythus or Cortona (X. 719), and so to that 'Etruscan home of Corythus' (VII. 209) whence sprang Aeneas' own forefather Dardanus before 'winning his way to the Idaean cities of Phrygia' (*Idaeas Phrygiae penetravit ad urbes:* VII. 207) together with his brother Iasius, the Etruscan-born 'father' of those Trojan Penates who, inherited by Aeneas from Dardanus, themselves in Crete itself instigated Aeneas' substitution of 'Corythus and the Ausonian lands' of Italy for 'the Dictaean fields' of Crete (III. 161-171).

It was, moreover, in very ruins of Minoan Knossos (III. 115, 121-123), itself the site both of Ariadne's Cretan dance as performed pictorially on Achilles' shield (*Iliad* XVIII. 591) and of Daedalus' Cretan labyrinth as surveyed pictorially by Aeneas on Apollo's temple-gates at Cumae (VI. 23, 27-30), that Aeneas earlier received those Cretan instructions for his Etruscan contacts; and it was also on the site of Minoan Knossos (III. 121-131), the pattern of whose labyrinth will be that of Roman performances of the Trojan game (V. 588-602), that Aeneas began mistakenly to build his city-walls under the name of Troy's own Pergamean citadel (III. 132-134) until he learnt through Dardanus' Penates in his Cretan-Trojan city that his walls must be built for them in Dardanus' Etruscan-Roman Italy.

In other words, Aeneas' Etruscan-Roman contacts, as Dardanus' lineal heir to the cult of Vesta, result directly from his Cretan-Trojan contacts as Teucer's lineal heir to the cult of Cybele (III. 94-115); while Virgil's application of the same terms (*penetravit ad urbes*) both to the Etruscan Dardanus' Trojan contacts (*Idaeas Phrygiae:* VII. 207) and to the Trojan Aeneas' Etruscan contacts (*extremas Corythi:* IX. 10) verbally suggests that mental vision, symbolized under the prophetic welcome of Tiberinus as personifying 'Etruscan Tiber' (VII. 242), which sees Aeneas as equivalent to a returning Dardanus (cf. III. 94-98) bringing back with him once more from Phrygia to Italy an originally Etruscan 'Troy-town' (*Troianam . . . urbem qui revehis nobis:* VIII. 36-37).

Not only does the Etruscan origin of Aeneas' 'Troy-town' recall the Etruscan version of Iulus' 'Troy-game' as represented on the Etruscan vase under its Etruscanized name of 'Truia' (='Troia'), but it further suggests Virgil's awareness of the fact that labyrinths or mazes are frequently called 'Troy-town' or simply 'Troy' — nomenclature which, although now apparently confined to north-western Europe, was probably of south-east European origin.

There are, in fact, definite indications that Virgil's mind associated the idea of Aeneas' Italian 'Troy-town' with that of the maze-pattern, and both of them with that of Aeneas' shield, in a specifically defensive context.

It will be remembered that the pattern of Iulus' 'Troy-game', both in Sicily and in Italy (V. 596-602), was the pattern not only of Daedalus' Cretan labyrinth (V. 588-593), and so also of Ariadne's Cretan dance as represented on the Homeric prototype of Aeneas' Roman shield, but also of dolphins gambolling in the waves (V. 594-595); and that the Greek name for this maze-pattern, as imitating the Cretan labyrinth, was the 'Crane' (γέρανος) — the behaviour of cranes upon the ground, no less than that of dolphins in the sea, being frequently labyrinthine in movement (E. A. Armstrong, *Bird Display*, Cambridge 1942, pp. 184-186).

Now Aeneas, during his visit to the site of Rome for the shouldering of his shield, has left Iulus behind in charge of his *Troia* (VIII. 546-550), off which are moored most of his ships. Meanwhile Turnus, informed of Aeneas' absence (IX. 6-13), seizes his chance of attacking the Trojan fleet (IX. 69-76); whereupon Cybele saves her own Idaean ships from the flames (77-122) by transforming them into sea-nymphs of dolphin-like behaviour (*delphinumque modo:* IX. 119) — a comparison whose defensive context at once recalls the similarly dolphin-like behaviour (*delphinum similes:* V. 594) of the performers of Iulus' labyrinthine *troia*.

But Virgil's Cybele embodies all those specifically Cretan-Trojan contacts which, inherited from Teucer (III. 103-117), are symbolized in the fabric of Aeneas' ship (X. 156-158); while the fabric of Aeneas' shield symbolizes all those specifically Etruscan-Roman contacts which, inherited from Dardanus (III. 94-98, 163-171), result in his return voyage to relieve Iulus of responsibility for the defence of that Trojan-Roman destiny whose fulfilment results from Cretan-Etruscan urgency — a voyage whose unforgettable description not only couples the symbolism both of the ship and of the shield with the behaviour both of dolphins and of cranes, but further associates all of them with the idea both of 'Troy'-defence and of

Aeneas' equivalence to a returning Dardanus who is now Teucer's heir.

For Virgil, after twice giving the name *Troia* (X. 27, 74) to 'the camp of Dardanus' sons' (*Dardanidum:* X. 4), who as 'Aeneas' sons' (*Aeneadum:* X. 120) vainly fight Turnus' fires under the leadership of Aeneas' son Iulus as 'the Dardan boy himself, Venus' most rightful care' (X. 132-133), continues:

'Thus had they clashed in stubborn warfare's conflicts, while Aeneas at midnight was cleaving the waters. For as soon as, leaving Evander and entering the Etruscan camp' (=Aeneas' Roman-Etruscan contacts), 'he meets the king, and to the king announces his name and race, the aid he seeks, and the aid he himself offers . . . then without delay Tarchon joins forces and strikes a treaty; then, freed from Fate, the Lydian (i.e. Etruscan) people embark under heaven's ordinance, entrusting themselves to a foreign leader' (=Aeneas' Trojan-Etruscan contacts). 'Aeneas' ship leads the van, with Phrygian lions yoked under her beak, with Mount Ida towering above them, sight most welcome to the exiled Teucrians' (=Aeneas' Trojan-Cretan contacts; cf. Teucer, Cybele, yoked lions, Mount Ida: III. 103-117). 'There sits great Aeneas, pondering the veering issues of warfare; while Pallas, clinging close to his left side, asks him now of the stars, their guide through darksome night, and now of his trials by land and sea' (=Aeneas' Trojan-Roman contacts; embodied in Evander's son Pallas, eponym of Pallanteum itself, who was the first to welcome Aeneas to the site of Rome (VIII. 97-125), through which he accompanied Aeneas during his topographical tour (VIII. 306-313; cf. 466) and from which he accompanied Aeneas as representing Evander's foundation of Rome's citadel (VIII. 313, 514-519, 558-591) . . . Then follows a list of the Etruscans who follow Aeneas and Pallas on their ships: (X. 163-212) . . . 'So many were the chosen chiefs who sailed in thrice ten ships to the succour of Troy (*subsidio Troiae:* X. 213-214) . . . Aeneas, for care allows no rest to his limbs, sits at his post, with his own hand guiding the tiller and tending the sails; when lo! in mid-course a dancing-band (*chorus*) of his own companions (*comitum*) comes to meet him; for the nymphs, whom gracious Cybebe (=Cybele) had bidden be sea-goddesses and turn from ships into nymphs, were swimming abreast and cleaving the waves (*secabant;* cf. *secant:* V. 595, of the dolphins)

— even so many as the bronzen prows that had lain moored to the shore' (of the *Troia*, when they behaved like dolphins: IX. 117-120). 'They recognize their king from afar, and encircle him with dances (*choreis*). From among them, Cymodocea . . . thus accosts him, to his astonishment: "Wakest thou, Aeneas, scion of gods? . . . We, Idaean pines from Ida's sacred summit, now sea-nymphs, we are thy fleet! . . . This shape the Mother (Cybele) gave us in pity . . . But thy boy Ascanius is hemmed in by wall and trench (of the *Troia*) in the midst of arms and of Latins bristling with war . . . Take thou the shield which (Vulcan) the Lord of Fire himself gave thee, even the shield invincible and rimmed about with gold. To-morrow's light, if thou deem not my words idle, shall look on mighty heaps of Rutulian carnage" . . . Marvelling, the Trojan son of Anchises is in amaze, yet cheers his spirits with the omen. Then, looking up at the vault above, he briefly prays: "Thou gracious Idaean Mother of the gods" (Cybele's Cretan-Trojan-Roman cult-title), "to whom Dindymus is dear, and tower-crowned cities, and lions twin-yoked at thy rein, do thou be now my leader in the fight!" . . . And now, as he stands on the high stern, he no sooner catches sight of his Teucrians and his camp (the *Troia*) than straightway he uplifts in his left hand his blazing shield. The sons of Dardanus from the walls raise a shout to the stars; fresh hope kindles wrath; they shower their darts amain — even as amid black clouds Strymonian cranes give signs, while noisily they skim the air, and flee before the south winds with clamour in their wake . . . On Aeneas' head blazes the helmet-peak, flame streams from the crest aloft, and the shield's golden boss spouts floods of fire' (X. 146-271).

Virgil, it will be noted, applies the same phrase, 'standing on the lofty stern' (*stans celsa in puppi*), both to Aeneas while uplifting Vulcan's shield (X. 261) and to Augustus as portrayed by Vulcan on that same shield (VIII. 680); a parallelism which extends to the environment of both scenes.

For the golden rim of Aeneas' shield, to which Cymodocea significantly refers (X. 243), represents the sea in blue-and-white enamelled gold (VIII. 671-672); 'and round about, shining in silver, dolphins were sweeping the sea-surface with their tails in circles and cleaving the tide' (*et circum argento clari delphines in orbem aequora verrebant candis aestumque secabant:* VIII. 673-674) — a memory of Herakles' Hesiodic shield as made by Hephaistos: 'In his hands he took his shield, all glittering; no one ever broke it with a blow or crushed it. And a wonder it was to see; for its whole circle was a-shimmer with enamel and white ivory and electrum, and it glowed with shining gold; and there were zones of cyanus drawn upon it' (i.e. concentric bands of deep blue glass-paste, in which were portrayed the scenes described by the poet) . . . 'And on the shield was a harbour with a safe haven from the irresistible sea, made of refined tin wrought in a circle, and it seemed to heave with waves. In the middle of it were many dolphins rushing this way and that, fishing; and they seemed to be swimming. Two dolphins of silver were spouting and devouring the mute fishes' (*Aspis* 139-143, 207-212, trans. H. G. Evelyn-White, in the Loeb Classical Library Ed., London 1936).

Thus Aeneas is another Hercules like Augustus (VI. 791-807), who is himself placed at the centre of this dolphin-patterned sea upon Aeneas' 'Herculean' shield: 'In the midst (*in medio*) could be discerned brazen ships with Actium's battle; one might see all Leucate aglow with War's array, and the waves ablaze with gold. Here Augustus Caesar (cf. VI. 792), leading Italians into battle, with peers and people, and the great Penates-gods, standing on the lofty stern' (*cum patribus populoque, Penatibus et magnis dis, stans celsa in puppi:* VIII. 675-680.)

Similarly Aeneas, 'standing on the lofty stern' (*stans celsa in puppi:* X. 261) of that same ship whereon he originally embarked 'with comrades and son, and the great Penates-gods' (*cum sociis natoque, Penatibus et magnis dis:* III. 12) when voyaging from the vain defence of his Phrygian *Troia* (*portusque relinquo et campos, ubi Troia fuit:* III. 10-11) past 'the storm-capped peaks of Mount Leucate' (III. 274) to those 'shores of Actium' on which were performed 'the games of Ilium' (III. 280), before reaching the site of Augustus' 'Victory-city' Nicopolis — mentally visualized as forming one *Troia* with Aeneas' Italian camp-city (*unam faciemus utramque Troiam animis:* III. 504-505) — now voyages to the sure defence of that same Italian *Troia* (*subsidio Troiae:* X. 214) through a sea in whose midst (*medio in spatio:* 219) his ship begins to be encircled by the dances (224) of those dolphin-like sea-nymph dancers (219) whose continual cleaving of the waves (222) recalls the *troia*'s labyrinthine convolutions (cf.

delphinum similes qui per maria umida nando Carpathium Libycumque secant luduntque per undas: V. 594-595).

Now Augustus, who elsewhere on Aeneas' dolphin-patterned shield is portrayed in a victoriously defensive context (VIII. 714-728) as reviving various Roman rites, including 'games' (*ludis:* 717), himself in 27 B.C., and so during Virgil's composition of the *Aeneid*, revived the 'Trojan game' (Dio Cassius xlix. 43; li. 22; liii. 1; liv. 26); this Augustan revival, as symbolizing in a victoriously defensive context the Venus-descended Trojan Roman ancestry of the Iulean-Julian clan, itself renewing Julius Caesar's celebration of the *troia* when, returning in triumph to Rome, he dedicated in his *forum Iulianum* that temple of Venus *Genetrix* which he had vowed to Aeneas' mother at the battle of Pharsalia in 48 B.C.

Virgil, that is to say, while consciously symbolizing these Julian performances of the *troia* under those Iulian performances of the *troia* which originated in the directions of Venus' son Aeneas (V. 545-602), at the same time unconsciously symbolizes Augustus' victoriously defensive fulfilment of the Julian destiny, under the figure of Aeneas' victoriously defensive fulfilment of the Iulean destiny, by mentally associating the idea of the *troia's* dolphin-like maze-pattern both with Augustus as central to Aeneas' shield and with Aeneas as uplifting that shield upon his ship — Aeneas' ship, moreover, like Augustus' ship upon the shield, bearing that same specifically Vestal burden of 'the great Penates-gods' as is borne pictorially on the specifically Vulcanic burden of his Augustus-centred 'Herculean' shield.

CHAPTER VIII

VULCAN AND VESTA

> Inde ubi prima quies medio iam noctis abactae
> curriculo expulerat somnum, cum femina primum,
> cui tolerare colo vitam tenuique Minerva
> impositum, cinerem et sopitos suscitat ignis,
> noctem addens operi, famulasque ad lumina longo
> exercet penso, castum ut servare cubile
> coniugis et possit parvos educere natos:
> hand secus Ignipotens nec tempore segnior illo
> mollibus e stratis opera ad fabrilia surgit.
>
> (*Aeneid* VIII. 407-415)

AENEAS' Vulcan-forged Virgilian shield, as being the poetically symbolic counterpart of Herakles' Hephaistos-forged Hesiodic shield (*Aspis* 122-321), is characterized by that epithet *invictus*, 'unconquered and unconquerable' (*clipeum . . . invictum:* X. 242-243) which belonged in Roman cult to Hercules, the Greek Herakles, himself.

As *Invictus*, Hercules was commemorated in the Roman calendar on two successive days of August, the 12th and the 13th; the foundation-myth of his cult under this title, with variants *Victor* and *Triumphalis*, being the immemorially ancient legend of Hercules' victory over Cacus on the Roman Aventine hill.

Between the Aventine and the Tiber stood the *porta trigemina*, or 'Triple Gate', through which one passed northwards into the *forum boarium*, or 'Cattle Market', with its *ara maxima*, 'Greatest Altar', and *aedes Herculis*, 'House of Hercules'; this latter resembling the *aedes Vestae* both in being called a 'house' instead of a 'temple', and also in being a round, domed building — a shape no less indicative of great antiquity than its name.

The *forum boarium* faced north-eastwards along the *Velabrum*, a valley between the Palatine hill to the right and the Capitoline hill to the left, towards the *forum Romanum*, or 'Roman Market'; so that the cult of Vesta in her *aedes rotunda* on the lower Palatine ledge and the cult of Vulcan in his *Volcanal* on the lower Capitoline ledge, confronting each other across the *forum Romanum*, were topographically neighboured by the cult of Hercules in his own *aedes rotunda* and his *ara maxima*, confronting each other within the *forum boarium* on the Tiber-bank near the Aventine *porta trigemina*.

Every August 12th, under the priesthood of two ancient patrician families, the Potitii and Pinarii, Hercules' mythical victory over Cacus was ritually celebrated at the *ara maxima* and *aedes Herculis* by a festival which began with a cattle-sacrifice in the 'Cattle Market' and ended with a cattle-'sacrament' in the form of a sacred meal partaken of by the worshippers while seated on the ground, as was the most ancient practice both in Italy and in Greece (W. Warde Fowler, *The Roman Festivals*, pp. 193-194). On the following day, August 13th, the annual rites of Hercules *Invictus* were concluded, in what manner remains uncertain, at the *porta trigemina;* near which, at the foot of the Aventine, stood the altar of Evander, himself long associated locally with the Hercules-Cacus myth.

Now Cacus' father was Vulcan, while Cacus' sister is recorded by Servius (on *Aen*. VIII. 190) as Caca, the betrayer of her brother to Hercules, who as such 'was worshipped as a goddess in a chapel where a perpetual fire was kept up and sacrifices were offered to her as a sort of Vesta. All this seems to suggest that Cacus and Caca were an ancient pair of Roman divinities of fire, of whom Cacus corresponded to Vulcan, and Caca corresponded to Vesta' (Frazer, *The Fasti of Ovid*, vol. II, p. 207) — a view now generally accepted (H. J. Rose, *A Handbook of Greek Mythology*, Ed. 2, London 1933, p. 325; Altheim, *op. cit*., pp. 204-206).

But Hercules, like both Cacus-Vulcan and Caca-Vesta, was himself traditionally associated by the Romans with fire; since he not only 'initiated the rites of sacrifice with unblemished victims burning on a pure fire' which his own hand kindled on the altar he had erected 'near the ascent leading from the *forum* (*Romanum*) up to the Capitol' (Dion. Halic. I. xxxiv. 4, xxxviii. 2), but also won his own immortality in the fire, kindled at his command on the Thessalian Mount Oeta, wherein he cremated himself — this latter incident being twice referred to by Ovid (*Fasti* I. 584; VI. 519) in connection with Hercules' visit to Evander for his victory over Cacus.

Virgil's appropriation of all these local links, both ritual and mythical, between Evander and Hercules, Cacus-Vulcan and Caca-Vesta, is characteristic of his symbolism.

For Aeneas' visit to the site of Rome covers just two days—by implication, August 12th and 13th; since he lands on the Tiber-bank (VIII. 101) below the Aventine (231) for immediate participation there in Evander's already-started yearly celebration (102-106, 172-178), with feasting on sacrificed cattle (179-184), of Hercules' victory over Cacus (185-267) by the Potitian and Pinarian priesthood (268-270) at the *ara maxima* (179, 186, 271-272) 'in a grove before the city' (104) which is clearly meant to be the site of the *forum boarium*, whose cattle stray from their own market up the *Velabrum* into the *forum Romanum* (360-361)—these two central markets being flanked by the Capitoline hill on the one side (347) and by the Palatine hill on the other (341; cf. IX. 9).

Virgil, moreover, particularly emphasizes the identity of the destructive fires of Cacus with the destructive fires of Vulcan—'This monster's father was Vulcan; his were the black fires he belched forth, as he moved in mighty bulk' (VIII. 198-199)—and so with those same destructive fires whose constructive employment by Vulcan (416-453) render Aeneas' shield *invictus* (X. 242-243) precisely during the one night between the two days of Hercules *Invictus*; a night significantly spent by Aeneas as Hercules' own successor in Evander's palace (VIII. 359-465), with its cults both of Hercules and of Vesta (542-544).

Finally, on the following day, by implication August 13th, Aeneas' visual recognition of 'Vulcan's weapons' (*Volcania . . . arma:* 535) immediately results in Aeneas' ritual coupling of Evander's cult of Vesta with Evander's cult of Hercules: 'Then, before all else, he rouses the slumbering altars with the fires of Hercules, and joyfully visits yesterday's Lar and little Penates'—

> *et primum Herculeis sopitas ignibus aras*
> *excitat hesternumque Larem parvosque Penates*
> *laetus adit* (VIII. 542-544).

In other words, the thunderous sky-epiphany of Aeneas' shield (520-540), as rendered *invictus* in the fires of Vulcan, Cacus' paternal self, at once suggests to Virgil's mind the kindling of those 'fires of Hercules' *Invictus* which to Virgil's contemporary readers were the ritual and domestic Roman counterpart of the mythical and crematory fires whose kindling meant the thunderous sky-epiphany of Hercules himself.

Nor is this all. For Virgil unconsciously reveals his train of associative thought by here employing phraseology reminiscent of two earlier passages — the one concerned with the idea of the mythically awakened fires of Vulcan, and the other with that of the ritually awakened fires of Vesta; the mentally connecting links being, once again, Hercules and Venus — Hercules, as Aeneas' predecessor both in Sicily and on the site of Rome; and Venus, as partnered both with Anchises and with Vulcan.

Thus, in Sicily, Aeneas' aerial vision of Anchises' spirit — whose description, be it noted, occupies exactly the same number of lines (V. 722-742) as those describing Aeneas' aerial vision of Vulcan's weapons on the site of Rome (VIII. 520-540) — is immediately followed by Aeneas' ritual renewal of Anchises' domestic cult of Vesta, itself the Pergamean-Trojan counterpart of Evander's Pallantean-Roman domestic cults of Vesta and Hercules: 'While so speaking, he stirs the ashes and slumbering fires, and with holy meal and full censer humbly worships the Pergamean Lar and hoary Vesta's shrine' —

> *haec memorans cinerem et sopitos suscitat ignis*
> *Pergameumque Larem et canae penetralia Vestae*
> *farre pio et plena supplex veneratur acerra* (V. 743-745).

Precisely the same terms, 'stirs the ashes and the slumbering fires' (*cinerem et sopitos suscitat ignis*), are later applied by way of domestic simile (VIII. 410) to Vulcan's own preparations, as *Ignipotens* (VIII. 423), for rendering Aeneas' shield no less 'unconquered and unconquerable' (*clipeum cape, quem dedit ipse invictum Ignipotens:* X. 242-243) than Hercules himself in relation to Cacus on the site of Rome:

'Then, so soon as repose had banished (Vulcan's) sleep, in the mid career of now waning night, what time a housewife, whose task it is to eke out life with her distaff and Minerva's humble toil, stirs the ashes and slumbering fires, adding night to her day's work, and keeps her handmaids toiling by lamplight at the long task, that she may preserve chaste her husband's bed, and rear her little sons: even so, and not more slothful at that hour, the Lord of Fire (*Ignipotens:* 414) rises from (Venus') soft couch to the work of his smithy' (VIII. 407-415) — Vulcan's smithy being a volcanic cave (416-424) where 'fire pants in the furnace' (421) under the bellows (449-450) of the Cyclopean smiths (424, 440) who forge Aeneas' shield (445-449) with metal-twisting tongs (451-453) upon the anvils.

The arresting incongruity of such a simile, combined with the Vestal associations of the sentence 'stirs the ashes and slumbering fires' (V. 743; VIII. 410), surely points to Virgil's mental association of the ritual and domestic fires of Rome's Caca-Vesta with those mythical and crematory fires of Rome's Cacus-Vulcan which in significantly similar phraseology (*sopitas ignibus aras excitat:* VIII. 542-543) he associates both explicitly with the ritually domestic fires, and implicitly with the mythically crematory fires, of that Hercules *Invictus* who at Rome was worshipped also as *Domesticus*.

The verbal evidence, in fact, suggests that Virgil — who transfers the traditional name 'Rhea' from Vesta's Alban priestess to a Roman priestess, presumably Caca's, who on Cacus' Aventine hill bore Hercules' son Aventinus (VII. 655-663) — mentally appropriated the old Roman ritual myth of Caca's betrayal to her lover Hercules of her brother Cacus; with the result that Hercules, *Domesticus* in relation to Caca, became *Invictus* in relation to Cacus.

But Virgil's appropriation of this ritual myth, no more than mentally implicit in regard to Hercules, becomes verbally implicit in regard to Aeneas, whose poetically symbolic relationship to Vulcan and Vesta in the *Aeneid* corresponds largely to Hercules' ritually mythical relationship to Cacus and Caca at Rome.

Now Vesta personifies the hearth-fire (*ardentem . . . Vestam:* G. IV. 384), while Vulcan personifies the earth-fire.

'Volcanus . . . was originally worshipped in the earth-fire, whether of volcanic or other origin. In this context Cacus, the enemy of Hercules, appears as his son; we are still able to prove that Virgil, in making him an underground demon, vomiting smoke and fire, has preserved the original account' (Altheim, *op. cit.*, p. 119); 'Vulcan made fire burn and destroy things . . . The only fire-spirit who has anything to do with the hearth in Italy is feminine, Vesta' (H. J. Rose, *Primitive Culture in Italy*, London 1926, pp. 44, 81).

In early Rome, moreover, there was a complementary relationship, centred in the *forum Romanum*, between the *ustrinum publicum*, or 'Public Incinerator', and the *Vesta publica*, or 'Public Hearth' — a relationship, that is to say, between the crematory fire of Vulcan and the domestic fire of Vesta.

'The cremation cemetery', writes Altheim, 'probably began just at the end of the Palatine city on the high back of the Velia, extended over the valley of the forum, and climbed up the opposite slopes of the Capitol and Quirinal . . . (On the Capitoline slope) from ancient times was the altar of Vulcan; Romulus himself is said to have founded it . . . It is hardly an accident that the god of fire had his seat inside a cremation cemetery. There is great probability in the suggestion that the oldest *ustrinum publicum* lay here, and that that was why the god was established on the spot. Even in later times the custom held that funeral processions should pass over the forum, and that the *elogia* on the dead should be delivered there; in this we recognize the after-effects of the old cemetery. Varro connected this custom with the grave of Romulus, which was localized in the forum . . . (Vulcan's) oldest place of cult lay within the cremating cemetery of the forum . . . Vesta had her seat in Rome on what was later the forum . . . Nor can it be accident that the altars of the two deities connected with fire, Volcanus and Vesta, lie on this side and on that of the old cremation cemetery on what was later the forum.

'The cult of Vesta, then, belongs to the cremating, that is to say, to the Latin race. And the Roman tradition points in the same direction, when it makes the goddess spring originally from the neighbouring Lavinium. The local (Lavinian) cult was in later times marked out as the mother-cult of the Roman . . . In Alba Longa, too, there was a very old cult of Vesta. It outlasted the destruction of the city and, like the Laurentine, was regarded as the mother-cult of the Roman. All traces of the goddess, then, lead us to Latium' (Altheim, *op. cit.*, pp. 94-95, 136, 140-141).

'*Tendimus in Latium*' (I. 205); for this prehistoric Lavinian-Alban-Roman cremating Latin race, with its complementary cults of Vulcan and of Vesta, respectively personifying the crematory earth-fire and the domestic hearth-fire, is precisely Virgil's *genus Latinum* (I. 6) whose members are Virgil's *Prisci Latini* (V. 598).

Servius, moreover, commenting on the *Vesta* entrusted by Hector to Aeneas while dreaming in Anchises' house in burning Troy (II. 296) explains the poetically symbolic meaning of this gift as follows: 'Vesta is the Earth . . . which has a fire within itself' — an explanation whose Vulcanic-Vestal implications are clarified by Servius' earlier comment on the *Vesta* coupled by Virgil with Romulus (I. 292; cf. G. I. 498) which, after identifying this Hearth as belonging to 'Assaracus' House' (I. 284) with the Earth as belonging to Augustus' Rome (I. 276-291), points both to Mount Aetna in particular and to volcanic phenomena in general as proving the correspondence of the fire inside the Earth to the fire inside the Hearth (Frazer, *The Fasti of Ovid*, vol. IV, pp. 201-202).

Servius, that is to say, interprets the *Aeneid* as implying that Virgil mentally symbolized Augustus' Roman Earth, together with its crematorily warlike fire of Vulcan, under the equivalent figure of that burden of Aeneas whose verbally explicit symbol is Assaracus' Trojan House together with its domestically peaceful fire of Vesta (cf. VI. 777-807; IX. 257-262).

This unconscious because hereditary Virgilian integration of Vesta's Hearth-fire with Vulcan's Earth-fire, moreover, was consciously facilitated by the contemporary Roman identification of the two; an identification, also unconsciously inherited from Early Latin ancestry, which is crystallized by Ovid in the otherwise somewhat startling assertion, based upon philosophic rationalization of an irrational instinct, that 'Vesta is the same as the Earth; under both of them is a perpetual fire; the Earth and the Hearth both symbolize the Home' —

> *Vesta eadem est et terra; subest vigil ignis utrique:*
> *significant sedem terra focusque suam* (F. VI. 267-268).

Ovid then goes on to record the contemporary idea that the round and sky-domed shape of the Earth is symbolized by the round and dome-roofed shape of Rome's *aedes Vestae* (F. VI. 269-282).

Similarly Dionysius of Halicarnassus, referring to Numa's foundation of Rome's *aedes Vestae*, observes: 'They think that the fire (on its Hearth) is dedicated to Vesta because the goddess, being the Earth and occupying the central position in the universe, kindles the celestial fires from herself (*Antiqu.*

Rom. II. lxvi. 3); while Festus (*s.v.* '*Rutundam aedem*', p. 320, ed. Lindsay) says that Numa 'seems to have consecrated a round temple of Vesta because he believed that she was the Earth by which the life of men is sustained, and he gave her temple the shape of a ball in order that the goddess might be worshipped in a temple like herself.'

Conceptions such as these, however philosophically disguised, are all traceable back to those of that Early Latin race whose cult of Vesta's domestically peaceful Hearth-fire was the complement of their cult of Vulcan's crematorily warlike Earth-fire — a ritual correspondence properly belonging to prehistoric Rome, but mentally transferred by Virgil to prehistoric Troy as being the mythical source of Rome's Vestal cult.

This correspondence, moreover, involves for Virgil's mind an imaginative contrast, discernible (as we shall find) throughout the *Aeneid*, between the fires and ashes respectively of warlike Vulcan and of peaceful Vesta; the former, whether mythical or crematory, symbolizing all the destructive associations of the outdoor Earth-fire, and the latter, whether ritual or domestic, symbolizing all the constructive associations of the indoor Hearth-fire.

Such a contrast is, for example, clearly discernible at the outset of Aeneas' narrative at Carthage (II. 250ff.); where Virgil, precisely at the point where Aeneas receives from Hector the first intimations of his destiny, implies a complementary antithesis between the crematory outdoor fire of death-dealing Vulcan, here associated with the warlike destruction of Hector's old Troy, and the domestic indoor fire of life-giving Vesta, here associated with the peaceful construction of Aeneas' new Troy oversea.

Out of doors Troy is burning, while Aeneas is asleep indoors. To him, peacefully dreaming in Anchises' house, Hector appears: '"Ah! flee, goddess-born", he cries, "and snatch thyself from these flames (*flammis*). The foe holds our walls; Troy falls from her lofty height. All claims are paid to fatherland and to Priam; if Troy's *Pergama* could be saved by strength of hand, by mine too they had been saved. Troy commits to thee her *sacra* and *Penates*: take them as the companions of thy destiny; for them seek the city-walls which in their greatness thou shalt at length establish when thou hast wandered oversea." So he speaks, and in his hands he brings forth from their inmost shrine chapleted and all-powerful Vesta (*Vestam*) and her undying fire (II. 289-297) . . . More and more, though my father Anchises' house lay far withdrawn and screened by trees, clearer grow the sounds and war's dread din sweeps on. I shake myself from sleep and, climbing to the roof's topmost height, stand with straining ears (299-303) . . . Even now Deiphobus' spacious house has fallen, as Vulcan (*Volcano*) towers above; even now his neighbour Ucalegon blazes (*ardet*); the fire (*igni*) is reflected in the broad Sigean straits (310-312) . . . "Our city is in flames!" (*incensa:* 327) . . . "Sinon, victorious, insolently kindles conflagrations" (*incendia:* 329) . . . I am driven into flames and weapons (*in flammas et in arma feror:* 337) . . . "Troy's *Pergama* are in flames!" (*incensa:* 374) . . . O ashes of Ilium! O funeral flames of my kin!' (*Iliaci cineres et flamma extrema meorum:* 431) — this last a distinctively crematory metaphor, implying the incineration of the Trojans in an *ustrinum* whose devouring flames are those of Vulcan's fire.

Aeneas has by this time reached Priam's palace, whose roof he climbs, only to find it the target of flames (*flammas:* 478) deliberately hurled at it by the foe. Looking down from the burning roof through the ruined building, 'I saw Hecuba and her hundred daughters, and amid the altars Priam, polluting with his blood the fires (*ignis*) that he himself had hallowed' (501-502) — domestically ritual fires which, at once coupled with Vulcan's crematory fire (*ignis:* 505), include by implication the perpetually burning fire of that Vesta the images of whose Penates (514, 517) are frantically clasped by Priam's wife and daughters: 'Such was the end of Priam's destiny; such the doom that by fate befell him — to see Troy in flames (*incensam*) and her *Pergama* laid low . . .' (554-556).

Then, after Aeneas' reference to the fires (*ignibus:* 566) that have incinerated so many of his companions, there follows that much-disputed passage (II. 567-588) whose Virgilian authorship is surely confirmed by its Virgilian antithesis, unconsciously but quite clearly implied as underlying the poet's mental visualization of the scene he describes, between Vesta's protective Hearth-fire within doors and Vulcan's destructive Earth-fire out of doors — an antithesis, moreover, whose metaphorical synthesis is implied, no less characteristically of

Virgilian symbolism, in Aeneas' own emotional heart-fire with its domestically fuelled but crematorily scorching flame:

'And now, now I alone was left when I saw, hugging Vesta's threshold (*limina Vestae*) and lurking silent in her withdrawn dwelling (*secreta in sede*), Tyndareus' daughter (Helen); the bright conflagrations (*incendia;* i.e. Vulcan's flames) give me light, as I wander and widely scan every detail of the scene ... Fires blazed up in my heart (*exarsere ignes animo*) ... Is Troy to have been ablaze with fire? (*Troia arserit igni?*) ... (and Helen go unscathed?) Not so ... It will be joy to have glutted my heart with the flame of vengeance (*ultricis flammae*), and to have sated (with Helen's blood) the ashes of my kin' (*cineres ... meorum*) — a repetition, be it noted, of Aeneas' earlier crematory metaphor (*Iliaci cineres et flamma extrema meorum:* 431).

Thus Virgil, to whom Rome's heart was the *forum Romanum* with its foundation-burial of Vestally-mothered Romulus, founder of Vulcan's altar therein, imaginatively figures Troy's heart, on the analogy of prehistoric Rome, as equivalent to an *ustrinum publicum* with its complementary *Vesta publica*; Aeneas' own correspondingly twin-fiery heart, whose 'blood of Assaracus' will run in Romulus' veins (VI. 778), beating accordingly in sympathetic unison with the twin-fiery hearts both of Troy and of Rome as thus mentally envisaged.

But Troy's state-cult of Vesta has already passed, through Vulcan's agency, to Anchises' house; whose hitherto private *sacra* — including, on the Lavinian-Alban-Roman analogy its household *Vesta* and *aeternus ignis*, its household *Lar* and *Penates* (II. 293-297; V. 743-745; IX. 258-260) — have now become, as Hector himself implied (II. 289-292), the henceforth public *sacra* of Troy itself.

'Anchises' house' (*Anchisae domus:* II. 300), in other words, as lineally equivalent to 'Assaracus' house' (*domus Assaraci:* I. 284) and containing in its *penetralia* (or *penus*) *Vestae* 'Assaracus' Lar' as now equivalent to the 'Pergamean Lar' (V. 744; IX. 259), has already become Troy's official *aedes Vestae*; whose hereditary guardians are henceforward successively Anchises and Aeneas and Iulus, as embodying respectively the past and present and future destinies of Troy and of its *Pergama* or citadel — Troy's citadel being under the divine protection of Apollo (II. 319), henceforth himself the divine protector of Anchises' Troy-representing house, as later of Augustus' Rome-representing house.

It is for this reason that, just as Aeneas is on the point of slaying Helen, his mother Venus suddenly intervenes: ' "Wilt thou not first see where thou hast left thy father, age-worn Anchises? whether Creusa thy wife and the boy Ascanius still live? All these the Greek battle-lines compass round on every side; and, did not my love prevent, the flames (*flammae*) ere now had swept them off and the hostile sword had drunk their blood (II. 596-600) . . . Haste thy flight, my son, and put an end to thy toil. Never will I leave thee but will set thee safe upon thy father's threshold" (619-620) . . . Then, indeed, methought all Ilium sank into the fires (*considere in ignis*) and Neptune's Troy was upturned from her base (624-625) . . . I descend and, with a god for my guide (*ducente deo*), I make my way amid flame (*flammam*) and foe; weapons give place and the flames (*flammae*) retire' (632-633).

This guiding 'god' (*deo;* not *dea*, 'goddess'), so powerful over flames and weapons, is clearly Venus as virtually identified with her divine husband Vulcan, himself the maker of flames and weapons; so that, both in protecting the household of her human husband Anchises from flames and weapons (596-600) and in guiding their son Aeneas through their midst (632-633), Venus appropriately relies on Vulcan's restraint of his own deadly artifacts as made within that 'House of Vulcan' (*Volcani domus:* VIII. 422) which bears the same symbolical relationship to the 'House of Anchises' (*Anchisae domus:* II. 300), now the 'House of Vesta' (cf. *limina Vestae:* II. 567) since Troy's fiery destruction, as that borne by Vulcan's mythically Troy-annihilating fire (311) to Vesta's ritually Troy-perpetuating fire (297).

Thus it is Venus herself who, as Virgil's consciously connecting link between her two husbands, Vulcan and Anchises, is at the same time Virgil's unconsciously connecting link between Vulcan and Vesta; with the result that he thinks of Venus as guiding Aeneas through Vulcan's handiwork directly from the *limina* of Vesta's *secreta sedes* (567-568) to the *limina* of Anchises' *secreta sedes* (299, 634), whose *penetralia* (665) recall to Aeneas' mind the *adyta penetralia* of Vesta (296-297) as so recently seen by him in his dream — a dream whose significance, now dawning upon him for the first time, has in reality been clarified by his yet more recent experiences. For, during his comparatively brief absence from Anchises' house, Aeneas has thrice witnessed the fiery destruction, either imminent or complete, of Troy's various Vestal sanctities in Vulcan's flames — first, those of Apollo's temple, rescued indeed by Panthus his priest (318-338) but only to share Panthus' own incineration (429-431); next, those of Priam's palace (502, 512-517), also doomed to cremation (478) with Priam's people (566); and then, finally, those of Vesta's own temple, already exposed to the general conflagration (567-570) which will shortly incinerate Troy (624-625).

Hector had urged Aeneas in his dream to rescue from Vulcan's fire (311) not only himself (289) but also Vesta's fire (297), together with Troy's other Vestal hallows (293-294); without, however, specifying their precise whereabouts — and all Troy's public Vestal hallows must by now have been destroyed in Vulcan's flames.

But the fiery doom of Priam's palace had already reminded Aeneas of the fiery doom awaiting Anchises' house (559-563), even before his restoration thereto by Venus as inseparable from Vulcan (632-635); so that the sight of Anchises in his house, refusing to be rescued from that doom (635-658), at once reminds Aeneas of Priam's death (659-670) beside his own Vestal fire (502) and his Vestal Penates (514) amid Vulcan's fire (555).

Aeneas doubts his dream no longer. 'All claims are paid to Priam', Hector had said (291), before entrusting him with Vesta's fire and Vesta's Penates for transportation oversea; thereby, as Aeneas now at last realizes, implying Anchises' succession by right of birth to his cousin Priam's official custody of Troy's Vestal hallows, now finally identified with those of Anchises' own house.

Thus Aeneas' first longing, to carry Anchises out of burning Troy (635-637, 657-658), is but the complement of Hector's longing to see Aeneas carrying Troy's Vestal hallows therefrom; but it takes a fiery portent, by implication at once Vulcanically alarming and Vestally comforting, to persuade Anchises himself (671-700) that his own domestic Penates are now henceforward those, not only of his ancestors and descendants, but also of Troy itself as represented by his House:

'"Now, now there is no delay; I follow, and where ye lead

there am I. Ye gods of my fathers! (*di patrii:* 700=*patrii Penates:* 717) save my House, save my grandson (*servate domum, servate nepotem*)! Yours is the omen, and in your divine power Troy yet lives (*Troia est:* 703; the antithesis of *fuit Ilium*: 325; cf. *ubi Troia fuit:* III. 11). Yea, I yield and refuse not, my son, to accompany thee." He ceased; and now through the city more loudly is heard the fire (*ignis*), and nearer its conflagrations (*incendia*) roll their waves of heat (701-706) . . . "Father, do thou take in thy hand our (Vestal) hallows and the Penates of our fathers" ' (*tu, genitor, cape sacra manu patriosque Penates:* 717; cf. Hector's *sacra suosque tibi commendat Troia Penates; hos cape fatorum comites:* 293-294).

Then follows that family flight through Vulcan's fire with Vesta's fire (297) which carries out Hector's instructions (289); a flight successful in rescuing all Anchises' household except Creusa, whose loss symbolizes the supersession of Priam's House: ' "Then I turn homeward (to Anchises' House), if haply, haply she had made her way back thither. The Danai had rushed in and filled all the dwelling. At once the devouring fire (*ignis*) rolls before the wind to its very roof; the flames tower above it (*exsuperant flammae:* 759; cf. *Volcano superante:* 311), the wave of heat roars skyward" ' (756-759).

So ends the material fabric of Anchises' House; already containing, since Priam's death as king, Troy's actual *Vesta publica* and now become Troy's figurative *ustrinum publicum.* So too, under the central symbol of Anchises' Troy-representing House, Virgil mentally integrates the two complementary aspects of his symbolism — the domestic, peaceful, constructive, life-giving aspect, embodied in Vesta; and the crematory, warlike, destructive, death-dealing aspect, embodied in Vulcan.

For Anchises' Vestal House, which Creusa has earlier implored Aeneas to guard as his first duty (*hanc primum tutare domum:* II. 677), although thus materially destroyed by Vulcan as representing Troy itself, has already been rescued immaterially by Aeneas, whose first duty is still to guard it as represented by the miniature *penetralia Vestae* (V. 744; IX. 259) containing its Penates, and Lar, together with its perpetually burning fire on Vesta's miniature hearth (II. 296-297; V. 743): ' "I am Aeneas the dutiful (*pius*), who carry with me in my fleet the Penates which I rescued from the foe" ' (I. 378-379).

Since, moreover, Anchises' House now immaterially represents Troy, Aeneas is carrying an immaterial Troy: 'carrying into Italy Ilium and its vanquished Penates' (I. 68) — a burden wholly inseparable, in Virgil's mind, from Anchises its first bearer (II. 717), himself borne by Aeneas (II. 707-708): 'Who, they say, carries about with him the Penates of his fathers, and who bore on his shoulders a father out-worn with age' (IV. 598-599).

But, since Anchises' immaterial House, as representing an immaterial Troy, symbolizes Anchises' material House as representing a material Troy, all the domestic and crematory, or Vestal and Vulcanic, symbolism of the latter belongs in Virgil's thought to the former also. Nor is this all.

For Virgil, who thus imaginatively associates Aeneas' Trojan-Roman burden with the idea of Vulcan and Vesta as linked by Anchises' wife Venus, yet further associates it with that of Cybele and Hercules; since Aeneas, by unconscious implication as earlier shown, carries his burden materially upon shoulders covered with Hercules' own skin of Cybele's own lion (II. 721-723) — this mentally connecting link, between Cybele and Hercules, being in fact that between Rhea and Hercules (VII. 655-669) upon the Roman Aventine, whose eponym wore his father Hercules' lion-skin as Rhea's son.

Now as Warde Fowler long ago insisted (*Aeneas at the Site of Rome*, Oxford 1918, pp. 72-73), the heart of Rome was bounded for Virgil by the Aventine, the Capitoline, and the Palatine hills; with the *forum Romanum* reaching centrally towards the *forum boarium* on the Tiber-bank, Aeneas' own landing-place as burden-bearer.

But the cult of Venus on the Capitoline hill, whose foot accommodated the cult of Vulcan, faced across the *forum Romanum* the cult of Cybele on the Palatine hill, whose foot accommodated the cult of Vesta; while the cult of Hercules in the *forum boarium*, whose *ara maximà* and round *aedes Herculis* correspond respectively to the *Volcanal* altar and the round *aedes Vestae*, was the ritual counterpart of the myth of Hercules associating him on the Aventine hill both with Vulcan's predecessor Cacus in a crematorily warlike context and with Vesta's predecessor Caca in a domestically peaceful context.

The cults of Venus and Cybele, moreover, meant for Virgil's contemporaries Rome's historical victory over Carthage; while the cults of Vulcan and Vesta meant for Virgil's 'Early Latins' that prehistoric connection of the *forum Romanum* with fire both crematory and domestic which was shared by the *forum boarium* in connection with Hercules' cult and myth.

It now remains to demonstrate Virgil's largely unconscious integration of all these localized traditions under the one symbol of Aeneas' Trojan-Roman burden, which is Anchises House.

CHAPTER IX

HUT AND HIVE

Romuleoque recens horrebat regia culmo.
(*Aeneid* VIII. 654)

AN Etruscan scarab of the early fifth century B.C. portrays Anchises on Aeneas' shoulders carrying his household *sacra* in a round receptacle (A. Furtwangler, *Die antiken gemmen*, Leipzig-Berlin 1900: i, pl. 20; ii. p. 96).

This was evidently an old Italian convention; for a similar representation occurs six centuries later in the already-mentioned *tabula Iliaca* found on the site of Bovillae and preserved in the Museo Capitolino at Rome (H. Stuart Jones, *Catalogue*, Oxford 1912, pp. 165ff; *Atti della reale Accademia dei Lincei*, 5th series, XIV, viii, 1909-1911 (1911), pp. 662-731; O. Jahn, *Griechische Bilderchroniken*, Bonn 1873, pl. 1).

The designs of Bovillae's 'Trojan picture', as reproduced on a now fragmentary earthenware tablet of the first century A.D., were drawn by one Theodoros, a Greek-speaking artist of Augustan date; who twice portrays Anchises carrying his household *sacra* in a round receptacle with a dome-like cover, whose general appearance recalls that of an old-fashioned beehive.[1]

In the one scene Anchises, framed within the doorway of his already fire-gutted house, sits on Aeneas' shoulders holding his beehive-shaped burden carefully on his knees; while little Ascanius (Iulus) steps manfully forward with his left hand in the right hand of Aeneas, whose wife Creusa follows reluctantly behind the family group, itself beckoned onward by Hermes (Mercury).

In the other scene Anchises, followed in turn by Aeneas and Ascanius and Misenus, is in the act of stepping on board a ship, still holding his beehive-shaped burden carefully in both hands, but this time sharing its weight with a sailor standing already on the deck.

Above Anchises runs the inscription ΑΓΚΙΣΗΣ ΚΑΙ ΤΑ ΙΕΡΑ, 'Anchises and his *sacra*'; above Aeneas, ΑΙΝΗΑΣ ΣΥΝ

[1] See Frontispiece.

ΤΟΙΣ ΙΔΙΟΙΣ ΑΠΑΙΡΩΝ ΕΙΣ ΤΗΝ ΕΣΠΕΡΙΑΝ, 'Aeneas starting with his charges for Hesperia'; above the quay, ΣΕΙΓΑΙΟΝ 'Sigeum'; and above the ship, ΑΜΟΩΛΟΥΣ ΑΙΝΗΟΥ, 'Aeneas' sailing'.

Thus the two episodes in question are those respectively of the family-departure from Anchises' house and of the family-embarcation at Sigeum — a fact surely significant in view of Virgil's own mentally visual coupling of Sigeum with Anchises' house in a fiery context at once Vulcanic and Vestal, crematory and domestic (II. 289-312; cf. VII. 294-297); a context, that is to say, reflecting Early Latin imagery.

Since, moreover, Bovillae meant for Virgil (as shown in the first chapter of this book) the Early Latin perpetuation of that Alban Julian-Vestal cult whose foundation-myth underlies the *Aeneid*, Bovillae's own *tabula Iliaca*, illustrating that myth, may very well graphically incorporate details which, mentally familiar to Virgil as traditional at Bovillae, were themselves verbally incorporable in the *Aeneid's* symbolism.

Now the foundation-myth of the Alban Julian-Vestal cult, as perpetuated into Virgil's own lifetime at Bovillae, included the identification of its perpetually burning Vestal fire with that which Aeneas brought from Troy to Lavinium, whence it was carried by Iulus to Alba Longa for eventual tendance by Romulus' Vestal-Virgin mother; an identification taken for granted by Virgil both when he gives the name 'Ilia', 'the Trojan maid', to Romulus' mother at Alba Longa (I. 274; VI. 778) and when he makes Hector entrust Aeneas with Vesta's perpetually burning fire for transportation oversea with Troy's other *sacra* (II. 293-297).

But Vesta's fire could neither be transported oversea nor kept alight during the long and often stormy voyage unless enclosed from wind and rain within some kind of easily portable container, so constructed as both to let out the smoke and to facilitate frequent tendance — a tendance attributed by Virgil to Aeneas himself after Anchises' death, when in Sicily 'he stirs the ashes and slumbering fires, and with holy meal and full censer humbly worships the Pergamean Lar and hoary Vesta's *penetralia*' (V. 743-745).

Virgil, in other words, reserves the specific term *penetralia Vestae* (V. 744; IX. 259) for the inmost part of some kind of receptacle which by implication contains throughout the

Aeneid all those *sacra* (II. 293, 717) of Anchises' Troy-representing house which, including its perpetually burning Vestal hearth-fire (II. 296-297; V. 743) no less than its Lar (V. 744; IX. 259) and its Penates (II. 293, 717, 747; III. 12; IV. 598; V. 62; IX. 258) will pass eventually from Lavinium through Alba Longa to the inmost part, called *penus* or *penetralia*, of Rome's *aedes Vestae*.

For the early migration of the Julian clan, Virgil's *Albani patres* (I. 7), from Alba Longa to Rome, its daughter-city, involved Rome's early inheritance of that Julian-Vestal cult whose Alban foundation-myth was the Aeneas-legend; an inheritance emphasized both implicitly by Virgil (I. 267-293) and explicitly by Ovid who, having first described Alba Longa's Vestal fire as 'Trojan' (*ignibus Iliacis:* F. III. 29), couples the Aeneas-legend with Augustus' guardianship of 'the perpetually burning fire' (*ignibus acternis*) on 'the Trojan hearth' (*Iliacis . . . focis*) of the *penetralia Vestae* at Rome (F. III. 417-428).

But the inmost part, specifically termed *penus* or *penetralia*, of Rome's *aedes Vestae* – itself a round structure with a dome-shaped roof – resembled an old-fashioned beehive, such as Virgil himself describes (G. IV. 34), being a round wattle-walled structure with a thatched dome-shaped roof, such as Virgil also describes (A. VIII. 654); in fact, what archaeologists aptly term a 'beehive-hut'.

'The Vestal fire of republican and imperial Rome', writes Frazer in a well-known passage, 'was strictly the successor or continuation of the fire which in the regal period had burned on the king's hearth . . . The little round building in which the sacred fire always burned was merely a copy of the round hut in which the king, like his subjects, had dwelt in days of old. Tradition preserved a memory of the time when its walls were made of wattled osiers and the roof was of thatch (Ovid, *Fasti* VI. 261-262); indeed, with that peculiar clinging to the forms of the past which is characteristic of royalty and religion, the inmost shrine' (of Rome's *aedes Vestae*) 'continued down even to late times to be fashioned of the same simple materials (Festus, *s.v.* '*penus*': p. 250, Ed. C. O. Muller; where for *saepius* we must obviously read *saeptus*).

'The hut of Romulus, or what passed for it, constructed of wood, reeds and straw, was always preserved and carefully repaired in the original style. It stood on the side of the Palatine hill facing the Circus Maximus (Ovid, F. I. 199; III. 183-184; Dion. Halic. I. lxxix. 11; Plutarch, *Romulus* 20). A similar hut, roofed with thatch, was in like manner maintained on the Capitoline hill, and traditionally associated with Romulus (Virgil, *Aeneid* VIII. 653-654; Conon, *Narrat.* 48; Vitruvius II. i. 5; Macrobius, *Saturn.* I. XV. 10). The so-called temple of Vesta in historical times stood, not on any of the hills, but in the Forum at the northern foot of the Palatine. Its situation in the flat ground is quite consistent with the view that the building represents the king's house . . . and that the hearth in it, on which burned the sacred fire, was originally the hearth of the king's house.

'That the so-called temple' (really 'Vesta's house', *aedes Vestae*) 'was built on the model of the round huts of the old Latins is proved by the discoveries made at an ancient necropolis near Albano. The ashes of the' (cremated) 'dead were here deposited in urns, which are shaped like little round huts with conical roofs, obviously in order that the souls of the dead might live in houses such as they had inhabited during life. The roofs of these miniature dwellings are raised on cross-beams, sometimes with one or more holes to let out the smoke . . . The prehistoric' (cremation) 'burial-ground lately discovered in the Roman forum has yielded several hut-urns of precisely the same shape as those of the Alban cemetery. Hence we may infer with tolerable certainty that the earliest Latin settlers both on the Alban hills and at Rome dwelt in round huts built of wattle and daub, with peaked roofs of thatch.

'If the storeroom (*penus*) of a Roman house was deemed so holy that its contents could only be handled by persons ceremonially clean' (cf. Virgil, *Aeneid* II. 717-720), 'the reason was that the *Penates* or gods of the storeroom dwelt in it (Cicero, *De natura deorum*, II. xxvii. 68). The domestic hearth, where the household meals were cooked in the simple days of old, was the natural altar of the *Penates* (Servius on Virgil, *Aeneid* XI. 211); their images' (cf. Virgil, *Aeneid* II. 517; III. 148-152), 'together with those of the *Lares*, stood by it and shone in the cheerful glow of the fire, when the family gathered round it in the evening (Horace, *Epod.* II. 65ff; Martial III. lviii. 3ff). Thus in every house Vesta, the goddess of the hearth, was intimately bound up with the *Penates* or gods of the storeroom; indeed, she was reckoned one of them (Macrobius, *Saturn.* III. iv. 11).

'Now the temple of Vesta, being nothing more than a type of the oldest form of Roman house' (i.e. the 'beehive-hut' of archaeology), 'naturally had, like an ordinary house, its sacred storeroom, and its *Penates* or gods of the storeroom (Festus, *s.v.* '*penus*': pp. 250-251, Ed. Muller). Hence, if in every common house strict chastity was, theoretically at least, expected of all who entered the storeroom, we can well understand why such an obligation should have been laid on the Vestals, who had in their charge the holiest of all storerooms, the chamber in which were popularly supposed to be preserved the talismans on which the safety of the state depended (Dion. Halic. II. 66; Livy XXVI. xxvii. 14).

'Thus on the whole we may regard it as highly probable that the round temple of Vesta in the Forum, with its sacred storeroom and perpetual fire, was merely a survival, under changed conditions, of the old house of the Roman kings, which again may have been a copy of the still older house of the kings of Alba' (Virgil's *Albani reges: Aeneid* XII. 826). 'Both were modelled on the round huts of wattled osiers in which the early Latins dwelt among the woods and hills of Latium' (Sir J. G. Frazer, 'The Magic Art', vol. II, *The Golden Bough*, pp. 200-206).

Since Frazer thus wrote, in 1911, his then somewhat tentative opinion has won general acceptance both by archaeologists and by classical scholars.

Dr. Randall-MacIver, for example, dealing with the archaeology of Latium and Etruria in the twelfth-eleventh centuries, and so precisely with the period and the locality of Virgil's own choice, writes as follows:

'We are enabled to understand the precise character of the dwelling-houses from models which have been found in the tombs. My frontispiece, which shows the house of a prehistoric Roman some three centuries before the time of Romulus' (it is a round structure with a dome-shaped top and an openable door), 'is taken from an example actually found in a grave in the Forum. Similar models have been found on several sites in Etruria, as well as at Grotta-ferrata and Castel Gandolpho. Some of the most interesting may be seen in the

Museo Preistorico at Rome, and others in the Vatican "Museo Etrusco". These houses' (i.e. 'beehive-huts') 'were evidently built of wattle and daub, with a roof of beams sometimes carved with decorative forms. The figure of a bird is occasionally used as the finial of a beam. Solid doors fastened with a bronze bar secured the entrance, and the smoke-hole in the roof formed quite an architectural feature. One hut-urn from Castel Gandolpho . . . has an external porch of wooden columns.

'There is evidence that this style of dwelling persisted for several centuries, so that we may fairly infer that the Rome of Romulus was composed of round houses looking like these huts . . . South of the Tiber, that is to say in Latium . . . the cremated ashes were usually placed in some form of hut-urn, which was enclosed with all the other tomb-furniture in an immense jar' (D. Randall-MacIver, *Italy Before the Romans*, Oxford 1928, pp. 66-68).

Warde Fowler, again, not only unreservedly embraced Frazer's views of the Vestal cult as originating in the simple conditions of primitive domesticity as centred in the King's representative dwelling (*The Roman Festivals*, pp. 36, 111, 114, 146-154), but himself further suggested 'that the *casae* of the Roman custom, made of branches at the Neptunalia and the feast of Anna Perenna' (worshipped both at Bovillae and at Rome), 'and made of *virgae* by the slaves on the farm, are a reminiscence of the earliest form of Italian dwelling, which survived to historical times in the round temple of Vesta, and of which we have examples in the hut-urns discovered in the necropolis at Alba. The earliest form of all was probably a round structure made of branches of trees stuck into the ground, bent inwards at the top and tied together' (W. Warde Fowler, *The Religious Experience of the Roman People*, London 1911, reprinted 1933, p. 477).

It is thus of particular importance that the same classical scholar should interpret Virgil as mentally visualizing both Evander's Pallanteum and Romulus' Rome as a primitive settlement of thatched, wattled and dome-roofed round huts resembling the cinerary hut-urns found in Alba Longa's cremation-cemetery; adding that Virgil, who describes Romulus' Capitoline *regia* as precisely such a hut (VIII. 654), must have been thinking of Romulus' Palatine beehive-hut when describing the humble guest-house of Evander's *regia* (VIII.

359-368), located by implication on the future site of the unpretentious *aedes* to which Augustus moved in 29 B.C., the very year in which Virgil began writing the *Aeneid* (Warde Fowler, *Aeneas at the Site of Rome*, pp. 72-78, 93).

But Romulus' beehive-hut was the recognized symbol of Rome's foundation, while Rome's foundation is the primary theme of the *Aeneid*; so that the *Aeneid*'s primary symbol for Virgil's mind, upon its level of unconscious relation to his own heredity, might well be a beehive-hut — a symbol all the more appropriate as suggesting, not only Romulean Rome, but also both the Roman *aedes Vestae* and the Roman *aedes Herculis*; a threefold fusion in point of fact suggested by Aeneas' return to Evander's guest-house, where Hercules had recently slept, in order to renew its twofold cult of Hercules and of Vesta (VIII. 541-544) upon the site of Romulus' Rome (VIII. 342-343).

It is further significant that Virgil, precisely when describing the shield-pictures fashioned by Vulcan during the very night of Aeneas' succession to Hercules in Evander's Vestal equivalent of Romulus' beehive-hut on the Palatine hill, has no sooner within the space of eleven lines identified the Roman people indifferently with the descendants both of Romulus (*Romulidis:* VIII. 638) and of Aeneas (*Aeneadae:* 648) than he at once goes on to include, amongst the symbols of Aeneas' Roman destiny as depicted on his shield (626, 731), Romulus' beehive-hut on the Capitoline hill (652-654), where it was treasured in the temple of Aeneas' divine grandfather Jupiter (Conon, *Narrat.* 48).

For it is on the Capitoline hill that Virgil shortly afterwards locates that 'House of Aeneas' (IX. 448) whose equivalence to the Roman people was earlier implied by Jupiter's divine son Apollo (III. 97); while this same *domus Aeneae*, as coupled by Virgil on the Capitoline hill with the *pater Romanus* (IX. 449) is lineally identical with the *domus Assaraci* as earlier coupled by Jupiter with the *Troianus Caesar* (I. 284-286).

Both the 'House of Aeneas' and the 'House of Assaracus', moreover, are themselves lineally identical with that 'House of Anchises' (*Anchisae domus:* II. 300) whose *adyta penetralia* (II. 297), now the *penus* or *penetralia Vestae* of Troy's *aedes Vestae*, contain Assaracus' Pergamean Lar as well as Vesta's Penates and perpetually burning hearthfire (II. 293-297; V. 743-745; IX. 258-260), and whose symbol on Bovillaes' *tabula Iliaca* closely resembles an old-fashioned beehive—a resemblance most naturally explicable on the assumption that Anchises' house is there symbolized, in accordance with Alban tradition, by the miniature representation of a beehive-hut such as once housed both the kings of Alba Longa and their Vestal hallows.

Hence it may well be that Virgil's mind, imaginatively fusing the two Roman beehive-shaped houses of Romulus, together with those of Vesta and Hercules, into that one conventionally beehive-shaped symbol of Anchises' Trojan house which he remembered as both Alban-Bovillensian and Etruscan, unconsciously appropriated the hereditarily familiar beehive-shape as uniquely symbolizing Aeneas' Trojan-Roman destiny.

Virgil, as an authority on bee-keeping, distinguishes very early in the *Georgics*' fourth book between the natural hive of the wild bees and the artificial hive of the tame bees:

'Then let the hive itself, whether it be sewn of hollow bark, or woven of pliant osier (*lento . . . vimine texta*), have its entrances narrow . . . Often, too, if report be true, bees have made a snug home in tunnelled hiding-places underground, and are found deep in the hollows of pumice-rock, or in the cavern (*antro*) of a decayed tree' (G. IV. 34-35, 42-44).

In other words, the natural hive of Virgil's wild bees is some kind of cave, recalling the Homeric cave-beehive (*Odyssey* XIII. 102-106); while the artificial hive of Virgil's tame bees is some kind of hut, recalling the Hesiodic hut-beehive (*Theogony* 594-596).

Virgil's hut-beehive, moreover, is a miniature house, constructed either of sewn bark or of woven osier; and it is significant that Ovid, when he wishes to describe an early Roman thatched and wattled beehive-hut, actually quotes Virgil's own description of a hut-beehive (*lento vimine textus: Fasti* VI. 262).

Nor was Virgil unfamiliar with the rustic beehive-huts of Italy, since he twice refers to them in the *Eclogues* (*pauperis et tuguri congestum caespite culmen:* E. I. 68; *humilis habitare casas:* E. II. 29).

Thus, whereas in the *Eclogues* Virgil has in mind a beehive-hut community of men who keep bees, in the *Georgics* he has in mind a hut-beehive community of bees kept by men; but both communities share alike that Vestal domesticity which belonged to the beehive-hut communities of Alba Longa and Rome.

In the *Eclogues*, for example, the rustic beehive-huts have hearths (E. V. 70) with perpetually burning fires (E. VII. 49-50), whose smoke rises visibly from the hut-clusters (E. I. 82); and these hut-hearths have their own Vestal shrines (E. VIII. 64, 105) adjoining the hearth-fire with its glowing flames and ashes (E. VIII. 101, 105-106). It is further suggestive that the rustic who describes his dwelling as a beehive-hut (E. I. 68) should in the same breath claim equivalence to a king (E. I. 69); as though Virgil were remembering Romulus' hut-palace (*regia:* A. VIII. 654) at Rome.

Similarly, in the *Georgics*' fourth book, the Virgilian hut-beehive is the *sedes augusta* (228) or *aedes* (258) of a *rex* (75, 106, 201, 212), with its *lar* (43) and *penates* (155); being a *domus* (133, 159) with *tecta* (104, 153, 189, 256), *limina* (188, 257), *portae* (78, 165, 185), *fores* (247), *thalami* (189), *cubilia* (243), and *thesauri* (229), in a *regnum* (202) of *Quirites* (201) whose *patria* (155) contains *oppida* (178), *castra* (108), and an *urbs* (154) with *moenia* (193).

Thus the Virgilian bee-world is a hut-beehive community which is the miniature counter-part of the beehive-hut community of Romulean Rome, its thatched and wattled *regia* being at the same time its *aedes Vestae*; so that the Virgilian hut-beehive poetically symbolizes what was popularly symbolized by the Romulean beehive-hut.

Nor is this unnatural when we remember two facts — first, that the early Italian bee-keepers deliberately built their hives as miniature copies of their own huts; and, secondly, that Virgil, as an Italian bee-keeper's son, will as a boy subconsciously have associated the idea of his father's hut-beehives with that of the beehive-huts in which dwelt many Italian bee-keepers in his father's neighbourhood.

From this subconsciously functioning because environmentally determined association of ideas, moreover, will have sprung an imaginative correspondence between the little world of the hive-dwelling bees and the large world of the hut-dwelling men; their identically constructed homes suggesting identically ordered lives, with one common home-life inseparable in the boy Virgil's poetic mind from the circumstances of his own home-life, including its nursery-tales of kings and battles.

Thus, while the man Virgil's epic theme, to 'sing of kings and battles', is referred to as early as his sixth *Eclogue* (3) in connection with his beehive-hut community, it is in connection with his hut-beehive community that he begins his epic song in the fourth *Georgics*.

But these kings and battles, witnessed by Virgil as a child, are on a tiny scale; belonging to the miniature world of bees: 'The wondrous pageant of a tiny world, great-hearted chiefs, a whole race's habits and interests and tribes and battles, I will in due order unfold to thee' (G. IV. 3-5) — a world, however, minutely comparable with that large world of men whose Trojan-Roman epic is already being planned (G. III. 8-39).

The fact is that the poet's mind, while consciously at work upon the epic symbolism of the last book of his *Georgics*, was all the time subconsciously so hard at work upon the epic symbolism of his next poem, the *Aeneid*, that his conscious composition of the *Aeneid* was subconsciously affected by the remembered symbolism of the fourth *Georgics*.

The result is that, whereas in the fourth *Georgics* Virgil compared bees with men through associating the idea of hut-beehives with that of beehive-huts, in the first *Aeneid* he compares men with bees through associating the idea of beehive-huts with that of hut-beehives; and he does so precisely because this particular kind of round and domed structure has long been associated in his mind with that Romulean foundation of Rome which itself sprang from Aeneas' and Iulus' successive foundations of an Early Latin regal city for the Vestal *sacra* of Anchises' Troy-representing house.

The scene in question is Carthage, whose suburb was called *Magalia* (Plautus, *Poenulus*, prol. 86), a Semitic word meaning the equivalent of our 'Beehive-huts' (*magalia aedificia quasi cohortes rotundas dicunt:* Cato, *Orig.* fragm. ap. Serv. ad Virg. *Aen.* I. 421) — its variant form *mapalia* being applied by Virgil (G. III. 340) to their Libyan portable counterpart.

Professor H. J. Rose has pointed out that the Italian beehive-huts do not differ in principle from the Libyan (*Primitive Culture in Italy*, London 1926, p. 33); while Osric Bates (*The Eastern Libyans*, London 1914, pp. 168-169), after describing and illustrating the Libyan beehive-huts, continues:

'On the outskirts of the Afro-Roman towns, groups of *mapalia*' (here the equivalent of the fixed *magalia*) 'were to be found collected . . . It was for this reason that the name *mapalia*, *mappalia*, came to be used to designate a native quarter . . . At Carthage was a *Via Mappaliensis* in the time of St. Cyprian Martyr' (A.D. *c.* 200-258); 'and, as this street was distant from the centre of the town, it probably ran through, and derived its name from, an old native suburb . . . A parallel is seen in modern Tripoli Town, where a long street . . . at last goes through a settlement of wattled huts.'

Bates further describes (pp. 169-170, *op. cit.*) certain Tunisian mosaics showing various types of the native Libyan round hut, including one of beehive-shape with 'wattled walls and a conical roof of thatch'; while a note (p. 168), quoting Festus (p. 258 Egger) for the statement that 'Punic huts are called *mapalia*', explains that 'a variant is *magalia*'.

Now it is a remarkable fact, yet further illuminating the unconsciously functioning because hereditarily determined profundities of Virgil's mind, that these primitive Libyan and Italian communities were in fact comparable with bees, not only in the shape and materials of their round huts, but also in the cell-like adjustment of one hut to another in communal groups or clusters, corresponding to the bee-like psychology of their prehistoric occupants.

Thus Altheim (*op. cit.*, pp. 28-29), analysing the significance of what he calls 'the ancient Mediterranean round house', points out that 'there are whole villages of huts, where the single buildings unite in a kind of scattered, yet huddled formation, to make swarm-like masses. The very word "swarm" seems to me to express the fact that the multiplicity here, by the manner in which it is inwardly combined, belongs to the order of nature . . . Where several round huts combine to form a continuous and regular whole, regulation of axis is entirely dispensed with. We have already used the simile of a swarm; a second simile, also drawn from nature, is now appropriate: I mean the combination of crystals or of a beehive. Hut-wall is fixed to hut-wall; separation into individual compartments is abandoned and the result is a system of cells, which is only interrupted by occasional approaches or narrowings . . . The close union of the lodgements, the natural combination and associated growth of the single round houses, must have something to correspond to them in the order of the inhabitants who chose this form . . . In other words, living together in a web of cells means in architecture what organization by families, brotherhoods, clans and tribes means in human society. The shape of the architecture and the organization of society both essentially coincide with the conditions of the life of nature.'

It is now easier to fathom the depths of Virgil's poetic symbolism when he suddenly brings Aeneas, reduced by shipwreck to the level of primitive livelihood (I. 157-222) but still the destined founder of the Roman race (223-304), to that old Libyan beehive-hut settlement whose Carthage-builders are both comparable with bees and the envied rivals of Aeneas, whose own city remains as yet unbuilt (419-438); and again later, when Aeneas is described as forfeiting his Roman destiny by beginning to build his city, in Libya instead of Italy, on the foundations provided by the same primitive beehive-hut settlement (IV. 259-276):

'Aeneas marvels at the massive buildings, once beehive-huts (*magalia quondam:* I. 421); marvels at the gates, the din and the paved highways. Eagerly the Tyrians press on: some to build walls, to rear the citadel, and roll up stones by hand; some to choose the site for a dwelling, and enclose it with a furrow. Laws and magistrates they ordain, and a holy senate. Here some are digging harbours, here others lay the deep foundations of their theatre and hew out of the cliffs vast columns, lofty adornments for the stage to be.

'Even as bees (*qualis apes:* 430) in early summer amid flowery fields ply their task in sunshine, when they lead forth the full-grown young of their race, or pack the fluid honey and strain their hive-cells to bursting with sweet nectar, or receive the burdens of incomers, or in martial array drive from their folds the drones, a lazy herd; all aglow is the work, and the fragrant honey is sweet with thyme. "Happy are they whose city-walls already rise!" cries Aeneas, lifting his eyes towards the city-roofs' (I. 421-438).

Analysis of these eighteen lines reveals their perfect balance. For the first two (421-422) combine with the two last (437-438) to form one integral statement both of Aeneas' experience and of his reaction thereto; while the intervening fourteen lines (423-436), illuminating that twofold statement, are themselves halved into two seven-line lengths, of which the former describes the doings of men (423-429) and the latter the doings of bees (430-436).

Nor is this all. For division of the whole passage into nine-line halves will show the former's first line as ending with the two words *magalia quondam*, 'once beehive-huts' (421) and the latter's first line as beginning with the two words *qualis apes*, 'even as bees' (430).

So elaborate a verbal proportionment implies a mental deliberation explicable only by the importance attached by Virgil to the passage as a whole; whose implicit concern is less with the idea of Carthage than with that of Rome, as is proved explicitly by that later passage which again associates Aeneas with the same prehistoric beehive-hutment in a foundational context:

'No sooner has Mercury with winged feet touched the beehive-huts (*tetigit megalia:* IV. 259) than he catches sight of Aeneas founding citadels (*fundantem arces;* cf. *Romanas . . . arces:* IV. 234) and building new dwellings . . . At once he assails him: "Art thou now laying the foundations of lofty Carthage, and building up a fair city, a wife's minion? Alas! of thine own kingdom and concerns forgetful! . . . (Jupiter) himself bids me bring thee this charge through the swift breezes: What plannest thou? or in what hope dost thou waste idle hours in Libyan lands? If the glory of so great concerns stirs thee not, if for thine own fame's sake thou shoulderest not the burden" (of thy destiny as founder of the Roman race) "at least have regard for growing Ascanius, even the promise of Iulus thine heir, to whom the kingdom of Italy and the Roman land are due" ' (IV. 259-276).

Now this passage at once recalls Bovillae's 'Trojan picture', where Mercury similarly urges Aeneas forward with Ascanius (Iulus) and with that shouldered burden which even now, despite Anchises' own material death, still remains immaterially Anchises' house as symbolized by a beehive-hut, itself the symbol both of Iulus' Alba Longa and of Romulus' Rome.

For Virgil, who begins the *Aeneid* by explicitly coupling the prehistoric foundation of Rome with the prehistoric foundation of Carthage in one complementary contrast of Mediterranean rivalry (I. 1-296), with Mercury as the link between the two rival foundations (297-304), not only goes on to symbolize implicitly both that rivalry and those foundations under the uniquely typical Mediterranean symbol of a beehive-hutment (421-438) such as formed the prehistoric foundations of both Rome and Carthage — a hutment, moreover, itself implicitly comparable in the *Aeneid*, and explicitly comparable in archaeology, with a beehive — but also brings Aeneas himself mysteriously into the very heart of that Mediterranean symbolism:

'Veiled in cloud, he enters — wondrous to tell — through their midst, and mingles with the (bee-resembling) men, yet seen by none of them' (439-440).

Aeneas, in short, is mentally visualized by Virgil as shouldering the burden of that Trojan-Roman destiny whose Mediterranean symbol is a beehive-hut as the counterpart of a hut-beehive; so that the eventual settlement of his Trojans in the Roman neighbourhood, explicitly symbolized by Virgil under the figure of a swarm of bees (VII. 64-70), implicitly results from Aeneas' final refusal, under Mercury's persuasion, to forfeit that equivalent share in the foundation of historical Rome, above its prehistoric Italian beehive-hutment, whose Mediterranean rival is his equivalent share in the foundation of historical Carthage above its prehistoric Libyan beehive-hutment.

CHAPTER X

URN AND HOUSE

hic tibi certa domus, certi (ne absiste) Penates.
(*Aeneid* VIII. 39)

VIRGIL, remembering what he had himself seen of Roman building-processes, employs similar terms both for Dido's deep foundational excavations amongst the remains of the old beehive-huts mentioned six lines earlier (*magalia . . . alta theatri fundamenta locant:* I. 421; 427-428) and for Aeneas' high foundational elevations amongst the remains of the same beehive-huts again mentioned exactly six lines earlier (*magalia . . . Karthaginis altae fundamenta locas?*: IV. 259; 265-266) — an equally-spaced verbal repetition obviously corresponding to some equivalent mental association between the idea of the remains of old beehive-huts and that of the 'deep foundations' of 'lofty Carthage' as the rival of 'lofty Rome' (*altae . . . Romae:* I. 7).

Now Augustus, portrayed on Aeneas' shield as dedicating three hundred votive temples throughout Rome (VIII. 715-716), dedicated a votive temple in the *forum Romanum* to his adoptive father Julius Caesar under the title *divus Iulius* in 29 B.C., the very year in which Virgil published his *Georgics* and began his *Aeneid*, upon the site of Julius Caesar's cremation.

Nor is it probable that Augustus' excavations in the *forum Romanum* for laying down the deep foundations of his temple to the there-cremated *divus Iulius* (cf. *Divi genus*: VI. 792) will have failed, in that overcrowded Early Latin cremation-cemetery where Roman tradition located Romulus' foundation-burial as the king who reigned from a beehive-hut palace overlooking his future grave, to disinter specimens of those Early Latin cinerary urns whose deliberate imitation of beehive-huts involved their accidental resemblance to hut-beehives.

Since, therefore, the *Aeneid*'s Libyan beehive-huts bear much the same foundational relationship to Carthage as that borne by the Italian cinerary hut-urns to Rome, it is reasonable to relate Virgil's mental vision of the Carthaginian excavations to his visual memory of their Roman counterpart as foundational to Augustus' cremation-sited temple of Aeneas' own Julian descendant—a memory giving point to Virgil's mention of Iulus as Aeneas' heir (*heredis Iuli:* IV. 274) in a foundational context linking the idea of beehive-huts both with Iulus' Roman destiny as founder of the Julian clan and with Aeneas' destiny as founder of the Roman race.

Virgil, moreover, as antiquary and poet enjoying Augustus' favour, will at once have recognized the uniquely symbolical significance of Rome's prehistoric hut-urns as implying precisely that Early Latin association of the domestic hearth (*focus*) with the crematory pyre (*pyra*) which correlated the cult of Vesta with the cult of Vulcan across their common area, the Roman forum, as the site both of the Public Hearth and of the Public Pyre—an associative correlation evidently so deeply implanted in Virgil's mind, at least upon its functionally unconscious because hereditarily determined plane, that when describing the mortuary customs of the Early Latins he actually fuses the idea of their crematory pyres with that of their domestic hearths:

'The Latins built innumerable pyres (*pyras*). Of their many slain . . . (the majority), a mighty mass of indistinguishable slaughter, they cremate (*cremant*); then, on all sides, emulous with close-clustering fires (*ignibus*), flare the broad fields . . . (On the third morning of incineration) they began mournfully to rake out the heap of ashes (*cinerem*) and the jumble of bones (*ossa*) from the hearths (*focis*), and to bury them under a still-warm mound of earth' (XI. 203-212).

Virgil, in fact, here implies just that imaginative equivaence, between the still warmly smouldering embers of the crematory pyres of the dead and the still warmly smouldering embers of the domestic hearths of the living, which underlies the life-after-death symbolism both of the Early Latin hut-urn and of the *Aeneid* itself.

Venus, for example, complaining to Neptune of Juno's frequently attempted frustration of Aeneas' Trojan-Roman destiny, exclaims: '"It is not enough that from the midst of the Phrygians' race she in her fell hate has consumed their city, and dragged through utmost vengeance the remnants of Troy; the ashes and bones of the perished (race) she still pursues" ' —

> *non media de gente Phrygum exedisse nefandis*
> *urbem odiis satis est nec poenam traxe per omnem*
> *reliquias Troiae; cineres atque ossa peremptae*
> *insequitur* (V. 785-788).

Superficially, of course, these Juno-pursued 'ashes and bones' are those of Anchises himself (*cineres . . . et ossa parentis:* V. 55), insulted by Juno's attempt to burn the Trojan fleet during his funeral ceremonies (V. 604-666); but they are much more than that.

For Venus' reference to the ashes and bones of the dead and incinerated Anchises as 'the ashes and bones of the perished race' (*cineres atque ossa peremptae* (sc. *gentis*): V. 787) implies the Virgilian equivalence of Anchises to the dead and incinerated Trojan race: ' "We Trojans are dead, Ilium is dead . . . our city is aflame" ' (*fuimus Troes, fuit Ilium . . . incensa . . . urbe:* II. 325, 327); ' "O ashes of Ilium! O funeral flame of my kin!" ' (*Iliaci cineres et flamma extrema meorum:* II. 431).

Thus, except for Aeneas' followers as representing Anchises' household, all the Trojans have shared in that figurative death and incineration of their 'perished race' whose representative symbol is the actual death and incineration of Anchises; so that not only is the 'race', described by Juno as 'carrying into Italy' Ilium itself and Ilium's Penates (I. 67-68), identical with what Venus calls 'the remnants of Troy' (*reliquias Troiae:* V. 787) as persecuted by Juno, but the only Ilium which that remnant-race can carry into Italy is those other remains of Troy which, called by Venus 'the ashes and bones of the perished race', are representatively symbolized by Anchises' 'ashes and bones'.

Now Virgil's contemporary Strabo (V. iii. 2=229) records a variant tradition of Anchises' death in Italy, whither he accompanied Aeneas; a tradition mentioned shortly afterwards by Dionysius of Halicarnassus (I. lxiv. 5).

Ovid, moreover, explicitly reflects one facet of Virgil's implicit symbolism when, visualizing Evander's Pallanteum as a beehive-hutment (*Fasti* I. 502), he puts into the mouth of Evander's mother a prophecy of Aeneas' Trojan-Roman destiny which implies that Aeneas brought to Italy, not only the Penates and Anchises actually, but also the ashes of Troy figuratively, in order to place them on the site of Augustus' Earth-equivalent Rome:

' "Howbeit, conquered Troy, thou shalt yet conquer and from thy fall shalt rise again; thy very ruin shall overwhelm the houses of thy foes. Ye conquering flames, consume Neptune's Pergama! Shall that prevent Troy's ashes from overtopping all the world? Anon Aeneas the dutiful shall bring hither his sacred burden and, burden no whit less sacred, his own father; Vesta, admit the gods of Ilium! The time will come when the same hand shall guard you and the world, and when a god shall in his own person hold the sacred rites. In the line of Augustus the guardianship of the fatherland shall abide; it is decreed that his House shall hold the reins of empire" ' (*Fasti* I. 523-532).

There are, in point of fact, indications that Virgil, while consciously locating Anchises' death (III. 707-711) and incineration (V. 28-57) in Sicily, unconsciously located both of them in Italy according to the variant tradition as known to his contemporaries; since Dido by implication attributes the theft of 'Anchises' ashes and ghost' (*nec patris Anchisae cineres Manisve revelli:* IV. 427) to that same Diomede whom Virgil locates in Italy (VIII. 9; XI. 226, 243) — an implication following, moreover, Aeneas' reference both to that 'city of Troy' (*urbem Troianam:* IV. 342) which is represented by Anchises' house (II. 289-335) and to those 'sweet relics' of Aeneas' kin (*dulcisque meorum reliquias:* IV. 342-343) which are represented by the 'relics and bones' of Aeneas' father (*reliquias divinique ossa parentis:* V. 47).

Nor is it without significance, not only that Dido's reference to Diomede's theft of 'Anchises' ashes and ghost' should itself be followed by her description of Aeneas' twofold burden as that both of an already dying Anchises and of the Penates of Anchises' house (IV. 598-599), but also that Turnus' appeal to Diomede in Italy should request his help against Aeneas as bringing into Latium those same 'vanquished Penates' (*adventum Aenean classi victosque Penates inferre:* VIII. 11-12) which Juno couples with Ilium as Aeneas' twofold burden (*Ilium in Italiam portans victosque Penates:* I. 68).

The evidence thus suggests Virgil's unconscious appropriation of the variant tradition about Anchises' death and incineration under the mentally transformed figure of warmly smouldering ashes from Vulcan's crematory fire (cf. VI. 226-228; XI. 211-212) which, symbolizing the Anchises-represented Trojan race as dead and incinerated (II. 325, 431) only for eventual Phoenix-like resurrection in Italy (I. 206), are carried thither by Aeneas, under the equivalent figure of those warmly smouldering ashes from Vesta's domestic fire (V. 743-745) which symbolize the undying life of Anchises' Troy-representing house (II. 296-297) — this symbolism, at once crematory and domestic, being facilitated by Virgil's appropriation also of that Hercules-legend which, deriving Hercules' attainment of divine immortality from his own self-incineration, belonged at Rome to his cult, at once crematory and domestic in its symbolism, as centred in the round and domed *aedes Herculis* which, no less than Rome's *aedes Vestae*, originated in a beehive-hut resembling a hut-beehive.

Virgil, that is to say, unconsciously envisaged Aeneas' Trojan-Roman burden as twofold; partly actual, and partly figurative — his figurative burden, described by Juno as *Ilium* (I. 68), being the still warmly smouldering because inextinguishably living ashes of the Trojan race as represented by Anchises; and his actual burden described by Juno as *Penates* (I. 68), being inseparable from those *sacra* of Troy (II. 293) as represented by Anchises' house (II. 717) which include not only the Pergamean Lar (V. 744) of Assaracus (IX. 259) but also the warmly smouldering ashes of the fire (V. 743) perpetually burning (II. 297) on the domestic hearth (II. 296) of the *penus* or *penetralia Vestae* (II. 297; V. 744; IX. 259).

Since, moreover, Anchises' actual house, whose explicit Italian artistic symbol was a beehive-hut resembling a hut-beehive, is finally seen by Aeneas as sharing in the figurative death and incineration (II. 756-759) of the Troy which it represents (II. 324-327), its implicit Virgilian poetic symbol should correspondingly represent Troy as figuratively dead and incinerated — a requirement uniquely satisfied by the conclusion that Virgil mentally visualized Anchises' Troy-representing House as carried by Aeneas into Italy under the poetically symbolic figure of a cinerary hut-urn whose imitation of a beehive-hut involves its likeness to a hut-beehive.

Since the Early Latin hut-urns of Alba Longa and Rome were not only easily portable but domestically complete, having always an openable door and often a smoke-hole in the roof, such a receptacle would be uniquely practicable for the purpose of transporting oversea (II. 294) an actually burning fire upon a *foculus*, or small removable hearth (*manibus . . . Vestam . . . aeternumque adytis effert penetralibus ignem:* II. 296-297), where the embers could be kept always aglow (*cinerem et sopitos suscitat ignis:* V. 743); as also for actually offering thereon 'pure gifts' (*munera libo intemerata focis:* III. 177-178) of 'holy meal and full censer' (*farre pio et plena supplex veneratur acerra:* V. 745) no less to an actual 'shrine of hoary Vesta' (*canae penetralia Vestae:* V. 744) than to those actual 'sacred images of the gods' therein (*effigies sacrae divum:* III. 148) which include both Troy's Penates (*Phrygiique Penates:* III. 148) and Troy's Lar (*Pergameumque Larem:* V. 744) — images, moreover, which share Aeneas' guardianship (*hanc primum tutare domum:* II. 677) of Anchises House (*di patrii, servate domum*: II. 702) as representing Troy (*vestroque in numine Troia est*: II. 703) in relation no less to the crematory fire of Vulcan (*quos mecum a Troia mediisque ex ignibus urbis extuleram:* III. 149-150; *nos te Dardania incensa tuaque arma secuti:* III. 156) than to the domestic fire of Vesta.

Since, moreover, Aeneas' cinerary hut-urn contains not only the Vesta of Anchises (II. 296) but also both the Lar of Assaracus (IX. 259) and the Penates of Dardanus (III. 167), it obviously symbolizes for Virgil's mind not only the Troy-representing House of Anchises (II. 300) but also both the Troy-representing House of Assaracus (I. 284) and that Troy-representing House of Dardanus which Aeneas carries back again once more to Italy as the native homeland no less of his cinerary hut-urn than of Dardanus himself:

> *o sate gente deum, Troianam ex hostibus urbem*
> *qui revehis nobis aeternaque Pergama servas,*
> *exspectate solo Laurenti arvisque Latinis,*
> *hic tibi certa domus, certi* (*ne absiste*) *Penates* (VIII. 36-39).

Now Aeneas, who for some reason clearly recoils at the word *certi* as following the phrase *certa domus*, is for some reason no less clearly expected by Tiberinus to find relief in the word *Penates* as following *certi* — a recoil and a relief alike explicable on the assumption that Virgil, having in mind the resemblance of Aeneas' urn to a hut-beehive, took for granted his readers' awareness both that the term *certa domus* was in Latin epigraphy applied conventionally to the tomb as the fixed dwelling of the incinerated and urn-housed dead (*Inscr.* Orelli 1174; 4525 ff.) and that the term *certi Penates* had in the fourth *Georgics* (155) been applied figuratively to the hive as the fixed dwelling of the domesticated and hut-housed bees.

It is further probable that Virgil — whose phrase *Hernica saxa* (VIII. 684) certainly assumes his readers' knowledge that *herna* was the Marsian equivalent of *saxum* (or perhaps of *saxa*; cf. Paul. ex Fest., p. 100 Muller: *Hernici dicti a saxis, quae Marsi herna dicunt*), and whose phrase *Atlantis duri* (IV. 247) surely assumes their knowledge not only that ἄτλας was the Greek equivalent of *durus* (W. F. Jackson Knight, *Roman Vergil*, London 1944, pp. 198-199) but also that *Duris* was the Libyan name for Mount Atlas (Strabo 825=XVII. iii. 2: ὄρος ἐστίν, ὅπερ οἱ μὲν Ἕλληνες Ἄτλαντα καλοῦσιν, οἱ βάρβαροι δὲ Δύριν[1] — likewise attributed to his readers his own linguistic derivation[2] of the name *Dardanus*, Δάρδανος, from the word *darda*, δάρδα, which in some as yet unidentified but probably then still surviving language meant 'bee' (Hesychius: δάρδα · μέλισσα).

This probability is indeed strengthened both by the identification in the *Aeneid* (VII. 68-70, 255-258) of 'Dardanus' sons' (*Dardanidae:* 195) with those 'bees' (*apes:* 64) which explicitly symbolize 'Aeneas' sons' (*Aeneadae:* 284, 334, 616), and also by the implied simultaneity (102-106) of the bees' arrival in Latinus' palace with the arrival of Dardanus' sons in Tiberinus river (29-80) — a simultaneity whose significance, explicitly based on the resemblance of a swarm of bees to a colony of men, is implicitly clarified for readers of the fourth *Georgics* by Tiberinus' beehive-recalling phrase *certi . . . Penates* (VIII. 39).

Virgil, in fact, clearly implies a parallel between the prophetically interpretative welcomes on Laurentine soil (*solo*

[1] See R. W. Cruttwell in *Classical Review* (May 1945), vol. 59, no. 1, p. 11.

[2] This derivation is approved by Sir William Ramsay, *Asianic Elements in Greek Civilisation*: the Gifford Lectures 1915-1916 (published, London, 1927), p. 83: '*Darda* meant, as Hesychius mentions, a "bee" . . . The town, the unity and assembly of human beings in a community, is modelled on the community of the bees in a hive . . . From *darda* is derived the name of the people, *Dardanoi*; of the hero, *Dardanus*; and the town *Dardanos*, on the Hellespont, between Troy and the Narrows . . . That bees in their hive should be a model of human life in a city is natural. Bees are regarded as peculiarly closely related to human beings, *viz.* those human beings that know and befriend and tend them; and it was an old custom in England to whisper to the hives the news of any important event in family history, a death or a birth.'

Laurenti: VIII. 38) given respectively by Tiberinus in his Laurentine river (*Laurentem . . . Thybrim:* V. 797) and by Latinus in his Laurentine palace (*Laurentis regia Pici*: VII 171) to the 'Laomedontian menfolk' (*Laomedontia pubes:* 105) who as 'Dardan menfolk' (*Dardana Pubes:* 219) are symbolized by laurel-swarming bees belonging to one hive — the word *Laurens*, 'Laurentine', conveying to Virgil the idea of that *laurus*, 'laurel' (63), which symbolized for his readers not only both oracular prophecy and victorious achievement but also the Iulus-descended Julian House as coupled by Virgil in a prophetically victorious context with the Rome-representing 'House of Aeneas' (IX. 446-449), itself identical with the Troy-representing House of Dardanus (VIII. 36-39).

Now the laurel, as Virgil doubtless knew, symbolized for the ancient Mediterranean world just that integration of Vulcan's crematory fire with Vesta's domestic fire which, implied by Virgil in Lavinia's self-conflagration under Latinus' bee-swarming laurel (VII. 52-80), belongs to Aeneas' Italian cinerary hut-urn as symbolizing the House of Dardanus; since the ancient Mediterranean custom of using laurel both to kindle fire ('Homeric' *Hymn to Hermes* 108-109) and for firewood (Tibullus II. V. 81) on the domestic hearth (Theocritus II. 23-26; Virgil, *Eclogue* VIII. 80-83) led to the belief that the laurel itself was full of natural fire (M. B. Ogle, 'Laurel in Ancient Religion and Folk-lore', *The American Journal of Philology*, vol. XXXI. 3; 1910; pp. 296-297) — a connection of ideas discernible in Virgil's comparison of Aeneas' fight with Turnus for Lavinia's hand to 'fires launched from opposing sides upon a dry forest and laurel-crackling thickets' (XII. 521-522); this fight being the fulfilment of the prophecy symbolized earlier by Lavinia's fire-crackling tresses (VII. 73-77).

When it is remembered that, before becoming the House of Anchises, the House of Dardanus had been that House of Priam whose laurel overhung both its central altar-fire and what were then still Dardanus' own Vestal Penates (II. 501-502, 512-514); and also that, while the birthday of Rome's new year was marked by the hanging of fresh laurel over and the kindling of fresh fire upon the Public Hearth of Vesta (Ovid, *Fasti* III. 141-143), the birthday of Rome itself was marked by rites including both the sprinkling of fresh water from a laurel-bough and the burning of fresh laurel on the private hearth (*Fasti* IV. 728, 742); it can hardly be doubted that Virgil's life-after-death symbolism of Aeneas' hut-urn involves the equivalence of the urn-represented Trojan House of Dardanus to that hut-resembling Roman House of Vesta whose hearth-fire was so closely associated with its laurel — the likeness of the House of Vesta's *penus* or *penetralia* to a thatched and wattled hut-beehive thus suggesting to Virgil an association, not only between the laurel as symbolizing the House of Latinus and bees as symbolizing the House of Dardanus (VII. 59-70), but also between both of them and the fire as symbolizing the war-effected union of the two Houses in the marriage of Lavinia with Aeneas (VII. 52-58, 71-80, 96-101); both bees and laurel being therefore connected in Virgil's thought with that crematory but domestic fire whose kindling symbolizes, not only the birth of that new Roman year which is but a rebirth of the old Trojan year, but also that birthday of Rome which is but the rebirthday of Troy:

'And now the sea was reddening with the rays of dawn . . . when lo! Aeneas, gazing forth from the flood, beholds a mighty forest through whose midst Tiberinus with pleasant stream leaps forth to the sea in swirling eddies and yellow with plenteous sand (VII. 25, 29-32)... He bids his comrades change their course and turn their prows to land, and joyfully enters the shady river (35-36) . . . Greater is the course of events that is brought to birth for my telling; greater is the task I take in hand. King Latinus, now old, was ruling over lands and towns in the calm of a long peace (44-46) . . . Alone, to preserve his House and noble home, was a daughter, now ripe for a husband, now of full age to be a bride (52-53) . . . In the midst of his palace, within its lofty *penetralia*, was a laurel (59) . . . on whose top, wondrous to tell, settled a cluster of bees, borne with loud humming across the liquid air, and with feet intertwined hung in sudden swarm from the leafy bough. Forthwith, prophetic, he cries: "I see a foreigner approach, and a troop seek the self-same region from the self-same region, and lord it on the citadel's top." Moreover, while with hallowed torch he kindles the altars, and while at her father's side stands the maiden Lavinia, she was seen (O horror!) to catch fire (*ignem*) in her long tresses, and to burn (*cremari*) with crackling flame (*flamma*) in all her headgear, her queenly hair ablaze, ablaze (*accensa* . . . *accensa*) her jewelled coronal; then, smoking, with yellow glare enveloping her, she scattered Vulcan's fire (*Volcanum*) throughout the palace. That, indeed, was noised abroad as an awful and a wondrous vision; for she, they foretold, would herself be glorious in fame and destiny, yet to her people she boded a mighty war. But the king, troubled by the portent, visits the oracle of Faunus, his prophetic sire (64-82) . . . Suddenly a voice sounded from the deep grove: "Seek not, my son, to ally thy daughter (with Turnus) in Latin wedlock, and put no faith in the bridal-chamber prepared. Foreigners shall come, to be thy sons-in-law, whose blood shall exalt our name to the stars, and the children of whose race shall behold, where the circling sun looks on either ocean, the whole world roll obedient beneath their feet." This answer of his father Faunus, and the warning he gave in the silent night, Latinus keeps not shut within his own lips; but Rumour, flitting far and wide, had already borne the tidings through the Ausonian cities when the Laomedontian menfolk moored their ships to the river's grassy bank. Aeneas and his chief captains and fair Iulus lay their limbs to rest under the boughs of a high tree (95-108) . . . Forthwith (Aeneas) cries: "Hail, O land destined as my due! and hail, ye Penates faithful to Troy! Here is our House, this is our father's (i.e. Dardanus') land! (120-123) . . . Come, then, and gladly with the sun's first light let us explore what places these may be, what men here dwell, where is the city of the race, and let us fare forth from the harbour in divers ways" (130-132). . . .

'Then Anchises' son commands a hundred envoys, chosen from every rank, to go to the king's august city (152-154) . . . A messenger, galloping up, announces to the aged king that mighty men are come in unknown attire. He bids them be summoned within the walls, and takes his seat in the midst on his ancestral throne (166-169) . . . Then, as they entered, he greeted them thus with gentle mien: "Ye sons of Dardanus (*Dardanidae*) — for your city and descent we know, and have heard of your voyage hither oversea — say, what seek ye here? (194-197) . . . Nay, indeed I well remember, though time has dimmed the tale, Auruncan elders telling how that in this land sprang Dardanus (*his ortus ut agris Dardanus*), and hence won his way to the Idaean cities of Phrygia and to Thracian Samos, now called Samothrace. It was hence he set forth from the Etruscan home (*hinc illum . . . Tyrrhena ab sede profectum*) of

Corythus, and now the golden palace of the starry sky admits him to a throne, and he increases the number of gods' altars." He ceased, and Ilioneus (Aeneas' ambassador) followed thus (205-212) . . . "From Jupiter (as Dardanus' father) is our descent (as 'Dardanus' sons': 195); in Jupiter as their ancestor (as the grandfather of Dardanus' sons) glory the Dardan menfolk; of Jupiter's sovereign race is our king himself, Aeneas of Troy, who (both as Jupiter's grandson and as 'Dardanus' son', *Dardanides:* X. 545; XII. 775) has sent us to thy doors (219-221) . . . We crave a scant home for our *di patrii* (229: i.e. for Dardanus' Penates; cf. II. 702, 717; III. 167: *hae nobis propriae sedes, hinc Dardanus ortus*) . . . Nor shall Ausonia (Italy) repent of having welcomed Troy (*Troiam . . . excepisse*) to her breast (232) . . . Hence Dardanus sprang; hither he returns (*hinc Dardanus ortus, huc repetit:* 240-241) . . . Further, to thee our king offers these poor tokens of his former fortune, relics snatched from blazing Troy (*reliquias Troia ex ardente receptas*). With this gold did his father Anchises pour libation at the altars; this was Priam's array when after his wont he gave laws to the assembled nations — the sceptre, the sacred diadem, and the robes wrought by Ilium's daughters." At these words of Ilioneus, Latinus (243-249) . . . revolves within his breast the oracle of ancient Faunus. "This", he thinks, "must be he who set forth from a foreign home (*hunc illum . . . externa ab sede profectum*) by the fates predestined to be my son-in-law, and called to kingship as my colleague here; from whom will come the offspring, glorious in valour" (i.e. the Roman race), "whose might is to master the whole world." At last he joyfully speaks (254-259) . . . "Trojan, thy wish shall be granted" (260) . . . The sons of Aeneas (*Aeneadae*) . . . return to him with news of peace' (284-285).

The implications of this episode are clear.

Aeneas, to begin with, has now at last carried into Italy his twofold burden, consisting both of Dardanus' Penates (VII. 121, 229) and of Dardanus' Troy (VII. 121, 232), in order to lay it down in Dardanus' native land (122, 206-207, 240). Aeneas himself, moreover, is equivalent to a returning Dardanus (241) — an equivalence further emphasized by Virgil's application of the same phrase, *illum . . . ab sede profectum*, first to Dardanus as leaving Italy for Troy (209) and then to Aeneas as leaving Troy for Italy (255).

Next, Aeneas has also carried into Italy those 'relics snatched from blazing Troy' (244) which, representing both Anchises' (245) and Priam's (246-248) Trojan kingship, recall not only those 'relics' (*reliquias:* V. 47) which are 'vainly rescued Anchises' ashes' (V. 80-81), snatched like Misenus' 'relics' from the lately blazing pyre for urn-burial (VI. 226-228), but also those 'Penates vainly rescued from the foe' (V. 632) which represent Anchises' succession to Priam's Trojan kingship (II. 291-295); this same Trojan-Vestal kingship being in either case that of Dardanus himself, whose *regia* (VII. 210) is now that 'starry sky' which, Atlas' burden as once borne by Hercules, is figuratively now the burden of Aeneas (VII. 98-101) as the descendant of Dardanus' grandfather Atlas (VIII. 134-137).

Finally, since the actual equivalence of the *Aeneadae* (VII. 284) to the *Dardanidae* (VII. 195), by right of racial descent, involves the figurative equivalence of Aeneas to Dardanus by right of hereditary kingship — a kingship significantly emphasized by Ilioneus in his speeches both to Dido in Libya (I. 544) and to Latinus in Italy (VII. 220) — the underlying conception is that of a race whose unbroken continuity is symbolized by the house of its king.

Now Virgil, who shared the general belief of Mediterranean antiquity that every beehive was ruled by its 'king'-bee (*rex:* G. IV. 68, 75, 95, 106), will have expected his readers to remember his memorable description of the bees' 'house' as ruled by the bees' 'king': 'Although the limit of a narrow life-span awaits the individual bees — for never does it stretch beyond their seventh summer — yet the race abides immortal (*genus immortale manet*), and throughout many years stands firm the fortune of the house (*multosque per annos stat fortuna domus*), and ancestors' ancestors are numbered on its roll. Moreover, neither Egypt nor mighty Lydia, neither the Parthian tribes nor Median Hydaspes, show such homage to their king (*regem*). While their king (*rege*) is safe, all are of one mind . . .' (G. IV. 206-212).

It will at once be noticed how the phrase *multosque per annos*, here applied to the stable fortune or 'luck' of the bees' house (G. IV. 208), is applied in the *Aeneid* (VII. 60) to Latinus' long preservation in his palace of that laurel which, destined to swarm with Troy-representing bees as the Italian counterpart of Priam's palace-laurel, foreshadows the 'luck' of Augustus' Rome-representing house as symbolized by Livia's laurel; and also how the long ancestral line of Latinus' house (*veterum effigies ex ordine avorum:* VII. 177) recalls that of the bees' house (*avi numerantur avorum:* G. IV. 209).

Since, moreover, Virgil's description in the *Georgics* (IV. 58-59) of the bees, when 'just sent forth from the hive', as a 'troop' (*agmen*) borne 'through the liquid summer air' (*per aestatem liquidum*) 'to the stars of the sky' (*ad sidera caeli*) is verbally echoed in the *Aeneid* with reference both to Aeneas' starry destiny (*ad sidera caeli:* I. 259) as shared by Latinus' own descendants (VII. 99) and to the laurel-swarming bees as borne 'across the liquid air' (*liquidum trans aethera:* VII. 65), Latinus' immediate interpretation of the bees' arrival as that of a 'troop' (*agmen:* VII. 69) led by 'a foreigner' (68-69) clearly implies the arrival of a 'king'-bee with the 'subject'-bees of his 'house'-hive.

But Latinus, be it noted, further interprets their arrival as a return to their original Italian starting-point; for he sees this 'troop' under this 'foreigner' as 'seeking the self-same region from the self-same region' (*partis petere agmen easdem partibus ex isdem:* VII. 69-70) — a poetically emphatic form of saying that the troop under the foreigner is seeking identically the same region from which it set forth (*partis petere agmen easdem a quibus profectum*); an idea later repeated, not only in Latinus' own application of the phrase *ab sede profectum* both to Dardanus' departure from Italy for Troy (209) and to Aeneas' departure from Troy for Italy (255), but also in Ilioneus' intervening statement as the Trojan king's ambassador to the Italian king: ' "Hence Dardanus sprang: hither he returns" ' (240-241).

Virgil, in short, remembering that *darda* means 'bee', interprets *Dardanus* as the 'king'-bee whose figurative equivalent is Aeneas; 'Aeneas' sons', the *Aeneadae*, being the actual equivalent of those *Dardanidae* whom he interprets as the 'king-bee's sons' — a typically Mediterranean system of royal and priestly nomenclature (G. Robert-Tornow, *op. cit. supr.* pp. 30 ff.) already implied by Virgil in the fourth *Georgics* when comparing the bees' homage to their 'king'-bee with the Egyptians' homage to their king (G. IV. 210-212).

For the king of Lower Egypt was officially styled 'Bee', and his kingdom 'Bee-land'; while Ephesus had a college of sacred men officially styled 'King-bees' ('*Essenes*', Ἐσσῆνες), and the name of a legendary Cretan king was Melissos, 'Male bee', or Melisseus, 'Bee-man' (Frazer, *Pausanias' Description of Greece*, London 1898, Vol. IV. p. 223; Vol. V. p. 239; and 'The Magic Art', Vol. II of *The Golden Bough*, pp. 135-136: cf. Cook, *Zeus*, Vol. I (Cambridge 1914), pp. 112, 443-444).

Nor, since the *Aeneadae* are the Trojan-Roman race (I. 157; VIII. 648), whose founding by Aeneas forms the *Aeneid*'s primary theme (I. 33; XII. 166), could the immortality of that unbrokenly perpetuated race be symbolized throughout the *Aeneid* more appropriately for readers of the fourth *Georgics* than by that House of its King whose poetic symbol is a hut-urn resembling the 'House'-hive of a 'King'-bee.

Virgil, then, in his mind's eye sees an Aeneas who, under that symbol, carries back again from Troy once more to Italy that hive-equivalent House of the bee-equivalent Dardanus which, lineally identical both with the House of Assaracus and with the House of Anchises, is now the House of Aeneas himself; its Troy-representing symbol (*Troianam ex hostibus urbem qui revehis nobis aeternaque Pergama servas:* VIII. 36-37) being that Rome-representing cinerary urn whose imitation of a bee-hive-hut, itself the symbol of Romulus' kingship (VIII. 654), involves not only its likeness to the symbol of Dardanus' kingship, a hut-beehive (*certi . . . Penates:* VIII. 39; cf. G. IV. 155), but also its suggestion of that materially limited life-after-death (*hic tibi certa domus:* VIII. 39) whose spiritually limitless counter part (*nulli certa domus:* VI. 673) is the Aeneas-visited Elysium of Anchises and Assaracus and Dardanus (VI. 650, 679).

Now the central mystery of Elysium, as revealed therein to Aeneas by Anchises (VI. 703-751) is precisely that doctrine of reincarnation whose coupling with the bees' marvellous intelligence in the fourth *Georgics* (213-227) is there no less logically than verbally inseparable from the coupling of the bees' racial immortality with the permanence of their 'king'-bee's 'house'-hive (206-212) — that 'august home' (*sedem augustam:* 228) whose epithet, since in the *Aeneid* it is as bee-symbolized 'foreign sons-in-law' (*externi venient generi:* VII. 98) that 'Dardanus' sons shall come into Lavinium's kingdom (*in regna Lavini Dardanidae venient:* VI. 84-85) under 'Dardanus' son' (*Dardanides:* X. 545; XII. 775) as Latinus' son-in-law (*Dar-*

danium Aenean generum: XI. 472), there appropriately belongs by anticipation both to Latinus' 'august palace' (*tectum augustum:* VII. 170) and to that 'king's august city-walls' (*augusta . . . moenia regis:* VII. 153); Latinus' Lavinian citizens, precisely as contrasted with 'Dardanus' sons' (*Dardanidis:* XII. 585), being themselves significantly comparable with the wild bees of a cave-hive (XII. 587-592) precisely as contrasted in the fourth *Georgics* (33-44) with the tame bees of a hut-hive.

Similarly, in the sixth *Aeneid* (703-709), Virgil compares with bees just those departed spirits of 'Dardanus' offspring' (*Dardaniam prolem:* VI. 756) which in Elysium await their reincarnation in Italy as Aeneas' offspring (*qui maneant Itala de gente nepotes:* 757) by Latinus' daughter, his 'wife Lavinia' (*Lavinia coniunx:* 764); thus not only identifying Aeneas' yet-unborn descendants by Latinus' daughter with Dardanus' long-dead descendants by Teucer's daughter, but also symbolizing that reincarnational Dardan-Latin identity under the figure of bees:

'Father Anchises, deep in a green vale, was surveying with earnest thought the souls there imprisoned (*inclusas animas*) before passing to the light above' (i.e. before being reincarnated in the world of the living on earth) 'and, as it chanced, he was then engaged in reviewing the full tale of his people and beloved descendants, their fates and fortunes as heroes, their ways and works (VI. 679-683) . . . Thrice (Aeneas) strove there to throw his arms about (Anchises') neck; thrice the form, vainly clasped, fled from his hands, even as light winds, and most like a winged dream. Meanwhile, in the retired vale' (where Anchises has been found reviewing the host of his as yet unborn descendants), 'Aeneas sees a sequestered grove and crackling forest-thickets, and the river of Lethe drifting past those peaceful homes. About it were hovering peoples and tribes unnumbered: even as when, in the meadows, in cloudless summer, bees light upon many-hued blossoms, and stream round lustrous lilies, and all the fields murmur with their humming. Aeneas is thrilled by the sudden sight and, knowing not, asks the cause — what is that river yonder, and who are the men thronging its banks in such a host? Then father Anchises: "Spirits they are, to whom second bodies are owed by fate; and at the water of Lethe's stream they drink the soothing draught and long forgetfulness. These spirits in truth I have long yearned to recount and to show thee to thy face; yea, to reckon up this my children's offspring, that so thou mayest rejoice with me the more at finding Italy" ' (700-718) . . . (Here, in reply to Aeneas' question, Anchises explains the reincarnational process). . . .

'Anchises ceased, and drew his son and, with him, the Sibyl into the midst of the concourse and murmuring throng' (of bee-like souls awaiting reincarnation); 'then he chose a mound (*tumulum*) whence, face to face, he might scan all the long array, and note their countenances as they came. "Come now, what glory hereafter shall attend Dardanus' offspring (*Dardaniam prolem*), what children of Italian race (*Itala de gente nepotes*) await thee, spirits illustrious and heirs of our name — this will I set forth, and teach thee thy destiny" (752-759) . . . (Anchises now identifies by name many both of Aeneas' Dardan-Italian descendants by Lavinia's son Silvius and of Aeneas' Dardan-Trojan descendants by Creusa's son Iulus, as their bee-like souls file past in chronological order of rebirth; an order successively Lavinian, Alban, and Roman, with Romulus and Augustus outstanding) . . . "And when Anchises has led his son over every scene, and has fired his heart with love of fame to be, he tells him then of the wars he must wage hereafter, and instructs him of the Laurentine peoples and Latinus' city, and how he is to flee or face each toil" ' (888-892).

It is characteristic of Virgil that he applies not only the same term, 'imprisoned', both to denizens of Elysium that resemble bees (*inclusas animas:* VI. 680) and to bees that resemble denizens of Lavinium (*inclusas . . . apes:* XII. 587-588), the context in either case being concerned with Dardanus' progeny (*Dardaniam prolem:* VI. 756; *Dardanidis:* XII. 585), but also the same term, 'mound' (*tumulum*) both to Anchises' barrow in Sicily (V. 76, 664) and to Anchises' viewpoint in Elysium (VI. 754)—verbal identities unconsciously revealing mental associations.

For Virgil, who thrice links the idea of 'Dardanus' sons' with that of Anchises' Sicilian cremation-burial (*Dardanidae:* V. 45, 386, 576), yet further links Anchises' Sicilian *tumulus* with its Elysian counterpart, and so also Anchises' ashes with his spirit, under the symbol of that apparition which calls Aeneas from the Sicilian to the Elysian *tumulus* precisely as the agent whereby the Dardan-Elysian are to be reborn as the Dardan-Lavinian denizens (V. 721-740).

CHAPTER XI

ASHES AND SPIRIT

> dixerat et tenuis fugit ceu fumus in auras.
> Aeneas, 'quo deinde ruis? quo proripis?' inquit,
> 'quem fugis? aut quis te nostris complexibus arcet?'
> haec memorans cinerem et sopitos suscitat ignis. . . .
> (*Aeneid* V. 740-743)

VIRGIL's mind instinctively associated the spirit of a dead person with his ashes or his tomb.

In Libya, for example, Anna speaks of Sychaeus' ghost as actually buried with his ashes (*id cinerem aut Manis credis curare sepultos:* IV. 34), while Dido disclaims having uptorn Anchises' ashes or ghost (*nec patris Anchisae cineres Manisve revelli:* IV. 427) from what she clearly regards as their common burial-place.

Similarly Aeneas himself, who in Thrace actually buries Polydorus' spirit in his tomb (*animamque sepulchro condidimus:* III. 67-68) and who in Italy sends Lausus to rejoin his parents' ghosts and ashes (*teque parentum Manibus et cineri . . . remitto:* X. 827-828), in Sicily addresses Anchises as though his spirit were actually buried with his ashes (*salve, sancte parens, iterum; salvete, recepti nequiquam cineres animaeque umbraeque paternae:* V. 80-81).

Now Virgil's imagery, in all these five passages, is precisely that of those Early Latins who, both at Alba Longa and at Rome, housed their cremated dead within an earth-buried urn whose shape was deliberately modelled, down to the minutest detail, upon that of their domestic dwellings during life — an imitation explicable only on the ground of their belief that the indestructible spirits of these dead would continue to live together with the ashes of their destructible bodies in the urn itself.

'When the custom of incineration, followed in Italy from the prehistoric period', writes Cumont, 'became practically general in Rome, the destruction of the body took place regularly before the eyes of those present. Thus men reached the belief that those near and dear to them, whom they sometimes saw again in their dreams or seemed to feel beside them, who were kept alive at least in memory, differed from the beings of flesh and blood whom they had known. From those material individuals, subtle elements detached themselves, filled with a mysterious force which subsisted when the human elements had crumbled to dust or been reduced to ashes. If this light essence did not leave a man at the moment of his death — whether or not it could escape from his body immediately, was indeed uncertain — it was set free by the funeral fire (Servius on *Aeneid* III. 68), but it still inhabited the tomb in which his remains rested. The idea that it was attached to his remains had taken root in men's minds, and even literature bears witness to the persistence of this deeply implanted popular belief' (Franz Cumont, *After-Life in Roman Paganism*, Yale and London 1922, pp. 46-47).

Thus it appears probable that, since this mysteriously inextinguishable life-force (*Manes*) could hardly belong to a body long-since cold, it will originally have been attributed, by a cremating people whose poetically symbolic art fashioned the hut-urns, to that glow of the still-hot ashes (*cinis*, *cineres*) which warmed the burial-mound (XI. 211-212) containing the cinerary urn (VI. 226-233); and later to the fire itself (cf. *igneus est ollis vigor:* VI. 730) as it became one with the breeze (cf. *aurai simplicis ignem:* VI. 747) during the process of incineration (cf. *exuritur igni:* VI. 742) — with the result that the shadows (*umbrae:* V. 81) cast by the breath-like (*animae:* V. 81) or wind-like (*par levibus ventis:* VI. 702) flame (*flamma:* VI. 226) and breeze-borne smoke (*ceu fumus in auras:* V. 740) from the embers (*favillam:* VI. 227) on the pyre (*pyram:* VI. 215) would, in their child-like because primitive fancy, come to form an image (*imago:* VI. 701) or likeness (*facies:* V. 722) of the departed such as came to visit them sometimes in a dream (*volucrique simillima somno:* VI. 702).

So deeply ingrained, however, will have been the ancestrally inherited and so unconsciously influential concept of the mound-buried hut-urn as the actual dwelling-place of the dead, that even the more sophisticated Romans of a much later period than the Early Latin must still have tended instinctively, like Virgil himself, to regard the spirit of a cremated person as sharing one habitation with his ashes, while at the same time attributing to his spirit all those intangible qualities (V. 740-742; VI. 697-702) of flame and smoke and shadows which belonged properly to their breeze-born appearance in the open air at the vividly remembered moment of actual incineration, and which continued to haunt the living eye-witnesses of their real appearance (*veris . . . umbris:* VI. 894) in the guise of unreal dreams about the spirits of the dead (*falsa ad caelum mittunt insomnia Manes:* VI. 896).

Thus Elysium, unconsciously viewed by Virgil as the immaterially limitless counterpart (*nulli certa domus:* VI. 673) of the materially limiting hut-urn (*hic tibi certa domus:* VIII. 39), is simultaneously both 'the place of shadows, of Sleep and drowsy Night' (*umbrarum hic locus est, Somni Noctisque soporae:* VI. 390) and also equivalent to those 'peaceful homes' (*domus placidas:* VI. 705) whose Early Latin symbols are hut-urns.

So it is that Dido, whose spirit is recognized in the Mourning Fields (*Lugentes Campi:* VI. 441) by Aeneas as 'dim amongst the shadows' (*adgnovitque per umbras obscuram:* VI. 452-453) through which he goes (*has ire per umbras:* VI. 461), flees from his grasp (*quem fugis?* 466) and rejoins those *Manes* of her husband Sychaeus (472-476) whose burial with his *cinis* (IV. 34) implies also the burial of Dido's own spirit with her ashes.

Such a conception, although unconscious because hereditary in Virgil, surely illuminates the poetic symbolism of Aeneas' relationship, as bearing the hut-urn symbol of his Trojan-Roman destiny, both to Dido in Libya and to Anchises in Sicily — Anchises' Sicilian incineration bearing the same symbolically representative relation to Troy's fiery destruction by Greece as is borne by Dido's Libyan incineration to Carthage's fiery destruction by Rome; with the difference that, whereas Anchises' Troy-representing spirit enjoys 'the happy places and green pleasaunces and blessed abodes of the Blissful Groves' (VI. 638-639), Dido's Carthage-representing spirit wanders for ever miserable 'in a great forest' (VI. 451).

The Libyan episode, accordingly, as symbolizing the historical rivalry between Carthage and Rome, concludes with a picture of Aeneas, whose duty is to found the Roman race (I. 33; XII. 166), in process of substituting a Dardan-Carthaginian foundation above Libya-representing beehive-huts (IV. 259-266) in place of that Dardan-Roman foundation (IV. 267-276) whose Virgilian symbol is an Italy-representing hut-urn; this picture, moreover, no less significantly including one of Mercury, father of 'the founder of Rome's citadel' (VIII. 138, 313), as visiting Aeneas with the *caduceus* or magic wand, 'wherewith he calls pale ghosts from Orcus and sends others down to gloomy Tartarus, gives or takes away sleep, and unseals eyes in death' (IV. 242-244) — this latter being an allusion, here significantly coupled with the ideas both of sleep and of ghosts, to the Roman custom of opening the eyes of the dead upon the incinerating pyre; a threefold concept, properly belonging to the magic of Mercury's wand as perpetuating the mortuary magic of the Early Latins and Greeks, characteristically appropriated by Virgil for his presentment of the moral struggle between Dido and Aeneas as crematory.

For Dido's reaction to Aeneas' sudden resolve to leave Libya for Italy, in consequence of Mercury's intervention, is fiery (*incensa:* IV. 300); while Aeneas, recalling 'the city of Troy and the sweet relics of my kin' (*urbem Troianam . . . dulcisque meorum reliquias:* 342-343), continues: ' "To me, as oft as night with dewy shadows (*umbris*) veils the earth, oft as the fiery stars (*astra ignea*) arise, in dreams (*somnis*) my father Anchises' troubled image (*imago*) brings me warning and terror (351-353) . . . Cease to fire (*incendere*) thyself and me with thy complaints!" ' (360).

Then Dido, all the more 'inflamed' (*accensa:* 364), replies: ' "No goddess was thy mother, nor was Dardanus the founder of thy line (*generis nec Dardanus auctor:* 365; cf. VI. 650, VIII. 134) . . . Alas! I am whirled on the fires (*incensa*) of frenzy (376) . . . Go, follow Italy down the winds; seek thy kingdom over the waves (381) . . . Though far away, I will follow thee with murky fires (*ignibus*) and, when chill death has severed soul and body, everywhere my shade (*umbra*) shall haunt thee. Shameless one, thou shalt repay! I shall hear, and the tale shall reach me down among the ghosts (*Manis*) in the nether world" ' (384-387).

Already Dido's mind is playing with the idea, not merely of fire and death, but of death by fire, and so of incineration; for, on the failure of her last appeal to Aeneas on the ground that it was not she who 'uptore the *cineres* or *Manes* of his father Anchises' (427), she requests her sister Anna to construct a pyre (*pyram:* 494), ostensibly for burning whatever may remind her of Aeneas, but really for her own self-cremation as unfaithful 'to the ashes of Sychaeus' (*cineri . . . Sychaeo:* 552) — the implication being that only so can Dido's spirit be reunited with Sychaeus' spirit (VI. 472-476) as buried with his ashes (IV. 34).

Meanwhile Aeneas, unaware of Dido's resolve to destroy

herself (IV. 415, 475-476) and sleeping on that same 'high stern' (*celsa in puppi:* 554) on which as Augustus' prototype (*celsa in puppi:* VIII. 680; X. 261) he will be standing wide awake after reaching Italy in consequence of Mercury's warning in Libya, dreams that Mercury again warns him; this time, however, of Dido's crematory thoughts against himself: ' "Wilt not flee hence in haste, while hasty flight is possible? Soon thou wilt see the water a welter of timbers, see fierce brands ablaze, and soon the shore flashing with flames, if the dawn find thee lingering in these lands" ' (565-568).

Dido next morning, finding Aeneas' fleet gone, exclaims: ' "Go, quickly fetch flames, serve out weapons, ply the oars! (593-594) ... Lo! this is the pledge and faith of him who, they say, carries about with him his ancestral Penates! who bore on his shoulders a father outworn with age! (597-599) ... I should have fired his camp, filled his decks with flames, blotted out father and son with the whole race, and flung myself on top of all (604-606) ... Do ye, O Tyrians, pursue with hate his whole stock and the race to come, and to my ashes (*cineri*) offer this tribute! Let no love nor league be between the nations. Arise from my bones, unknown avenger! to chase with fire and sword the Dardan settlers" ' (622-626).

With this prophetic reference to Hannibal, and to Rome's Punic wars (627-629), Dido 'then briefly spoke to Barce, nurse of Sychaeus; for the pyre's black ashes (*cinis*) held her own nurse in her olden land: "Dear nurse, fetch me Anna my sister hither (632-634) ... I am minded ... to give over to the flames the pyre of that Dardan wretch" ' (640) — an excuse to be left alone for a moment while 'she mounts in madness the high pyre, and unsheathes the Dardan sword, a gift besought for no such end' (645-647).

Virgil then leaves his readers in doubt no longer that the end of Dido symbolizes the end of Carthage itself; for Dido's utter destruction by sword and fire is at once bewailed by her women 'even as though all Carthage or ancient Tyre (the mother-city of 'ancient Carthage': I. 12-13) were falling before the inrushing foe and fierce flames were rolling over the roofs of men, over the roofs of gods' (IV. 669-671), and by her sister as though the 'pyre' (*rogus*) and 'fires' (*ignes*) of Dido's self-cremation (676) were in fact annihilating (*exstinxti*) her entire 'people and senate and city' (682-683) — the phrase *populumque patresque* being significantly echoed by Virgil in that phrase *patribus populoque* (VIII. 679) which, there coupled with the phrase *Penatibus et magnis dis* in an Augustan-Roman context of victory in war, itself echoes the phrase *cum sociis natoque, Penatibus et magnis dis* (III. 12) wherewith Aeneas related to Dido at Carthage his oversea departure from a fallen and fierily smoking Troy (*ceciditque superbum Ilium et omnis humo fumat Neptunia Troia:* III. 3-4) which, like the future Carthage, once was but is no more (*campos ubi Troia fuit:* III. 11) after finally 'sinking into the fires' (*considere in ignis:* II. 624) of its incineration (*Iliaci cineres:* II. 431).

Thus Virgil, unconsciously influenced by the hereditarily remembered association of the *ustrinum publicum* with the *Vesta publica* in the hut-urn period of Early Latin Rome, and consciously influenced by that identically derived 'king-bee' interpretation of Dardanus' name whose poetically symbolic counterpart is Dardanus 'house-hive' or Aeneas' hut-urn, brings Aeneas directly from the Libyan scene of Dido's cremation, the flames of whose self-kindled and distantly blazing fire he sees but does not understand (V. 1-5), to the Sicilian scene of Anchises' cremation the previous year:

' "Could any land be more welcome to me, any whereto I would sooner steer my weary ships, than that which holds my Dardan kinsman Acestes, and enfolds in her embrace my father Anchises' bones?" This said, they make for harbour (28-32)' . . . (Whence, on the following morning, Aeneas calls those same *socii* (42-44) whom at Carthage he coupled with Anchises' own grandson and Penates as embarked upon his ship at the Trojan harbour of Sigeum III. 8-12) 'and addresses them' (like a Roman commander) 'from the mound provided by the barrow' (*tumulique ex aggere fatur:* 44) wherein lie Anchises bones and ashes: ' "Great sons of Dardanus (*Dardanidae*), born of heaven's high blood! (i.e. the blood of Atlas' daughter Electra as fertilized by the seed of Venus' father Jupiter). With the passing of the months the circling year draws to an end since we buried in the earth the relics, even the bones (*reliquias . . . ossa*) of my divine father, and hallowed the altars of grief (45-48) . . . We are now actually in the presence of my father's own ashes and bones (*nunc ultro ad cineres ipsius et ossa parentis . . . adsumus*) not, methinks, without the purpose and will of the gods (55-57) . . . Come, then, let us all join in joyful solemnization of his funeral rites (58) . . . Fetch to his feast the Penates (*adhibete Penates . . . epulis*), both those of our own ancestors and those worshipped by our host Acestes (62-63) . . ." So saying (72) . . . he took his way from the assembly (gathered at the *agger*, or outer earth-work, surrounding Anchises' central *tumulus*) to the barrow (*ad tumulum*), together with many thousands, himself the centre of the great accompanying throng' (75-76: the suggestion clearly being that Aeneas now stands at the top of the barrow, whose foot is encircled by the 'sons of Dardanus') . . . '"Hail, holy parent, once again!" he cries; "hail, my vainly rescued father's ashes and spirit and shade!"'—

Salve, sancte parens, iterum; salvete, recepti
nequiquam cineres animaeque umbraeque paternae (V. 80-81);

an invocation, clearly implying Anchises' integrally simultaneous habitation both on the material and on the immaterial planes of poetic symbolism, whose significantly appropriate answer is the immediate manifestation of that sevenfold-coiling because labyrinthinely-defensive snake whose presence at the barrow containing Anchises' ashes at once suggests to Aeneas' mind, as representing Virgil's, the presence there also of Anchises' spirit (84-99).

It follows that, since Anchises' mortuary rites are to be solemnized at his barrow (*tumulo referunt sollemnia:* V. 605), the Penates of Anchises' Troy-representing house are there brought into the very presence (*adhibete Penates . . . patrios:* 62-63; cf. *quem secum patrios aiunt portare Penates:* IV. 598) both of Anchises' 'spirit and shade' (*animaeque umbraeque paternae:* V. 81) and also of those 'ashes' (*cineres:* 81) and 'bones' (*divinique ossa parentis:* 47) which, precisely because belonging simultaneously both to Anchises himself really (*nunc ultro ad cineres ipsius et ossa parentis . . . adsumus:* 55, 57) and ideally to the Trojan race as represented by Anchises (*cineres atque ossa peremptae insequitur:* 787-788), are singled out by Dardanus-hating Juno for an insult (781-795) explicitly described by Virgil as involving 'the mothers of Dardanus' sons' (*Dardanidum . . . matribus:* 622) in the outrageously unnatural use of Vesta's domestic fire (*rapiuntque focis penetralibus ignem:* 660) as Vulcan's crematory fire (*furit immissis Volcanus habenis:* 662) for the purpose of substituting Sicily in place of Italy (626-631) as the 'fatherland' of Anchises' Dardanus-inherited 'Penates vainly rescued from the foe' (*o patria et rapti nequiquam ex hoste Penates:* 632) — this last phrase significantly echoing Aeneas' Sicilian invocation of his 'vainly rescued father's ashes and spirit and shade (*salvete, recepti nequiquam cineres animaeque umbraeque paternae:* 80-81), since Aeneas rescued from the crematory fire of Vulcan that domestic fire of Vesta which Anchises himself was carrying when vainly rescued by Aeneas.

Now the full enormity of Juno's insult, as symbolically equivalent to using an occasion of peace for the making of war (cf. VII. 45-46, 80) instead of using an occasion of war for the making of peace (cf. XI. 362-363), lies in the fact that Vulcan's crematory fire should properly be used either as Vesta's domestic fire (cf. VIII. 407-415) or else for that incineration of the dead which is but preliminary to the housing of them in a cinerary urn (cf. VI. 212-228); Virgil's own mind upon this matter being sufficiently clear from his application to the domestic use of Vulcan's fire (*dulcis musti Volcano decoquit umorem et foliis undam trepidi despumat aeni:* G. I. 295-296) of that noun *aenum*, 'bronze cauldron' (*litore aena locant alii flammasque ministrant:* A. I. 213), whose corresponding adjective he applies to the 'bronze urn' (*cado . . . aeno:* VI. 228) which houses the ashes of the dead as now identical with the ashes from the pyre's flame (VI. 226-228) — the phrase *aena locant alii* being repeated (V. 102) in connection with Anchises' mortuary rites (cf. VI. 218).

Nor should it be forgotten that Virgil, at the very outset of the *Aeneid*, himself unconsciously reveals one of the postulates of its poetic symbolism when he applies the term *Penates*, strictly belonging to the gods of the domestic *penus* or 'store of provisions', to Dido's domestic hearth itself as kindled by the implied use of Vulcan's fire for Vesta's fire (*penum struere et flammis adolere Penates:* I. 704); nor yet that Dido's 'Penates', thus connoting her fire-kindled hearth, have been bespattered by the lifeblood of that same Sychaeus (*miseri post fata Sychaei coniugis et sparsos fraterna caede Penates;* IV. 20-21) whose ghost, although described by Anna to Dido as buried together with his ashes (*cinerem aut Manis . . . sepultos:* IV. 34), those ashes to which Dido has been unfaithful (*non servata fides cineri promissa Sychaeo:* IV. 552), is described by Venus to Aeneas as an 'image' haunting the dream of Dido 'in her sleep' (*ipsa sed in somnis inhumati venit imago coniugis:* I. 353-354) because she has not yet buried her husband — an apparent contradiction explicable only on the supposition, surely implied by Anna's own words (*id cinerem aut Manis credis curare sepultos?:* IV. 34), that Sychaeus' spirit, although buried with his ashes in the cinerary urn (IV. 34), has not been buried with them in the ground (I. 353) precisely because Dido, following that frequent Roman custom which originated no doubt in the prehistoric custom of hearth-burial, has been keeping Sychaeus' cinerary urn, containing both his spirit and his ashes, beside Sychaeus' blood-bespattered Penates of her hearth-fire.

Similarly in Sicily the fetching of Anchises' 'Penates' to the barrow (V. 62-63), followed by the invocation thereon of Anchises' ashes and spirit (80-81) and its answer under the symbol of a barrow-dwelling and spirit-suggesting snake (84-101), implies the fetching to Anchises' barrow of that symbol of Anchises' house which is a cinerary hut-urn containing within its *penetralia Vestae* the ashes from the undying fire of Vesta (743-745); this again being followed by the implied use of Vulcan's fire for the domestic purpose of cooking Anchises' funeral meats in 'bronze cauldrons' (100-103) whose name *aena* is applicable also adjectivally to cinerary 'bronze urns'.

The undercurrents of Virgil's mind are nowhere more clearly revealed than in his coupling, within a seven-line space, both of the improper use of Vesta's fire for Vulcan's fire and of Anchises' barrow as the scene of mortuary rites in honour of his spirit and ashes: '(The mothers of Dardanus' sons) cry aloud, and snatch fire from the hearths within; some strip the altars, and throw on leaves and twigs and brands. With free rein Vulcan riots amid thwarts and oars and hulls of painted pine. To Anchises' barrow with its theatral seats Eumelus bears tidings of the burning ships; and, looking back therefrom, their own eyes see the black embers floating in a smoky cloud' —

conclamant rapiuntque focis penetralibus ignem;
pars spoliant aras, frondem ac virgulta facesque
coniciunt. furit immissis Volcanus habenis
transtra per et remos et pictas abiete puppis.
Nuntius Anchisae ad tumulum cuneosque theatri
incensas perfert navis Eumelus, et ipsi
respiciunt atram in nimbo volitare favillam (V. 660-666).

Not only does the first of these seven lines verbally echo that which described how Hector 'brings forth, from the shrines within, the perpetually burning fire' of Vesta (*aeternumque adytis effert penetralibus ignem:* II. 297), not for use as, but for rescue from, the fire of Vulcan (II. 289, 311), but also the use of *favilla* in the last of these seven lines for the ashes from Vulcan's ship-burning fire is verbally echoed in the use of *favilla* for the ashes from Vulcan's corpse-cremating fire (*cineres . . . flamma . . . reliquias . . . favillam . . . ossa:* VI. 226-228) which are housed within a cinerary 'bronze urn' (*cado texit . . . aeno:* VI. 228) for burial by Aeneas at Cumae (VI. 232-235) precisely as the condition preliminary to his descent into Elysium for that meeting with Anchises' spirit (VI. 149-155) which involves a survey of Aeneas' Dardan-Italian bee-resembling descendants (VI. 703-759) from Anchises' Elysian *tumulus* (VI. 754); while Virgil's description of the ashes from Vulcan's ship-burning fire as 'floating in a smoky cloud' (V. 666) would be no less applicable to the ashes from Vulcan's corpse-cremating fire as witnessed a year earlier by the same eyes, during Anchises' own cremation for urn-burial under his Sicilian *tumulus* (V. 42-50) — these witnesses being in either case called 'Dardanus' sons' (*Dardanidae:* V. 45; *Dardanidum:* V. 622) as inheriting from Dardanus his cult of Vesta with her Penates (III. 147-168), Lar (V. 744), and never wholly dying fire (V. 743).

Thus the phenomena of Anchises' Sicilian cremation, characteristically implied by Virgil under the equivalent figure of Misenus' Cumaean cremation as preliminary to Anchises' Elysian manifestation, should be borne in mind when analysing Virgil's description of the Sicilian burning of Aeneas' ships as itself preliminary to Anchises' Sicilian manifestation — the unconsciously connecting link in Virgil's thought being the idea of a *tumulus*, common both to Sicily and to Elysium, from which is viewed that aspect of Aeneas' Dardan-Italian destiny whose poetic symbolism is Vulcanic-Vestal as belonging to his cinerary hut-urn, itself the symbol of Anchises' Troy-representing house.

In other words, the 'flame' (*flamma:* V. 680; *flammam:* 689) whose 'conflagration' (*incendia:* 680) while burning (*uritis:* 672) Aeneas' ships (*incensas . . . navis:* 665) sends up into the sky a floating cloud of black ashes (*atram in nimbo volitare favillam:* 666), slowly belched smoke (*vomens tardum fumum:* 682) and smouldering heat (*lentus . . . vapor:* 682-683), until quenched at Aeneas' prayer by Jupiter's thunder-rain (685-699), represents Juno's insult to those 'ashes and bones' of the Trojan race (787-788) whose representative equivalents are the 'ashes and bones' of Anchises himself (55) as cremated to the accompaniment of precisely similar aerial phenomena.

The immediate consequence of Juno's crematory insult is described by Virgil in terms unconsciously communicating the inherited undercurrents of his poetic symbolism. For it is just at the critical point where Aeneas, himself 'burning' (*incensus:* 719) at Nautes' suggested remedy for the ships' burning (*incensas:* 665), suddenly sees the aerial phenomenon of Anchises' 'likeness' (*facies:* 722) in the black night-sky (721), hovering by implication over the *tumulus* within which lie his own ashes from Vulcan's crematory fire (55) together with his own spirit as temporarily released from Elysium (80, 98-99), and upon which lie his own 'Penates' (62-63) as including his own ashes from Vesta's domestic fire (743) together with Assaracus' Pergamean Lar (744; cf. IX. 258-259) within the *penetralia Vestae* of Aeneas' cinerary urn.

Anchises' Sicilian manifestation over his Sicilian *tumulus*, moreover, significantly calls Aeneas to witness that Elysian manifestation of Anchises (V. 723-735) whose unfolding of Aeneas' destiny (737) upon Anchises' Elysian *tumulus* (VI. 754) is conditional upon Aeneas' preliminary visit to Cumae (V. 735-736) with its crematory prelude (VI. 149-235); while the aerial phenomenon of Anchises' Sicilian manifestation concludes with its 'passing like smoke upon the breezes' (*fugit ceu fumus in auras:* 740) — a description whose crematory suggestions are unmistakable when compared with the phenomena of the recently smoking ships (682).

Aeneas' immediate reaction to this smoke-like and breeze-born disappearance of his father's spirit, thus preceding him to Elysium, is deeply significant of Virgil's own unconsciously inherited poetic imagery. For Aeneas, unable to touch Anchises' urn-housed ashes from the crematory fire of Vulcan, any more than he can touch Anchises' smoke-like spirit, instinctively touches their ritual counterpart, Anchises' urn-housed ashes from the domestic fire of Vesta; since there is always, in Virgil's mind, an intimate correspondence between the undying fire of Vesta (*aeternum . . . ignem:* II. 297) and that undying citadel of Troy (*aeterna . . . Pergama:* VIII. 37) whose personification is the undying spirit of Anchises:

'He spake, and passed like smoke upon the thin breezes. "Whither art thou rushing now?" cries Aeneas; "whither hurriest thou? Whom fleest thou, or who bars thee from our embraces?" While speaking thus (*haec memorans*), he is all the time engaged in rousing the ashes and slumbering fires; then, with holy meal and full censer, he humbly worships the Pergamean Lar and hoary Vesta's shrine' (V. 740-745); in other words, that cinerary urn whose imitation of a beehive-hut, the symbol of Anchises' house, involves its resemblance to the symbol of Dardanus' house, the 'house'-hive of a 'king'-bee, and whose contents include Anchises' ashes from Vesta's fire as the ritual counterpart of Anchises' ashes from Vulcan's fire.

Comparison with the circumstances attending Aeneas' earlier visit to Buthrotum will clarify the unconscious implications of Virgilian symbolism at this point.

In Buthrotum, on the anniversary of that same Hector who gave Vesta's undying fire to Aeneas for transportation oversea with the other hallows of Anchises' Troy-representing house, his widow Andromache 'was offering her yearly feast and mourning gifts to his ashes (*cineri*) and was calling his ghost to Hector's barrow (*Manisque vocabat Hectoreum ad tumulum*), an empty mound of green turf hallowed by her with altars twain, where she might shed her tears' (III. 301-305).

Thus at Buthrotum, as in Sicily, there is a cremation-burial mound whereat is kept the solemn anniversary of the dear departed by means of mortuary feast and rite. But the barrow at Buthrotum, unlike that in Sicily, knows the presence neither of ashes (*tumulum . . . inanem:* III. 304) nor of ghost (*Hector ubi est?:* III. 312); so that these yearly celebrations at the cremation-burial mound of a Hector whose own Vestal hallows of Priam's house have been superseded by those of Anchises' house as entrusted to Aeneas are, from the poetically symbolic standpoint, the failure which Virgil explicitly means them to appear.

In Sicily, on the other hand, Virgil implicitly means Anchises' yearly celebrations to appear, from the poetically symbolic standpoint, the success which they certainly are; since here not only does the barrow know the presence of ashes (V. 55-81), of ghost (V. 721-740), and of Vestal hallows (V. 62-63, 743-745), but the apparition of Anchises' ghost is the final ratification of the rites paid both to his ashes and to his ghost (V. 80-81, 94-103); so that Aeneas, having no need to ask 'Where is Anchises?', at once acknowledges his ghost's appearance above his ashes by performing those royal rites of Vesta (V. 743-745), entrusted to him by Hector (II. 293-297), which compensate for its disappearance (V. 738-742) after calling him by way of Cumae to Elysium.

Now Venus, whose temple on Mount Eryx is founded by Aeneas when assigning to her husband Anchises' Sicilian barrow both a priest and a sacred grove (V. 759-761), combines in her complaint to Neptune references, not only to Juno's persecution of Anchises' urn-buried 'ashes and bones' as representing those of the Trojan race (V. 781-788) by means of a crematory attack upon the Trojan fleet (793-795), but also to Juno's earlier vain reliance on the storms of the wind-god Aeolus (789-792) for her persecution of those few 'remnants of Troy' (781-787) whom Aeneas is carrying into Italy (796-798).

Neptune, in answer to Venus' denunciation of that anger of Juno whose centrality in the *Aeneid*'s symbolism is clearly implied by its centrality in the *Aeneid*'s prelude (I. 1-7), promises that all Aeneas' Trojan remnants (cf. I. 29-32; III. 85-87) — except one — shall without further loss reach Cumae, the gate of Elysium (V. 799-815); and he follows up his promise of fair voyage, despite Juno's increasing fury, by himself calming the tempest which has already begun to swell the waves and darken the sky (816-821); this sea-storm being by implication (789-792) roused off Sicily by that same Juno-persuaded Aeolus who off Libya wrecked the Trojan fleet (I. 50-123).

Meanwhile Aeneas pursues his course for Italy (V. 827-834), during which he loses his helmsman Palinurus (835-871); since, as Neptune has warned Venus, 'one life shall be given for many' (815) — but not the only life.

For at Cumae, whither the remnants of the Trojan fleet at length arrive in safety from Juno's unremitting persecution, Apollo's Sibyl, appealed to by Aeneas for that guidance into Anchises' Elysian dwelling-place (VI. 106-118) which was foretold in Sicily by Anchises' own spirit (V. 731-737), grants his request only on condition that he first performs the customary funeral rites for the corpse of an as yet unmissed friend (VI. 149-152), who turns out to be 'Misenus, perished by an untimely death' (162-163) — that same Misenus, be it noted, whose importance in the Alban-Bovillensian tradition is proved by his being singled out from all other of Aeneas' followers for verbally identified portraiture on Bovillae's *tabula Iliaca*; his portrait there representing him as embarking on Aeneas' own ship at Troy's Sigean port with an Anchises who is carrying his Vestal hallows in a miniature beehive-hut, the Alban-Roman symbol of his house as king.

Virgil's Misenus, moreover, is a trumpeter, the 'son of Aeolus' (*Misenum Aeoliden:* VI. 164) and once 'Hector's comrade' (*Hectoris . . . comes:* 166) before becoming 'fellow to Dardan Aeneas' (*Dardanio Aeneae . . . socium:* 169-170); and his death is attributed to the jealousy of the divine trumpeter Triton, who feared the skill of his human rival (171-174).

There is, of course, a human Aeolus amongst Aeneas' Trojan followers (XII. 542), whose son Misenus might conceivably be; but, as Conington long ago pointed out, there would be not only plenty of Homeric precedent for making one of the Trojans a god's son but also some propriety in ascribing to a trumpeter so illustrious as Virgil's Misenus a divine father, Aeolus, god of the very winds which both Misenus and Triton blew from their trumpets.

Misenus, then, is best taken as the son of that wind-god Aeolus whom, at the very beginning of the *Aeneid*, Juno charged with wrecking Aeneas' fleet off Libya (I. 50-141); in which case there is even more propriety both in his birth and in his death. For Aeolus then gave way to that same Neptune (I. 142-156) who would later promise Venus that only one of Aeneas' crew should be lost during the voyage from Sicily to Italy (V. 799-815) — a prophecy referring obviously to Palinurus, drowned so shortly afterwards (V. 827-871).

It would, therefore, be typical of the Virgilian Juno's vengeful irony to punish both Neptune and Aeolus at a single blow: Aeolus, by the death of his son Misenus, for preferring Neptune's orders to her own; and Neptune, by that unpredicted loss of Misenus which would surely discredit him as a prophet in the eyes of her rival Venus, for saving from Aeolus' destructive winds that Juno-hated because Dardanus-descended Teucrian race (*genus invisum:* I. 28; *gens inimica mihi:* I. 67) whose ship-borne cargo includes the symbol of Jupiter's conjugal unfaithfulness (*Ilium in Italiam portans victosque Penates:* I. 68).

Thus Triton is by implication no less Juno's agent in destroying Misenus by water than was Iris explicitly her agent (V. 604-663) in destroying by fire some of the Trojan fleet whose flagship was transporting from Dardanus' Troy to Dardanus' Italy the Juno-hated symbol, at once crematory and domestic, of Dardanus' house.

Misenus, in other words, no less than the ships, is destroyed by Juno as a symbolic substitute for Dardanus' entire house; being sacrificed no less truly to Juno's wrath at Jupiter's infidelity to her than was Palinurus to Neptune's wrath at Laomedon's infidelity to him (V. 810-815). They are both of them innocent scapegoats: 'One life shall be given for many' (*unum pro multis dabitur caput:* 815).

For Misenus represents in Juno's eyes, not merely those *Dardanidae* (I. 560) who are to Dardan Aeneas (*Dardanio Aeneae:* I. 494) his *genus Aeneadum* (I. 565), but specifically that *gens Hectorea* (I. 273) whose Trojan-Vestal kingship of Iulus' Alba Longa shall one day threaten Juno's Carthage by linking Aeneas' Lavinium with Romulus' Rome, as promised by Juno's faithless husband Jupiter to her envied daughter Venus (I. 257-296); since Misenus, once *Hectoris comes* (VI. 166), became at the death of the *lux Dardaniae* (II. 281) *socius* to Dardan Aeneas (*Dardanio Aeneae sese fortissimus heros addiderat socium, non inferiora secutus:* VI. 169-170), thereby representing for Juno those *Hectorei socii* who became at Troy's death Aeneas' *comites* (V. 190-191) — this transference of Misenus, from Troy-representing Hector to Aeneas, thus also symbolizing for Juno the transference from Hector to Aeneas of those other *comites* (II. 294) which are the Vestal hallows of Dardanus' kingship.

Juno, that is to say, sees Aeneas as transporting into Dardanus' Italy two kinds of *comites*, both of which are his *Hectorei socii* — the Troy-representing members (*gens inimica mihi:* I. 67) and the Troy-representing symbols (*Ilium . . . victosque Penates:* I. 68) of Dardanus' hated house; so that Juno, in destroying Misenus through Triton, regards herself as destroying the embodiment of all that she failed to destroy through Misenus' father Aeolus.

Misenus himself, apart from one earlier mention as Aeneas' trumpeter (III. 239-240), means hardly more to Virgil than does Caieta, Aeneas' nurse; herself, like Misenus, a mere geographical eponym (VI. 234-235, 900; VII. 1-4). Nor can great importance have been attached either by Aeneas (VI. 150) or by his crew (VI. 160-162) to a comrade whose loss they do not even notice.

Only Misenus' representative importance to Juno, combined with his portrayal on Bovillae's *tabula Iliaca*, can fully account for the mystery and elaboration given by Virgil to Misenus' episode, which occupies no less than eighty-seven lines (VI. 149-235) — an elaboration and mystery wholly explicable when Misenus' death and incineration are interpreted as symbolizing the fate, already achieved for Troy and for Anchises, which is desired by Juno for Dardanus' house from the very outset of the *Aeneid*; Juno being of a crematory turn herself.

For it was in her blazing anger (*accensa:* I. 29), burning to reduce to mere ashes (*exurere:* I. 39; cf. *exussit:* V. 794) the fleet which carried both the symbols and the members of Dardanus' Troy-representing house (I. 67-68), that Juno 'with heart aflame' (*flammato corde:* I. 50) first pointed them out to Misenus' father Aeolus as the target of her fiery hatred (I. 65-66).

Aeolus off Libya having failed entirely, and Iris in Sicily having failed largely, to destroy them, Juno remembers that self-cremation of Dido on Aeneas' account which symbolized the future destruction of Carthage itself by his Roman descendants (I. 19-33; IV. 622—V. 5); so that her own cremation of Misenus at Cumae (VI. 212-228) through the unwitting agency of 'Dardanus' sons' (VI. 85) fittingly avenges her both for Aeneas' unwitting cremation of Dido at Carthage and for her own failure in Sicily to cremate Aeneas' entire fleet (V. 606-699, 792-795) through the unwitting agency of the 'mothers of Dardanus' sons' (V. 622) — a failure whose only consequence is Aeneas' foundation of two more Troys for Juno's hatred; first, after Anchises' Sicilian cremation-burial rites as preliminary to the Sicilian manifestation of Anchises' spirit, Aeneas' Sicilian *Troia* (V. 755-758); and then, after

Misenus' Cumaean cremation-burial rites as preliminary to the Elysian manifestation of Anchises' spirit, Aeneas' Italian *Troia* (VII. 157-159).

Against Aeneas' Dardan-Italian 'infant Troy' (*nascentis Troiae:* X. 27; *Troiam . . . nascentem:* X. 74-75) Juno now concentrates all the crematory fire of her anger: 'She has espied the rejoicing Aeneas and his Dardan fleet. She sees them already constructing houses, already trusting in the land, their ships deserted. She has paused, pierced with sharp grief; then, shaking her head, she pours forth from her breast these words:

' "Ah! hated race, and Phrygian fates that cross my own! Could they perish on the Sigean plains? Could they, captured, suffer captivity? Did the burning of Troy cremate them? (*num incensa cremavit Troia viros?*). Lo, through the midst of armies, through the midst of fires (*mediosque per ignis*) they have found a way . . .' " (VII. 288-297).

But Juno is not beaten yet. Calling Allecto the Fury to her aid, as she has earlier called Aeolus and Iris and Triton, she kindles yet further conflagrations, exclaiming: ' "Nor did (Hecuba) Cisseus' daughter alone conceive a firebrand (*face*) and give birth to nuptial fires (*ignis*). Nay, Venus has the like in (Aeneas) her own child, a second Paris, another funeral torch (to kindle the incinerating fire) for reborn Pergama" ' (VII. 319-322).

Allecto, as the furious Juno's no less fiery agent, first increases the already hot-glowing (*ardentem:* VII. 345) anger of Latinus' wife Amata against Aeneas as Turnus' rival for Lavinia's hand (323-345) by means of snake-venom (346-355) whose 'flame' (*flammam:* 356) 'envelopes her bones with fire' (*atque ossibus implicat ignem:* 355)—a phrase recalling that 'flame' (*flamma:* I. 673) of Dido's original love for Aeneas whose bone-enveloping fire (*atque ossibus implicet ignem:* I. 660) led later to the bone-enveloping fire of Dido's incineration as the Phoenix-like cause of Hannibal's vengeance (IV. 622-629) in succession to Turnus' vengeance (IV. 612-621) under the patronage of Juno and the Furies (IV. 608-611).

Then, visiting Turnus on Juno's behalf and in accordance with Dido's last curse upon Aeneas, the Fury Allecto 'blazed forth into anger' (*exarsit in iras:* VII. 445), 'rolling her flame-like eyes' (*flammea torquens lumina:* 448), and 'hurled at the youth a fire-brand (*facem*), fixing in his breast the torch all-smoking with lurid light' (456-457); whereupon Turnus himself began to burn for battle against Aeneas (458-462), his ardour being elaborately compared by Virgil with the flame (*flamma:* 462) under a 'bronze cauldron' (*aeni:* 463) whose 'black smoke pours on to the breezes' (*volat vapor ater ad auras:* 466) — an explicitly domestic simile whose crematory implications should by now be clear.

Allecto now kindles (*accendit:* 482) the whole countryside to war, returning then to Juno with offers of yet further kindling (*accendam:* 550); but Juno prefers to carry on the crematory work in person (552-560), until Turnus' fire (*igni:* 577) is matched by all Italy's blaze (*ardet:* 623); Turnus himself volcanically personifying Juno's own warlike conflagration:

'His lofty helmet, crested with triple plume, upbears a Chimaera, breathing from her jaws Aetnaean fires (*Aetnaeos . . . ignis*), lo! raging the more, and madder with baleful flames (*flammis*), the more blood is outpoured and the fiercer waxes the fight' (785-788).

It is this volcanically fiery Turnus, now Juno's unwitting agent, who sends to Diomede what is really Juno's own complaint — 'that Aeneas is come with his fleet, bringing to them his vanquished Penates (*victosque Penates:* VIII. 11; a repetition of Juno's complaint to Aeolus: I. 68) and proclaiming himself a king (*regem:* VIII. 12; a repetition of Juno's complaint to herself: I. 38) summoned by the fates (*fatis:* VIII. 12; so Juno: I. 39); that many tribes are joining the Dardan hero (cf. Juno's espial of "Aeneas and his Dardan fleet": VII. 288-289), and that his name spreads far and wide in Latium' (VIII. 11-14).

Juno, in other words, desires the help of the Greek Diomede's personal experience in attacking Trojans, in what she hopes may become another Trojan war resulting in a second death and incineration of Troy; this time, however, on Italian soil — the birthplace of her husband's bastard, Dardanus.

For Virgil, who has earlier implied Dido's acceptance of the tradition that Diomede 'uptore Anchises' ashes and ghost' from their common tomb (IV. 427), significantly couples Diomede's rejection of Turnus' Juno-inspired appeal (XI. 213-295) with the death and incineration of Trojans and Italians whose cremation-customs are described (XI. 184-212) no less elaborately than those of the Trojans who cremated Misenus (VI. 175-184, 212-235); a coupling suggestive of Juno's failure to secure Diomede's expert services in renewing on Italian soil that death and incineration of Troy whose symbolic continuance is her own persecution of the 'ashes and bones' of the Trojan race (V. 787) as represented on Sicilian soil by the 'ashes and bones' of Anchises (V. 55).

Meanwhile, until she learns Diomede's answer, Juno employs the services of Turnus for her own crematory attack upon Aeneas' Italian Troy and Dardan fleet, combining her Libyan motive with her Sicilian method. For it is once more Iris whom she sends down, this time to Turnus with the news that Aeneas, far both from his fleet and from his Troy, is already enlisting allies in Dardanus' Etruscan birthplace (IX. 1-11): '"Why hesitate? Now, now is the hour to call for steed and chariot; break off delay, and seize the bewildered camp!"' (IX. 12-13).

Turnus' reaction is crematory: 'As he scans wall and camp, the Rutulian's wrath grows fiery (*ignescunt irae*); resentment burns hot (*ardet*) within his iron bones (*ossibus*). By what device shall he essay entrance? (IX. 65-67) . . . Hard by the camp's side lay the fleet, fenced about with mounds and flowing river; this he assails, calling to his exulting comrades for means of fire (*incendia*), and with burning haste (*fervidus*) fills his hand with a flaming (*flagranti*) pine-brand. Then indeed they fall to, spurred on by Turnus' presence, and all his menfolk arm themselves with murky firebrands (*facibus*). Lo! they have stripped the hearths (*focos*); smoking torches fling a pitchy glare, while Vulcan (*Volcanus*) flings a blend of glowing ashes (*favillam*) up to the stars' (IX. 69-76).

Juno, in fact, repeats in Italy that outrageous use of Vesta's fire for Vulcan's fire which characterized her Sicilian attack upon Aeneas' fleet during his absence; a repetition verbally emphasized by Virgil's use of closely similar terms.

Although Cybele, as divine patroness of Teucer (III. 94-115), the grandfather of Dardanus' sons and eponymous ancestor of Dardanus' Teucrians (IX. 68, 77, 114), rescues the fleet of Dardan-Aeneas (*Dardanio iuveni:* IX. 88; *Dardanium . . . ducem:* IX. 100) from Vulcan's Vesta-stolen flames (73-122), Turnus voices Juno's own continued determination to cremate the Teucrians (130): '"Have they not seen Troy's Neptune-built walls collapsing into fires? (*considere in ignis:*

144-145; cf. II. 624-625)... I need not Vulcan's weapons nor a thousand ships to meet the Teucrians (148-149)... To surround their ramparts with fire (*igni circumdare muros*) is my fixed purpose" ' (153).

Having given orders 'to encircle the walls with flames' (*moenia cingere flammis:* 160) of brightly burning fires (*conlucent ignes:* 166), Turnus takes it for granted that escape is impossible from Aeneas' Italian Troy, which he himself later sets on fire with the flame of a blazing torch (535-536); until, with Juno in person joining in the attack (745, 764) against the *Aeneadae* (735) as equivalent to *Dardanidae* (660), 'straightway a new light flashes from Turnus' eyes, and his armour rings terribly; the blood-red plumes quiver on the crest' (of Turnus' volcanically fiery helmet: VII. 785-788), 'and lightnings shoot glittering from his shield' (IX. 731-733).

But, despite all Juno's efforts (802-803), the hated Teucrians (779, 805) — themselves now no less blazing with anger (*accensi:* 788) than was Juno (*accensa:* I. 29) at first seeing their approach to Dardanus' Italian homeland — temporarily extinguish Turnus' ardour in the Tiber, to whose waters he is driven by them for refuge (IX. 801-818).

Meanwhile Jupiter, as Dardanus' father, 'surveys the camp of Dardanus' sons and the Latin peoples' (X. 4): ' "I had forbidden Italy to clash in war with the Teucrians. What feud is this, in face of my command?" ' (8-9).

Venus, with her eye on Juno, replies: ' "Once more a foe threatens the walls of infant Troy (26-27)... Why should I recall the ships burnt to atoms" ' (*exustas:* 36; cf. Juno's *exurere classem:* I. 39, and Venus' *exussit... puppis:* V. 794) ' "on the strand of Eryx? Why the king of storms (Aeolus) and his raging gales roused from Aeolia, or Iris wafted from the clouds. Now she (Juno) even stirs the ghosts" ' (*Manis... movet:* 39-40; an oblique reference, surely, to Dido's threat: '*omnibus umbra locis adero*': IV. 386), ' "a quarter of the world as yet untried; and Allecto, launched of a sudden on the upper world, raves through the midst of the Italians' cities (36-41)... If there be no country for thy relentless wife to give the Teucrians, then, by the smoking ruins of overturned Troy, I beseech thee, my father, let me dismiss Ascanius from arms unscathed, let my grandson still live! (44-47)... What has it availed the Teucrians, in their quest for Latium and reborn

Pergama, to escape the plague of war, to have fled through the midst of Argive-kindled fires, to have exhausted all the perils of sea and desolate lands? Were it not better for them to have settled on their fatherland's last ashes (*cineres patriae . . . supremos:* 59; cf. *Iliaci cineres et flamma extrema meorum:* II. 431) and the soil where once was Troy (*solum, quo Troia fuit:* 60; cf. *fuimus Troes, fuit Ilium:* II. 325; *campos, ubi Troia fuit:* III. 11). Restore, I pray, Xanthus and Simois to a hapless people, and let the Teucrians (cf. *fuit . . . ingens gloria Teucrorum:* II. 325-326) retrace once more the woes of Ilium!" ' (X. 55-61).

Thereupon, Juno, furious with Venus for thus forcing her 'to publish abroad' her 'hidden sorrow' (62-64), Jupiter's intrigue with Dardanus' mother, bitterly blames Venus' son Aeneas both for his designs upon Latinus' kingship from an Iulus-defended Italian Troy and for his recruitments in that scene of her own shame, Dardanus' Etruscan birthplace (65-71); ironically inquiring how she is to blame (72-73): '"Ay, it is shameful that Italians should swaddle infant Troy with flames (*Troiam circumdare flammis nascentem*), and that Turnus should set foot on his native soil! (74-75) . . . But what of the Trojans assailing the Latins with murky firebrands?" ' (77).

Jupiter's declaration that destiny must take its course (100-117) leaves Turnus continued freedom to attack Juno's hated foes the *Aeneadae* (120) by 'encircling their walls with flames' (*moenia cingere flammis:* 119) until as *Dardanidae* (263) they at last welcome Aeneas' return with his Etruscan recruits 'to the help of Troy' (*subsidio Troiae:* 214) — a return whose eventual consequence is Juno's inability further 'to kindle the fire of war' (*accendere bellum:* XII. 804), despite her own declared readiness to girdle herself in flames (*flammis cincta:* XII. 811) and to stand thus fiery on Turnus' behalf against the Teucrians close to the very battle-line (XII. 791-812).

The fact is that Virgil mentally visualizes the entire Juno-kindled Latin-Dardan war in terms of Vulcan's fire:

'Even as in summer, when the winds he longed for have risen, some shepherd kindles fires (*incendia*) here and there among the woods; on a sudden the mid-spaces catch fire, and Vulcan's bristling battle-line (*horrida . . . acies Volcania*) spreads over the broad fields unbroken, while he from his seat gazes down victorious on the revelling flames (*flammas*): even so all thy comrades' chivalry rallies to one point in aid of thee, O Pallas' (X. 405-411).

So, too, Aeneas and Turnus in their final struggle for Lavinia's hand resemble two-forest fires whose fuel is that laurel whose connection both with fire-kindling and with Lavinia has already been pointed out (XII. 521-528); while Aeneas' final destruction of Latinus' Lavinium by means of fire is compared by Virgil with a shepherd's destruction of a cave-beehive by means of fire (XII. 554-592).

Since, moreover, these wild cave-dwelling bees are associated in Virgil's mind with that warlike fire of Vulcan whose complement is the peaceful fire of Vesta as associated in Virgil's mind with the tame hut-dwelling bees who symbolize the *Dardanidae* (VII. 195; XII. 585), the marriage of Aeneas with Lavinia, Lavinium's fire-kindled eponym (VII. 71-80), will symbolize an integration of Dardanus' house with Latinus' house, of peaceful reconstruction with warlike destruction, and of Vesta's domestic hearthfire-spirit and hearthfire-ashes with Vulcan's crematory earthfire-spirit and earthfire-ashes — this integration corresponding to the final reconciliation of Venus with Juno (XII. 786-842) through the intervention of Dardanus' father, Jupiter, Aeneas' own grandfather.

CHAPTER XII

TOMB AND WOMB

pandere res alta terra et caligine mersas.
(*Aeneid* VI. 267)

Aeneas, fresh from the urn-burial of Misenus' ashes near Cumae, is now as eager to renew contact with Anchises' spirit in Elysium as ever he was to re-visit his ashes in Sicily; for Virgil thinks of Anchises as dwelling, after his death and incineration, upon two simultaneously existent and mutually complementary planes — that of the ashes, now in Sicily, with their poetically symbolic counterpart near Cumae only just housed within a cinerary urn; and that of the spirit, now in Elysium, awaiting the arrival of Aeneas.

Figuratively, moreover, the spirit of Anchises — released at the moment of incineration, like Misenus' spirit, by the crematory fire of Vulcan — is the immaterial complement of that domestic fire of Vesta whose undying flame perpetuates the undying life of Troy; just as the ashes both of Misenus and of Anchises, collected from Vulcan's fire, are the material complement of those ashes from Vesta's fire whose stirring poetically symbolizes the Phoenix-like resurrection of a dead and incinerated Troy.

Consequently, since both the fire and the ashes of Vesta are housed actually, while the fire and ashes of Vulcan are both housed figuratively, within that symbol of Anchises' Troy-representing house whose counterpart is Misenus' earth-buried cinerary urn, it follows that Aeneas' hut-urn also houses figuratively both the spirit and the ashes of the Trojan race as represented by Anchises and Misenus; so that Aeneas, when he descends into the Underworld, is in fact fathoming the depths of that life-after-death symbolism which belongs also to his hut-urn.

As Virgil puts it, Aeneas is about 'to pass beneath earth's secrecies' (VI. 140) into the inner mystery of 'things submerged in the depth and darkness of the earth' (VI. 267) — that fire-containing Earth whose Roman equivalent is the fire-containing Hearth (Ovid, *Fasti* VI. 267: the identical numeration, VI. 267, both in the *Aeneid* and in the *Fasti*, is at least curious).

It is indeed not so much Aeneas as his creator, Virgil himself, who is now on the point of descending into those dreamlands of the unconsciously functioning because hereditarily determined mind-plane wherein are woven the underlying patterns of his poetic symbolism with all their kaleidoscopic surprises; and we shall find the poet, as the maker of those changing patterns, attributing to the immateriality of the Underworld precisely that integration, of the crematory with the domestic, which we have already found him attributing to the materiality of Aeneas' hut-urn as symbolizing Anchises' Troy-representing and Dardanus-founded house.

The crematory has, indeed, for some time been manifested, in the naturally volcanic region around Cumae, by the incineration of Misenus as preparatory to the meeting with Anchises; but it now reappears in another form under the figure of that volcanically mephitic cave (VI. 236-242), itself the entrance to the Underworld, before whose sulphur-breathing mouth the Sibyl kindles fires (*ignibus:* 246) and Aeneas kindles flames (*flammis:* 253); the blaze (*ardentibus:* 254) of this oil-fed and flesh-fuelled conflagration gradually merging into that of the rising sun (252-255) whose reflected glow accompanies Aeneas and the Sibyl into the night-resembling, colourless darkness of the cave (256-272).

This cavernous gloom, the abode of Sleep and Dreams, of Death and Fears (273-284), is soon somewhat lightened by the distant blaze of Phlegethon, that underground river of fire upon which Virgil appropriately calls for enlightenment through what otherwise would remain a chaotic nightmare of terrifyingly monstrous forms (264-294); as also by a sudden glimpse of 'Chimaera armed with flames' (*flammis:* 288), herself the personification of a Lycian volcanic fire; by the flaming stare of Cerberus' eyes (*stant lumina flamma:* 300); and finally by the torrent flames (*flammis:* 550) of the river of fire itself (*Tartareus Phlegethon:* 551), forming a perpetually blazing moat around the triple walls of Tartarus, that eternal Bastille of the damned (541-627) whose very domesticity produces 'the sounds of volcanic action, the hissings and rumblings and explosions of subterranean forces, interpreted into a new meaning' (J. W. Mackail, *The Aeneid*, Oxford 1930, p. 521).

But Elysium, not Tartarus, is the home of Anchises' fire-freed spirit; and the Sibyl therefore urges Aeneas forward to the right (cf. 540-543), along the road leading to those Cyclopaean ring-walls whose gate is Elysium's only entrance:

' "Let us hasten", she says; "I descry the walls upreared by the forges of the Cyclopes and the arched gateway in front of us, where the divine ordinances require us to lay our gifts." She ended speaking; and, advancing side by side along the dusky way, they hasten over the mid-space and draw nigh to the doors. Aeneas wins the entrance, sprinkles his body with fresh water, and plants the (golden) bough full on the threshold. This at length performed and the goddess' duty fulfilled, they find themselves arrived in a land of joy, the green pleasaunces and happy homes of the Blissful Groves. Here an ampler ether clothes the meadows with roseate light, and they know their own sun and their own stars' (630-641).

This, then, is Elysium at last; that interior of the fire-containing Earth whose equivalent is the interior of Rome's *aedes Vestae* with its fire-containing Hearth.

But the ring-walls of Elysium are described by Virgil in terms (*Cyclopum educta caminis moenia:* VI. 630-631) applied almost identically to those volcanic caves (*Cyclopum exesa caminis antra Aetnaea:* VIII. 418-419) which form the very 'house of Vulcan' himself (*Volcani domus:* VIII. 422) as 'Lord of fire' (*Ignipotens:* VIII. 423); a fire whose crematory flame and ashes, compared by Virgil with the domestic flame and ashes (VIII. 407-415), are those also of incineration as preparatory to urn-burial (VI. 226-228).

Thus since it is the subterranean abode of Venus' divine husband Vulcan which provides ring-walls for the subterranean abode of Venus' human husband Anchises, now himself 'divine' (V. 47) and dwelling both materially and spiritually (IV. 427) inside the Earth (V. 48; VI. 140, 267) as symbolically equivalent to that Hearth of the *Anchisae domus* (II. 296, 300) the Vestal stirring of whose hut-urned flame and ashes during the smoke-like return of Anchises' spirit from his ashes to Elysium (V. 731-745) is described in terms (*cinerem et sopitos suscitat ignis:* V. 743) identically applied by way of simile (VIII. 410) to Vulcan's stirring of his own cave-housed and smoking flame and ashes (VIII. 417, 421, 432), it follows that Virgil's Elysium so integrates the crematory nature of the earthfire-containing *Volcani domus* with the domestic nature of the hearthfire-containing *Anchisae domus* as to reproduce unconsciously on the spiritual plane the integrally Vulcanic-Vestal symbolism of that material hut-urn whose life-after-death meaning for Virgil is the House of Dardanus, Teucer's son-in-law and heir.

For here, in the very heart of Elysium, 'is Teucer's olden line, offspring most fair, high-souled heroes born in happier years — Ilus and Assaracus and Dardanus, Troy's founder' (VI. 648-650); just as, in the *penetralia Vestae* of Aeneas' hut-urn, is that Lar or household-spirit of Assaracus (IX. 259) which, invoked by an Iulus whose original name was Ilus (I. 267-268), perpetuates the ancestral life of Dardanus in company with his Penates (III. 147-168).

The inmost secret of Elysium, moreover, is at once crematory and domestic.

For those imperfect *Dardanidae*, who, unlike Dardanus and Assaracus, Ilus and Anchises, there await reincarnation (*inclusas animas:* VI. 680) within their 'peaceful homes' (*domos placidas:* VI. 705), have already passed through some purgatorial process such as having their guilt 'burnt to atoms by fire' (*exuritur igni:* 742), leaving their spirit's own fire (*ignem:* 747) no longer tainted, and so fit for their rebirth in a new body (751).

Since, therefore, this spiritual equivalent of material cremation takes place outside the Cyclopean ring-walls (743-744) and so by implication near the fire-moated Tartarus (548-551), Virgil gives his Elysium a Vulcanically crematory environment which is both destructive of what is bad, as looking outwards to the fiery river Phlegethon, and reconstructive of what is good, as looking inwards to that peaceful river Lethe about whose Vestally domestic banks hover innumerable bee-resembling *Dardanidae* awaiting their rebirth or resurrection in Italy as *Aeneadae* (703-759).

For both the *domus placidae* (VI. 705) and the *sedes beatae* (VI. 639) of Dardanus' Elysium are to have their material equivalent in those *sedes quietae* of Latium wherein Troy itself will be reborn as Dardanus' kingdom in his Italian homeland:

tendimus in Latium, sedes ubi fata quietas
ostendunt; illic fas regna resurgere Troiae (I. 205-206);

so that, since this 'resurrection' or rebirth of Dardanı
is equivalent to the 'birth' of Aeneas' Troy (*nascenti.*
X. 27; *Troiam nascentem:* X. 74-75) as foreshadowing
Lavinium, Iulus' Alba Longa and Romulus' Rome, the
'conception' of Aeneas' Troy as their archetype is equivalent
to the 'reconception' or 'death' of Dardanus' Troy.

Virgil's Elysium, that is to say, is the spiritual equivalent both of a tomb, wherein Dardanus' 'dead' Troy awaits 'resurrection', and of a womb, wherein a 'reconceived' Troy awaits 'rebirth'; this Elysian tomb-womb having its material counterpart in that cinerary urn, shaped to resemble the Romulean beehive-hut symbol of Rome's birth, wherein Dardanus' 'dead' Troy awaits her phoenix-like resurrection from the ashes of her own incineration (*Iliaci cineres:* II. 431; *cineres patriae:* X. 59) — this same phoenix-metaphor being significantly implied by Virgil-echoing Ovid precisely when, having first explicitly equated Rome's birth with Troy's resurrection from her ashes on the very site of Rome, he goes on to describe Aeneas as bearing from the recent site of Troy both Anchises and the Vestal symbols of Anchises' Troy-representing house for Pallantean welcome both by Evander and by the Vestal symbols of Evander's Rome-representing house upon the future site of Rome (*Fasti* I. 523-528).

Virgil himself, moreover, in a revealing because unconscious play upon mentally associated words, characteristically transfers this phoenix-metaphor to Dido, who as *Phoenissa* (I. 670; IV. 348, 529; VI. 450) and wife of a *Phoenix* (I. 343-344) whose spirit is buried with his ashes (IV. 34) but still lives inside the earth (VI. 472-474), will herself by implication rise again from the ashes of her own incineration under the reincarnational form of Hannibal (IV. 622-629) as personifying Phoenicia-founded Carthage in rivalry with Troy-founded Rome; while another Phoenix, the Greek son of Amyntor, is no less significantly described by Virgil as guarding 'Troy's treasures, torn from blazing shrines', within the Trojan sanctuary of Juno, guardian of Carthage, in a context describing the fiery incineration of Anchises' Troy-representing house (II. 756-764).

In the last analysis, therefore, the *Aeneid*'s symbolism implies the reincarnational equivalence of the entombment of Dardanus' Troy for eventual resurrection to an enwombment of Romulus' Rome for eventual birth; this Trojan-Roman tomb-womb equivalence, poetically symbolized by Virgil both explicitly under the figure of an Earth-equivalent Elysium which spiritually manifests the Earth-hidden secrets of Aeneas' Dardan-Romulean destiny and implicitly under the figure of a Hearth-equivalent hut-urn which materially manifests the Hearth-hidden secrets of Aeneas' Dardan-Romulean destiny, belonging properly to the Hearth-equivalent Earth herself as that All-Mother (*Terra parens:* IV. 178; *Terrae omniparentis:* VI. 595) and that First of Gods (*primamque deorum Tellurem:* VII. 136-137) who is at once the universal tomb of the past and the universal womb of the future, and whose fertility-symbol amongst the Early Latin makers of hut-urns for earth-burial was a sow with young.

Thus Altheim, after describing the prehistoric hut-dwellings and urn-burials of Palatine Rome, continues:

'What can we deduce from this earliest stratum of the (cremation-) cemetery (in the *forum Romanum*) for the religion of the Palatine city? Important, in the first place, are the numerous remains of food; above all, the bones of young pigs and swine, which have been found in the funeral urns or in special dishes beside them. The rite, recorded in literature, has been rightly brought into account here, by which at a burial the sacrifice of a sow took place at the open grave. This sacrifice of the *porca praesentanea* was due to Ceres . . . (as) the Earth-Mother. To the same context belong in all probability the remains of wheat and beans, which have been found on the remains of bones in the urn for ashes. The custom recurs elsewhere in similar form; through Cicero (*de leg.* 2, 63), we hear of an old Athenian custom, of strewing seed on the fresh grave. The earth meets us here in the extremes of her functions; she is, as everywhere in ancient belief, not only the queen of the dead, guardian of that which has perished — she is, at the same time, the power which makes the new shoots of life emerge from her bosom. . . .

'Soon after the cremating people had settled beyond the Tiber on the Palatine, the eastern hills were occupied by an inhumating race (such as the Sabine) . . . Above the oldest cremating stratum (in the *forum Romanum*) has been found an inhumating, the age of which is considerably later than the other . . . The grave-offerings, which permit of some inference about the cult of the dead, are not much different from those of the cremating stratum: wheat and fruit-kernels, bones of cattle and sheep. It is of importance that in one case the bones of a small pig too were found lying at the feet of the dead. Here, too, then, the *porca praesentanea* was sacrificed at the open grave, here too was Mother Earth worshipped . . . The realm into which the dead has passed is not to be distinguished from that out of which the seed pushes its shoots and new life springs. . . .

'A group of feminine deities — Ceres, Tellus, and Flora — remind us by their very names of Demeter. She herself was none other than Δα-μάτηρ "Mother Earth" . . . Ceres is certainly not merely the goddess of growth in plants, as has been maintained. Like Demeter she has two sides — she makes all life spring from her bosom, and takes back the dead and lost to herself again. In this second function Ceres appears in a number of cases. To her, as to Dionysus, the lord of souls, worship is paid by the suspension of masks (*oscilla*); we are at once reminded of the well-attested use of masks in the cult of Demeter. Here too belongs the sacrifice of the pig, whether for the departed in general (*porca praecidanea*) or, especially, at the open grave (*porca praesentanea*); we have already met with it more than once before. Of both rites it is expressly recorded in our tradition that they were due either to Ceres alone or to her in conjunction with Tellus. Similarly, the *mundus*, the seat of the cult of the dead and the link between the underworld and the world above, is placed in connection with her. In the description as Panda Cela — as the power that reveals (*ea quae pandit*) and that conceals (*ea quae celat*) — this connection found its special expression. For the *mundus* itself can be conceived of from these two opposite points of view. On the few days of the year on which it is opened it too reveals the hidden secrets of Hades, which at other times are shut up in darkness and withdrawn from human view. On the Greek side equally can this conception of the earth that opens and closes be attested. . . .

'What is true of Ceres is equally true of . . . Tellus or Terra Mater. She again is identical with Demeter. First of all, she too appears as giver of the vegetation, as goddess of the sown field, "that takes the seed and lets it develop in her bosom". But, besides, Tellus appears again as queen of the dead; the sacrifice of the *porca praecidanea* is due to her in common with Ceres and, in the formula of "devotion", the army of the enemy is dedicated *Telluri ac dis manibus*. Here, then, appears again that contrast between the giving birth to the living and the concealing of the dead, that we have already encountered in the case of Ceres and, on the Greek side, of Demeter' (Altheim, *op. cit.*, pp. 94-121).

Now Virgil, as has been already demonstrated, had an 'Early Latin' mind.

He describes, for example, how the army of the Sabine-descended king Latinus, like the later inhabitants of prehistoric Rome, practised both cremation and inhumation:

'Nor less, elsewhere, the hapless Latins built pyres innumerable. Of the many bodies of their slain, some they bury in the earth (*terrae infodiunt*), some they lift and carry to the neighbouring fields or send home to the city; all the rest, a mighty mass of indistinguishable slaughter, they burn (*cremant*) unreckoned and unhonoured: then on all sides, emulous with close-clustering fires, flare the broad fields' (XI. 203-209).

It is, moreover, to the fruitful bosom of the earth-mother as a tomb-womb that Apollo in Delos surely refers in that same Dardan-Romulean reincarnational sense which Anchises emphasizes in the Underworld:

' "Ye enduring sons of Dardanus! the earth (*tellus*) which bare you first from your parent stock shall welcome you as returning once more (*reduces*) to her fruitful bosom (*ubere*). Seek out your ancient mother (*matrem*). There the House (*domus*) of Aeneas shall lord it over all lands, even his children's children (*nati*) and they which shall be born of them" ' (III. 94-98).

In the same Dardan-Romulean reincarnational sense must be interpreted Aeneas' similarly worded welcome by Tiberinus to that same earth-mother's fruitful bosom, whose symbol as 'Earth, the first of deities' (VII. 137) is precisely a sow with young:

' "O seed of a race divine! thou who from foemen's hands bringest back once more (*revehis*) to us the city of Troy, and preservest her Pergama perpetual, O thou long looked-for upon Laurentine ground (*solo*) and Latin fields! Here is thy fixed House (*domus*), fixed (draw not back!) Penates. Nor be scared by threats of war; all the swelling wrath of heaven has abated. Even now, lest thou deem these words the idle feigning of sleep, thou shalt find a huge sow lying under the holm-oaks on the shore, just delivered of a litter of thirty young, the mother reclining on the ground (*solo*) white (*alba*); white, too, the young (*nati*) about her teats (*ubera*). By this token in thirty returning years (*redeuntibus annis*) shall Ascanius found a city, Alba ('White') of glittering name" ' (VIII. 36-48).

Thus each piglet of the mother-sow's brood symbolizes one year's completed revolution (cf. *annus:* G. II. 516), or return to its original starting-point, of the earth-mother's seasonal twelve-month circle (cf. *triginta magnos volvendis mensibus orbis:* A. I. 269) — precisely the idea underlying Anchises' Elysian account of that thousand-year reincarnational wheel (*ubi mille rotam volvere per annos:* VI. 748) whose completed revolution will bring the House of Dardanus back to its original Italian starting-point as the House of Aeneas (VI. 756-759), itself identical with the House of Romulus (VI. 760-787) and the House of Augustus (VI. 788-807).

It is further significant that Tiberinus, although identically repeating Helenus' earlier description of the mother-sow with her brood (III. 390-392=VIII. 43-45), should substitute this time-revolving symbolism in place of Helenus' prophecy that ' "There shall be the city's site, there a fixed rest from thy toils" ' (III. 393) — a substitution, moreover, involving also that of Romulus' birthplace and Rome's mother-city, Iulus' Alba Longa (VIII. 48) in place of Aeneas' Lavinium (III. 387) as the city whose foundation is symbolized by the mother-sow.

On the other hand, Tiberinus' '*hic tibi certa domus, certi* (*ne absiste*) *Penates*' (VIII. 39) precisely corresponds to Helenus' '*is locus urbis erit, requies ea certa laborum*' (III. 393); since not only does Aeneas' House (*domus*) represent his city (*urbs*), which is Dardanus' Troy as brought back once more to its Italian starting point (*Troianam . . . urbem qui revehis nobis:* VIII. 36-37) by Aeneas as Dardanus' offspring (*O sate gente deum:* VIII. 36), but the idea of fixity as complementary to that of movement, of the static as contrasted with the dynamic, is common to both sow-symbolized localities.

But the mother-sow herself is lying in either case upon that part of the Tiber-bank which is also the sea-shore, and so upon the actual site neither of Alba Longa nor of Lavinium, but of that Italian *Troia* which foreshadows both of them; so that, since Aeneas' Troy will be the mother-city of his Lavinium, itself the mother-city of Alba Longa, itself in turn the mother-city of Rome (I. 258-277), all four of these foundations are together symbolized by that one mother-sow whose piglets symbolize the earth-mother's annually recurrent seasons of animal fertility as both caused by vegetable fertility and causing human fertility.

For, since the three inseparable conditions of animal fertility are those of feeding, breeding and heeding, the sow became a widespread fertility-symbol as being not only a great feeder, and a great breeder, but also a great heeder both of her brood and of her food. Since, moreover, the interior of the sow is at once a rapacious tomb for her greedily swallowed food and a capacious womb for her lustily seeded brood, she came in time to symbolize that equivalence of tomb to womb which in her case meant the birth of her jealously heeded brood as resulting from the death of her jealously heeded food.

So it is that Aeneas, finding the mother-sow with her litter on the seaside Tiber-bank, sacrifices them all together to Juno (VIII. 81-85) not merely in consequence of Helenus' and Tiberinus' instructions to honour Juno in order to avert her threats and win her help (III. 437-440; VIII. 59-61) but specifically because pigs were the proper Roman sacrifice no less to Juno as *Lucina*, goddess of birth (Warde Fowler, *The Roman Festivals*, p. 105), than to Ceres and Tellus as goddesses of death — the Virgilian synthesis of birth and death, corresponding to this Roman sacrifice of swine, being that reincarnational return to life which, as the resurrection of Troy in Rome, involves the rotatory return to rest.

It will also be noted how Virgil, in accordance with the Early Latin association at Rome of hut-dwellings and urn-burials with those pigs which, sharing both the huts during life and the urns after death, thus came to symbolize the same life-after-death belief as belongs to the hut-urn, himself associates the idea of pigs (VIII. 42-45) with that of Dardanus' Troy-representing House as symbolized by a beehive-shaped hut-urn (VIII. 36-39), itself the symbol of Romulean Alba Longa and Rome.

Since, moreover, in the Gaulish dialect largely spoken in Virgil's own native Cisalpine Gaul, the word *troia* probably meant 'mother-sow', while Aeneas' mother-sow belongs to his *Troia*; since, too, Aeneas' *Troia*-belonging mother-sow symbolizes that foundation of Alba Longa by Iulus (VIII. 48) which involves Iulus' performance of the labyrinthine *troia* as taught to the 'Early Latins' and by them to the Romans (V. 596-602); it can hardly be doubted that in some language, once common to the Mediterranean coastlands of Gaul, of Italy, of Phrygia, and perhaps of the whole Balkan peninsular including Epirus and Greece generally, the term *troia* originally conveyed that notion of 'going round' which statically belongs to ring-walls or enclosures of any kind, and which dynamically belongs not only both to the wheeling maze-game and to the rolling mother-sow (W. F. Jackson Knight, *Cumaean Gates*, pp. 111-114) but also to that reincarnationally rolling wheel which, by Virgilian implication, brings back Dardanus' Italian *Troia* full-circle to its original starting-point.

It is here that the Cyclopean ring-walls of Elysium become important as the static counterpart upon the spiritual plane both of the ring-walls of Alba Longa as dynamically strengthened (*longam multa vi muniet Albam:* I. 271) upon the magical plane by the labyrinthine *troia* (*Longam muris cum cingeret Albam:* V. 597) and of the ring-walls of Dardanus' *Troia* as represented by those of Aeneas' hut-urn.

For the name 'Cyclops' comes from the adjective 'Cyclopean', which means little more than 'circular', and is applied to 'ring-walls'; while the ring-walls of Rome's *aedes Vestae*, as also represented by those of Aeneas' *Troia*-representing hut-urn, were regarded as 'hierocentric' in the sense of ritually symbolizing by their roundness not only Vesta's labyrinthine because defensive attributes, but also the central Hearth's equivalence both to the Earth and to the city of Rome (W. F. Jackson Knight, *Vergil's Troy*, Oxford 1932, pp. 137, 152-153; *Cumaean Gates*, Oxford 1936, pp. 3, 38-41, 97, 124, 157-158).

Virgil's own mental appropriation of this idea of 'going round', both in its Vestal and in its Vulcanic aspects, both in its static and in its dynamic form, is sufficiently clear from three passages: the first, where the ring-walls of Tartarus, thrice encircling it as the crematory counterpart of domestic Elysium, are themselves encircled by that fire of Vulcan (VI. 548-551) which, forging the ring-walls of Elysium (VI. 630-631), is in Virgil's mind complementary to the fire of Vesta (II. 296-297) as ring-walled by Aeneas' *Troia*-representing hut-urn (V. 743-745) and as stirred after the performance of that *troia* whose labyrinthine ring-walls dynamically strengthen Anchises' cremation-burial (V. 575-605); the second, where the cremation of Misenus is similarly followed by a threefold encirclement of his cremators by the same Corynaeus who has just housed Misenus' ashes within the ring-walls of a cinerary urn (VI. 226-231); and the third, where the Trojans and Etruscans in Italy, after cremating their dead, similarly 'thrice, girt in glittering armour, ran their course around the blazing pyres; thrice circled on horseback the mournful funeral-fire' (XI. 188-190).

Now this idea of 'going round'—which, be it noted, belongs also to that immemorial and widespread custom of 'going the rounds' for the purpose of 'beating the bounds' whose Roman equivalent was the *troia*-like dance of the warlike because labyrinthinely defensive *Salii* (Knight, *Cumaean Gates*, pp. 85-88) — was expressed in Greek by the verb περιπολεῖν, *peripolein*; a term applicable not only both to the reincarnational transmigration of souls and to the cosmic revolution of the heavenly bodies (cf. περιπόλησις, *peripolesis*) but also to the defensive patrolling of a limited area, such as a city or a district; so that the Athenians gave the name περίπολοι, *peripoloi*, 'goers round', to the youthful armed patrol who guarded the frontier.

Since, moreover, the Greek word περιπόλιον, *peripolion*, 'belonging to the goers round', came to mean specifically their headquarters, which themselves required careful guarding by the 'goers round'; and since the city of Troy itself began as the carefully guarded headquarters of those who thence carefully guarded the entrance to the Hellespontine Straits (W. Leaf, *Troy*, London 1912, *passim*); it is probable that the name Τροία, *Troia*, originally given to the entire district belonging to and patrolled by the 'goers round', Τρῶες, *Tröes*, who guarded that narrow sea-entrance, came also to mean their city or fortified headquarters as guarded by them for that purpose — a linguistic interpretation of the name Τρώς, *Tros*, suggested quite independently and from a different angle by Mr. G. D. Hornblower (*Antiquity*, vol. VII, no. 25, March 1933, pp. 94-95) and, although doubted by Mr. W. F. Jackson Knight, wholly consistent with his own convincing interpretation of the *troia*-principle as one of defensive closure against unauthorized penetration (*Cumaean Gates*, p. 113).

This interpretation is, indeed, strongly supported both by

the situation of Aeneas' Italian *Troia* precisely at the sea-entrance to the Tiber, on the site of Ostia (Jerome Carcopino, *Virgile et les Origines d'Ostie*, Paris 1919, *passim*) and by the fact that the name *Ostia* means precisely 'Entrance' (cf. Virgil's *Tiberina ostia:* A. I. 13-14).

Thus, since there were several places in Italy called *Troia*, while the mazes of north-western Europe have always been called 'Troy', it is likely that the place-name *Troia* originally everywhere signified 'belonging to the goers round' or *Troes*; whether their 'going round' was of a tactical or a ritual character or both combined, for the defence either of a district or of a city, or even of a burial regarded as itself foundationally defensive of the place thus guarded (Knight, *op. cit.*, pp. 78-90).

In that case, the Tiberine *Troia* would originally have been so-named as the carefully guarded headquarters, or camp-city, of a youthful armed patrol whose main duty, whether on foot (as earlier) or on horseback (as later), was defensive closure of the Tiber-mouth against piracy or invasion, or even mere smuggling, and whose cadet-drill or *troia*, 'belonging to the goers round', may well have taken the form of a defence-rehearsal whose maze-like manœuvres publicly advertised their task, for purposes of recruitment, as one of 'going round'— an interpretation supported by Virgil's close correlation of a Sicilian *Troia* (V. 756) with that *troia* (V. 602) whose performance is itself closely correlated with a foundation-burial (V. 605, 760-761).

In that case, too, the Latin diminutive of *Tros*, a fully qualified 'goer round' or trained patrol in contradistinction to a mere *tiro*, would naturally be *Trossulus*, a 'young goer round' or recent recruit, attracted by the *troia*-drill at the *Troia*-headquarters — whence the later application of the name *Trossuli*, not without an occasionally slighting connotation (cf. Seneca, *Ep.* lxxvi. 2; lxxxvii. 2), to the Roman cavalry (Pliny, N. H. xxxiii. 35); while the recruiting-headquarters would naturally be a *Trossulum*, as belonging to the 'young goers round' or recruits to the local patrol — whence the survival of that term as a place-name in Etruria (Aeneas' own recruiting-ground; IX. 10-11, precisely as a *Tros:* X. 250) having traditional cavalry-associations (Pliny, *loc. cit.*, Festus, *s.v.* '*Trossuli*').

This explanation would satisfactorily explain Virgil's significant coupling of Aeneas' Italian *Troia*, as the fortified headquarters of his subordinate *Troes* (VII. 157-159), with Latinus' fortified city before which 'boys and youths in their early bloom are being trained in horsemanship' (VII. 162-163) — a typically Virgilian reference to the Italian *troia* as revived both by Julius Caesar and by Augustus for the purpose of thereby reviving the old Italian manliness in the new Roman youth (Professor Lily Ross Taylor, '*Seviri Equitum Romanorum* and Municipal *Seviri*: A Study in Pre-Military training among the Romans'; article in *The Journal of Roman Studies*, vol. XIV. (1924), parts i and ii, pp. 158-161).

Again, this explanation would account for the alternative name *Flexuntes* or *Flexumines*, 'benders round', sometimes given to the *Trossuli* as Roman cavalry (Pliny, *loc. cit.*; cf. Knight, *Cumaean Gates*, p. 117), being clearly referred to by Virgil in the phrase *flectere ludus equos* (IX. 606) precisely when coupling Aeneas' Italian *Troia* (IX. 598-599) with the training in manliness of the Italian youth (IX. 600-608); this old Italian 'sport' (*ludus*) of 'bending round' (*flectere*), as further coupled with the 'shaking of towns in war' by the Italian 'youth' (*iuventus . . . quatit oppida bello:* IX. 607-608), being clearly identical with that 'game' (*lusus*) of 'going round' (*troiae*) which 'in sport awoke a mimicry of war' (*ludo . . . belli simulacra ciebat:* V. 674) when performed by the *Troiae iuventus* (V. 555) under the leadership of the young Iulus as a 'boy' (*puero . . . Iulo:* V. 569).

This interpretation, moreover, lends an entirely new force to Apollo's immediately-following eulogy of the 'boy' Iulus' 'manliness' (*macte nova virtute, puer:* IX. 641) in defending the *Troia* which 'cannot contain' him (*nec te Troia capit:* IX. 644) any more than can the *troia* of his Alban ring-walls (V. 597); since Iulus' starry destiny (*sic itur ad astra:* IX. 641), soaring above the world of war (*omnia bella:* IX. 642) as destined to become a world of peace under the race of Assaracus (IX. 642-643), will mean Iulus' participation in the cosmic revolution or 'going round' of the starry firmament, instead of his confinement to that rolling reincarnational wheel (VI. 748) whose 'going round' is the spiritual counterpart beneath the earth to that of the *troia* upon the earth as correlative to the *Troia*.

Finally, this interpretation would account for the Greek place-name Τροιζήν, *Troizen* — uniquely surviving in Argolis, as *Trossulum* in Etruria — as originally that of the headquarters of those responsible locally for guarding both sea-entrances of the narrow strait between the mainland of the Peloponnese and the island of Kalaureia — a strait whose tactical importance as the sea-gateway to Argolis is comparable with that of the Solent as the sea-gateway to Wessex; while at the same time suggesting a probable source for that fourfold Greek tradition which connected Theseus, son of the Aegean sea-god Poseidon-Aigeus, not only both with Troizen as his seaside-birthplace and with the *troia*-equivalent maze-dance called the 'Crane', but also with the penetration both of the Cretan labyrinth and of the Underworld, itself the labyrinth-equivalent interior of the earth-mother as both tomb and womb (Knight, *Cumaean Gates*, *passim*) — since that same *Tros* or 'goer round' who thereby tactically or ritually guarded conditionally penetrable entrances, whether of district or of city, was himself conditionally penetrative of those entrances.

Now the term *Tros*, as distinct from *Troius*, *Troianus* and *Troiugena*, is used by Virgil in the *Aeneid* thirty-five times, but only four times other than generically; and it is significant that on each of these four occasions (VI. 52, 126; X. 250; XII. 723) it should be precisely Aeneas who is termed *Tros* because of Virgil's mental association of his legend with that of Theseus.

Thus, at the very beginning of the sixth book, Virgil's coupling of the idea of the Cretan labyrinth as penetrated by Theseus (VI. 14-33) with that of Aeneas' own obsession therewith (33-41), as being himself in the Sibyl's eyes a *Tros* ('*cessas in vota precesque, Tros*', *ait*, '*Aenea? cessas?*': 51-52) who as such is conditionally entitled to penetrate entrances ('*neque enim ante dehiscent attonitae magna ora domus*': 52-53), is followed by Virgil's coupling of the idea of the Underworld as penetrated by Theseus (122-123) with that of Aeneas' own obsession therewith (106-124), as being himself in the Sibyl's eyes a *Tros* ('*Tros Anchisiade*': 126) who as such is conditionally entitled to penetrate entrances ('*facilis descensus Averno*': 126): ' "Night and day the door of gloomy Dis stands open; but to recall thy steps and to pass out to the upper air, this is the task, this the toil!" ' —

> *Tros Anchiade, facilis descensus Averno:*
> *noctes atque dies patet atri ianua Ditis;*
> *sed revocare gradum superasque evadere ad auras,*
> *hoc opus, hic labor est* (VI. 126-129);

an obvious reference to Theseus, who, as contrasted with Hercules (VI. 122-123, 392-397), failed to fulfil those conditions (*dominam Ditis thalamo deducere:* 397) which would qualify him to penetrate outwards (*sedet aeternumque sedebit infelix Theseus:* 617-618) that Underworld which he so easily penetrated inwards (*facilis descensus Averno:* 126).

The Sibyl's use of the word *labor* (129), moreover, in connection with the outward penetration of the Underworld, at once recalls Virgil's use of the word *labor* (27) in connection with the outward penetration of the Cretan labyrinth; Ariadne, as 'Queen' (*reginae:* 28), bearing the same relationship to Theseus' success in escaping from the *labor* of the Cretan labyrinth (27-30) as that borne by Persephone as 'Lady' (*dominam:* 397) to Theseus' failure in escaping from the *labor* (*Labos:* VI. 277) of the Underworld.

Nor is this all.

For the Sibyl's use here of the word *labor*, in connection with Aeneas' obsession with the idea of Theseus' penetration of the Underworld (VI. 122-129), is Virgil's own characteristically subtle reminder that Aeneas' obsession with the idea of Theseus' penetration of the Cretan labyrinth (VI. 24-37) is an obsession with precisely that twofold idea of *labor* and *error* (*hic labor ille domus et inextricabilis error:* VI. 27), which, as belonging to the labyrinthine *troia* (*irremeabilis error:* V. 591), Aeneas himself associates immediately afterwards with his own *Troia* (*Troiae . . . labores:* VI. 56; *errantisque deos . . . Troiae:* VI. 68); so that all those 'toilings' and 'wanderings' of the *Troes*, together with their *Troia* and their *troia*, which are elsewhere repeatedly emphasized from the very outset of the *Aeneid* — *labores:* I. 10; *errabant:* 32; *laborum:* 241; *laborem:* 330; *erramus:* 333; *laborum:* 373; *laboris:* 460; *Troiae . . . labores:* 597; *labores:* 628; *errores:* 755; *errantem:* 756; *Troiae . . . laborem:* II. 11; *pererrato:* 295; *laborum:* III. 145; *laborem:* 160; *erramus:* 200; *erramus:* 204; *labores:* 368; *laborum:* 393; *laborem:* 459; *labor:* 714; *Iliacos . . . labores:* IV. 78; *laborem:* 233, 273; *laborem:* V. 617; *labores:* 688; *laborem:* 769 — all these will henceforth be associated in Aeneas' memory, as representing Virgil's mind, both with Theseus' success in outwardly penetrating the Cretan labyrinth and with Theseus' failure in outwardly penetrating the Underworld.

It is Virgil himself, moreover, as Aeneas' creator, who —

having first significantly coupled the phrase *Troiae . . . labores* (IX. 202) with the idea of the training in manliness of the Trojan boy Euryalus (IX. 179-206), and the generic term *Tros* (X. 108) with the phrase *errore . . . Troiae* (X. 110) — goes on not only to couple the idea of *Troia*-defence (*subsidio Troiae:* X. 214) with that of Aeneas himself as a *Tros* (*Tros Anchisiades:* X. 250; cf. VI. 126) but also to associate both of them with that threefold idea of the dolphin-like *troia* (X. 219-224; cf. IX. 119 and V. 594), of the *troia*-like shield (X. 242-243; cf. VIII. 448-449 and V. 584-585), and of the maze-like crane-dance (X. 264-266) whose labyrinthine implications, already suggested in an earlier chapter, are in Virgil's mind connected with the legend of Ariadne's share in Theseus' penetration of the Cretan labyrinth both from without to the centre and from within to the circumference.

Finally, it is Virgil, as Aeneas' creator, who — having first significantly coupled the generic term *Troes* (XII. 704) with the idea of an attempted penetration of defensive walls (XII. 705-706) — goes on not only to apply the term *Tros* specifically to Aeneas himself (*Tros Aeneas:* XII. 723; cf. VI. 52), as representing all the other *Troes* in his single combat with Turnus (XII. 692-790, 887-952), but also to describe that *Troia*-combat (XII. 828) on behalf of the *Troes* (XII. 824) by the representative *Tros* (XII. 723) in maze-like terms (XII. 743, 753, 763-765) reminiscent of those comparing the *troia* with the Cretan labyrinth (V. 575-595).

When it is remembered that this single combat between Aeneas and Turnus is fought for Lavinia's hand in marriage as personifying Latinus' city of Lavinium, the penetration of whose defensive walls is thus correlative symbolically to the penetration of Lavinia's own defensive maidenhood by right of victory in that combat, it can hardly be doubted that Virgil is thinking of that single combat between Theseus and the Minotaur (VI. 24-26) which meant Theseus' penetration of the Cretan labyrinth by means of Ariadne's Daedalus-provided clue (VI. 27-30) as correlative symbolically to the penetration of Ariadne's maidenhood (Knight, *Cumaean Gates*, pp. 93-96, 125-141); Virgil's elaborate comparison of Aeneas and Turnus to two singly combating bulls (XII. 710-724) — a comparison, be it noted, whose description of Aeneas as a *Tros* (723) is followed by the attribution of labyrinthine movements (742-765) to these two singly combating bull-like men — being unconsciously reminiscent of that bull-like man, the Minotaur, whose death inside the Cretan labyrinth at Theseus' hands was preceded by the necessarily labyrinthine movements of both combatants therein.

Whence, then, arose this evidently deep-seated Virgilian association of Aeneas with Theseus?

The answer lies in the second book of the *Georgics*: 'The sons of Theseus (*Thesidae*; i.e. the Athenians) set up prizes for wit in their villages and at the crossways, and gaily danced in the soft meadows on oiled goat-skins. Even so the tillers of Italian soil, a race sent from Troy (*Troia gens missa*), sport with rude verses and laughter unrestrained' (G. II. 382-386).

Virgil, that is to say, quite early in his literary life associated the idea of the *Aeneadae* with that of the *Thesidae*, and so the Aeneas-legend with the Theseus-legend, because of that early literary association of Aeneas' Rome with Theseus' Athens which was eventually, after his completion of the *Aeneid* in 19 B.C., to send him from Rome to Athens on his way to Troy.

But at Athens he met Augustus, who persuaded him to return with him to Rome — a journey which ended prematurely in his death at Brundisium without the opportunity of those revisions of the *Aeneid* which, further clarifying its symbolism, must surely have resulted from a visit to the site of Troy (*campos, ubi Troia fuit:* III. 11; *solum, quo Troia fuit:* X. 60).